The Romantic Heroic Ideal

The Romantic Heroic Ideal

James D. Wilson

Louisiana State University Press
Baton Rouge and London

Designer: Rod Parker
Typeface: Janson
Typesetter: Graphic Composition
Printer and Binder: Thomson-Shore

Library of Congress Cataloging in Publication Data
Wilson, James D. (James Darrell), 1946–
The romantic heroic ideal.

Bibliography: p.
Includes index.
1. Romanticism. 2. Romanticism—United States.
3. American literature—19th century—History and
criticism. 4. Heroes in literature. I. Title.
PR751.W57   809'.9145   82–58
ISBN 0–8071–1030–2   AACR2

To the memory of my father

Contents

Preface and Acknowledgments

This study began several years ago as an attempt to write a tightly focused study of modes of heroism characteristic of the romantic period. Though the romantic hero had received considerable scholarly scrutiny, the amorphous body of relevant scholarship presented a fragmented picture. An effort to draw academic writing on this fascinating subject into a coherent whole would, I thought, prove helpful to those interested in romanticism. But the many divergent and often contradictory aspects of romantic heroism resisted my attempts at neat categorization; I soon discovered that to examine the nature of romantic heroism was to open the entire movement to close analysis.

An exhaustive classification of all the types of romantic heroes in Western literature from 1770 to 1860 lies beyond the scope of this study. Instead, I offer a series of essays that treats representative heroes from French, German, English, and American romanticisms as reflections of themes characteristic of the movement in general. Though certain major heroes receive extended analysis (*e.g.*, Werther, René, the Visionary of "Alastor," Faust, the Ancient Mariner, Ahab), the focus of my study falls on the intellectual context that produces these and other heroes. In the process, I have tried to call attention to what I think are prevalent misconceptions about the nature of the romantic movement. Ultimately the study is an attempt to define what I call the romantic heroic ideal.

Emphasis in this study falls on American romanticism. Two excellent recent books explore aspects of the relationship between American literature and Continental romanticism: Frederick Garber's *Thoreau's Redemptive Imagination* (New York University Press, 1977) and James Engell's *The Creative Imagination: Enlightenment to Romanticism* (Harvard University Press, 1981). Though Garber concentrates on the single writer, Thoreau, and Engell limits his discussion of American literature to the period prior to 1825, and though neither offers any sustained discussion of the idea of heroism, both document convincingly the resemblances and connections between American and Continental romanticisms in the important area of the aesthetic imagination. Others have, on a more limited basis, drawn connections between certain of Hawthorne's or Melville's heroes and their English or Continental prototypes (especially Goethe's Faust or the Byronic hero), but no one has as yet examined in detail the concept of American romantic heroism in light of the broader, international movement. In many ways the romantic movement culminates in America during what F. O. Matthiessen called the American Renaissance; all of the American romantic writers had read and were influenced by the European and English romantic writers, and much of their fiction was written in response to or in reaction against romantic theory as it developed on the Continent. More specifically, the central conflict between the solipsistic tendency of the hero and his recognition of social obligation becomes especially pertinent in American romanticism as a result of the emerging nation's persistent attempt at self-definition and the preoccupation of its artists with the cultural and political implications of the "experiment" in democracy. Still, in all examination of American writers I have tried to locate the authors within a romantic tradition of largely European origins and, consequently, to stress the essential unity of the romantic movement as a whole.

Obviously any study of international romanticism will rely heavily on material written in languages other than English. Whenever I quote from French or German primary texts, I provide English translations in the body of the essay; most of these translations come from scholarly sources that I identify in the notes. In all instances, however, the original language material is available in the notes.

I would like to thank Lewis P. Simpson of Louisiana State University and Lilian R. Furst of the University of Texas at Dallas for the inspiration and training that made this study possible; their friendship, guidance, and considered reading of large portions of the manuscript proved indispensable. The encouragement, patience, and practical suggestions of my colleagues at Georgia State University were also of great help; I would like to mention specifically Paul G. Blount, Jack I. Biles, and Robert D. Jacobs. Professor Jacobs has proved an especially valuable resource; not only has he read portions of this manuscript with great care, but he has also assisted and stimulated my thinking through many hours of discussion of the subject of romanticism. Finally, to my wife Mary Ann I owe the greatest debt. A colleague at Georgia State University, she has offered many valuable suggestions in the preparation of this manuscript. Without the love, encouragement, and patience she has given, the considerable personal sacrifices she has made, this study could never have been completed.

Portions of the manuscript have appeared earlier in scholarly journals: Chapter II, originally titled "Goethe's *Werther*: A Keatsian Quest for Self-Annihilation," originally appeared in *MOSAIC: A Journal for the Comparative Study of Literature and Ideas*, published by the University of Manitoba, Volume IX, No. 1 (Fall, 1975), 93–109; Chapter V, "The Romantic Love Object: The Woman as Narcissistic Projection," originally appeared in *Comparative Literature Studies*, published by the University of Illinois Press, Volume XV, No. 4

(December, 1978), 388–402; and Chapter VI, "Incest and American Romantic Fiction," first appeared in *Studies in the Literary Imagination*, published by the Department of English, Georgia State University, Volume VII, No. 1 (Spring, 1974), 31–51. In all three instances, however, the present chapters differ from the original essays.

The Romantic Heroic Ideal

I

Toward an Understanding of the Romantic Heroic Ideal

A survey of the many manifestations of the chameleon-like romantic hero, coupled with a critical evaluation of the various scholarly attempts to locate a common denominator sufficiently broad to include the multiple types of romantic heroes, might well bring one to A. O. Lovejoy's assessment that, because of the sheer number and bewildering diversity of academic approaches, the term "'Romantic' has come to mean so many things that, by itself, it means nothing. It has ceased to perform the function of a verbal sign."[1] The serious problems of definition posed by the concept of the "romantic" hero in large part result from the nature of the hero himself, or at least his conception and presentation of himself. When Rousseau in his *Confessions* proclaims his self as subject, he insists that the soul exhibited is unlike any the reader is likely to encounter elsewhere: "I want to show my fellows a man just as he is, true to nature; and this man will be myself. Myself alone. . . . I am not made like any of those I have come across. I venture to believe that I am not made like any

---

1 A. O. Lovejoy, "On the Discrimination of Romanticisms," *PMLA*, XXXIX (1924), 232.

other existing man. If I am not better, at least I am different."[2] The mere fact that Rousseau would offer himself as sole subject of an extensive prose work in 1764 is striking; to argue that the self presented is unlike "any other existing man" is revolutionary in an age that prizes the depiction of universal truth in art. But Rousseau's formula soon becomes the pattern in romantic art: central to the conception of most individual heroes—especially those offered and accepted as expressions of the artist who creates them—is a firm conviction that the character revealed is unique. As in any age of mass or fashionable nonconformity, however, the nonconformists begin to assume typical and rigid modes of living that render them remarkably uniform, and the rush of romantic heroes in the *mal du siècle* and satanic traditions ultimately produces a familiar pattern. Rousseau, Werther, Harold, and Manfred both reflect and influence traditions of romantic heroism and hence become "typical" in fundamental ways. But in most instances the creators of these heroes perceive themselves as outside the dominant literary tradition and sorely at odds with established conventions of their day; hence they seek for their heroes special consideration and sympathy from an audience whose sentimental proclivities might make them responsive to the "exceptional" individual whose behavior and sensitivity of soul render him hopelessly at variance with prevailing social convention.

Even if we view with suspicion each romantic hero's claim to originality, perceiving instead a "family likeness" linking Rousseau, Werther, René, Childe Harold and others,[3] we are nevertheless thwarted in our search for a common denominator uniting the various heroes by their sheer number and variety. The noble primitive of Fenimore Cooper's novels, the innocent child of infinite natural

2   Jean-Jacques Rousseau, *Confessions* (Paris, 1879), 1. "Je veux montrer à mes semblables un homme dans toute la vérité de la nature; et cet homme, ce sera moi.

Moi seul. . . . Je ne suis fait comme auçun de ceux que j'ai vus; j'ose croire n'être fait comme auçun de ceux qui existent. Si je ne vaux pas mieux, au moins je suis autre."

3   Lilian R. Furst, *Romanticism* (London, 1969), 54–55.

wisdom in Wordsworth's "We Are Seven," the rejected orphan wandering hopelessly in a world insensitive to his needs (Werther, René, Harold, Alastor, Ishmael), satanic figures embarked on monomaniac quests like Manfred or Ahab, melancholy figures suffering from ennui and satanic curiosity (Lermontov's Pechorin or Musset's "enfant"), and redemptive figures struggling for the salvation of mankind (Prometheus or Joan of Arc) do not, in fact, make comfortable companions. As Edmond Estève asks, "Le romantisme, qu'était-ce? *Le Genie du christianisme* ou *Manfred*?"[4] And when we remember that the creator of the two fundamental heroes of the age—Werther and Faust—was considered by his countrymen as a classicist hardly representative of the native romantic movement, or try to isolate characteristics separating "romantic" heroes from such predecessors as Marlowe's Tamburlaine, Milton's Satan, Shakespeare's Hamlet, Molière's Alceste, or Dryden's Almanzor, we are apt to fall into a veritable maze of seemingly irreconcilable contradictions. Traditionally, scholars who persisted in an attempt to categorize or document the nature of the romantic rebellion have had to content themselves with a delineation of what Michael Cooke disparagingly labels "a bouquet of mental tendencies and literary terms."[5]

Certainly the most prevalent common denominator used to link romantic heroes is their emphasis on the primacy of self. Though admittedly the celebration of self-consciousness is hardly unique to romanticism, only during the romantic period does self-assertion become an explicit artistic credo: "An artist is one who has his center of gravity within," F. Schlegel writes; according to Novalis, "the supreme task of human development is to take possession of one's transcendental self, to be, in a sense, the quintessential ego of one's ego."[6] The romantic artist rebelled against an empiricist tradition

---

4   Edmond Estève, *Byron et le romantisme française* (Paris, 1929), 132.

5   Michael G. Cooke, *The Romantic Will* (New Haven, Conn., 1976), ix.

6   Friedrich Schlegel, "Ideen," in *Kritische Schriften*, ed. Wolfdietrich Rasch (Munich, 1964), 94. "Ein Künstler ist, wer sein Zentrum in sich selbst hat." Novalis (pseudonym of Friedrich von Hardenberg), *Novalis Schriften*, eds. Paul Kluckhohn and Richard Samuel (4 vols.; Stuttgart, 1977), II, 424. "Die höchste Auf-

which had bequeathed to the mid–eighteenth century an impersonal, mechanistic world order, adopting instead an epistemological subjectivism which gave him the godlike power to remake the world in his own image.[7] When Rousseau surrenders in *Les Rêveries du Promeneur Solitaire* to "the ecstasy of communing with my soul," portraying an individual "absorbed in myself" in search of the answer to the question, "what am I within myself?",[8] he establishes a pattern which many have come to see as the trademark of romantic heroism. For Fichte this pattern becomes the central philosophical imperative: "Heed only yourself: turn your gaze away from all around you, and inwards on to yourself; this is the first requirement that philosophy makes of its apprentice. Nothing outside of you matters, solely yourself."[9] "The taproot of romanticism," writes H. N. Fairchild, "is an eternal and universal and primary fact of consciousness: man's desire for self-trust, self-expression, self-expansion."[10] George Ross Ridge, after a comprehensive survey of

---

gabe der Bildung ist—sich seines transscendentalen Selbst zu bemächtigen—das Ich ihres Ichs zugleich zu seyn."

7 Wylie Sypher, *Loss of Self in Modern Literature and Art* (New York, 1962), 21. Sypher points to the influence of Schopenhauer. James Engell too highlights the emphasis that fell on the introspective imagination during the formative stages of Continental romanticism: "The creative imagination had also become . . . an ideal to believe in wholeheartedly, a goal, a state of mind or being toward which to aspire—something it had never been before." James Engell, *The Creative Imagination: Enlightenment to Romanticism* (Cambridge, Mass., 1981), viii.

8 Jean-Jacques Rousseau, *Les Rêveries du Promeneur Solitaire* (Paris, 1949), 1; 46. "la douceur converser avec mon âme"; "enlacé de moi-même"; "que suis-je moi-même?"

9 J. G. Fichte, *Sämtliche Werke*, ed. J. H. Fichte (8 vols.; Berlin, 1845), I, 422. "Merke auf dich selbst: kehre deinen Blick von allem, was dich umgiebt, ab, und in dein Inneres—ist die erste Forderung, welche die Philosophie an ihren Lehrling thut. Es ist von nichts, was ausser dir ist, die Rede, sondern lediglich von dir selbst." M. H. Abrams provides a helpful discussion of Fichte's epistemology as it relates to romantic literature in *Natural Supernaturalism: Tradition and Revolution in Romantic Literature* (New York, 1971), 358; see too James Engell, *The Creative Imagination*, 225–31.

10 Hoxie Neale Fairchild, *1780–1830, Romantic Faith*, vol. III of *Religious Trends in English Poetry* (6 vols.; New York, 1939–68), 3.

nineteenth-century French literature, concludes that "the Romantic hero is essentially the same man . . . in spite of the most seeming variations . . . [H]e is the self-conscious hero."[11] Indeed, few would dispute Lilian R. Furst's claim that the romantic artist establishes a "principle of order . . . in terms of the inner world of the individual,"[12] or that the romantic heroic personality develops from the artist's exploration of that inner world. Harold Bloom, in an excellent and influential essay, writes that "in the Romantic quest the Promethean hero stands, finally, quite alone, upon a tower that is only himself, and his stance is all the fire there is."[13]

But recent scholarship has amply demonstrated that the theme of acute self-consciousness in romantic literature is infinitely more complex than it was once assumed to be. Michael Cooke writes, "Perhaps, then, it is not enough to adopt the truism that for the romantic poet self-concern and self-consciousness are paramount. . . . For this truism may obscure what the problematical status of self-knowledge should convey: the way the question of self-knowledge is bound up in the way the poet and man realize themselves in time."[14] Not all the romantics discovered the solipsistic excursion into the recesses of consciousness to have redemptive effect. Though Musset asserts, "I burrowed into the depths of my heart to feel its pangs of torture"—suggesting a consciously chosen, masochistic voyage—he eventually discovers himself "imprisoned in my solitude."[15] Werther, René, Alastor, and the various heroes of Poe's short stories provide ample testimony to the dangers posed by self-absorption; and, as Michael Hamburger points out, Hölderlin exposes in his fragmentary *Empedocles* the "Fichtean solipsism that

11 George Ross Ridge, *The Hero in French Romantic Literature* (Athens, Ga., 1959), x.

12 Lilian R. Furst, *Romanticism in Perspective: A Comparative Study of Aspects of the Romantic Movements in England, France, and Germany* (New York, 1970), 56.

13 Harold Bloom, "The Internalization of the Quest Romance," in Harold Bloom (ed.), *Romanticism and Consciousness: Essays in Criticism* (New York, 1970), 9.

14 Cook, *The Romantic Will*, 10.

15 Alfred de Musset, *Le Confession d'un Enfant du Siècle* (Paris, 1937), 86; 163. "Je descendais jusqu'au fond de mon coeur, pour le sentir se tordre et se serrer"; "renfermé dans ma solitude."

transforms a holy cosmos into the meaningless creation of the individual mind, All into Nothing."[16] Hence, though Victor Brombert might, with specific reference to Hugo, refer to the self as the "happy prison," most romantic artists were hardly so sanguine; as Wylie Sypher contends, "the romantics themselves often found the self to be an intolerable burden, and heroism often collapsed into tedium, ennui, if not despair or cynicism."[17] If consciousness is, as Cooke claims, "largely the bringing to light of passional, emotional, spiritual, perhaps even psychological data that may be kept private even from the self,"[18] then there always remains the possibility that what the self-conscious hero discovers will devastate him. One of the few flaws in Abrams' excellent *Natural Supernaturalism* is his failure to account for the despair characteristic of the considerable number of romantic heroes and artists who fail to complete what Abrams labels "the circuitous journey."[19] Ultimately we are led back to the distinction drawn by Morse Peckham between positive and negative romanticism, the latter category including those artists like Byron who fail to participate in the movement away from an initial condition of despair and alienation on to one of affirmation and assimilation into vital life forces—the progression that Peckham claims to be typical of romantic art.[20]

Though the primacy of self forms a convenient common denominator in discussing the romantic hero, it has unfortunately given rise to a number of misleading distortions of romanticism in general. Irving Babbitt, for example, wants to find in romantic self-

---

16 Michael Hamburger, *Contraries: Studies in German Literature* (New York, 1970), 14.

17 Victor Brombert, "The Happy Prison: A Recurring Romantic Metaphor," in David Thorburn and Geoffrey Hartman (eds.), *Romanticism: Vistas, Instances, Continuities* (Ithaca, N.Y., 1973), 62–79; Sypher, *Loss of Self in Modern Literature and Art*, 20.

18 Cooke, *The Romantic Will*, 3.

19 Abrams, *Natural Supernaturalism*, 141ff.

20 Morse Peckham, "Toward a Theory of Romanticism," *PMLA*, LXVI (1951), 5–23. H. A. Korff discusses the concept of "negative romanticism" in some detail. See his *Geist der Goethezeit* (Leipzig, 1940), 204–18.

assertion the source of all modern social and political ailments; the individual's will to power, initiated by Rousseau and developed to its logical extreme by Nietzsche in the late nineteenth century, contributes to the breakdown of mediating social institutions and makes possible the rise of the political demigod who tyrannically molds whole civilizations in his own image. F. L. Lucas sees modern fascism as "Romanticism gone rotten," arguing that Hitler "remained . . . a perverted romantic, who hated reason, boasted of marching to his goal like a somnambulist, and intoxicated both himself and his countrymen with megalomaniac dreams."[21] Though provocative, Babbitt's work suffers from its failure to consider the ambivalence exhibited by romantic artists toward Rousseauistic self-assertion and ultimately presents so distorted a view of romanticism as to become ineffectual; rarely does modern scholarship pay heed to his once influential work. In assuming romantic self-consciousness to be mere blind self-indulgence—"an abandonment to feeling or wallowing in it"—Lucas likewise oversimplifies a complex phenomenon.[22]

More dangerous than Babbitt or Lucas—because they are more influential—are those who follow the lead of Mario Praz and locate the seeds of romantic heroism in a satanic sensibility. Focusing his discussion of romanticism on figures who—like the Marquis de Sade, Monk Lewis, or members of the *fin de siècle* groups—are only bastard children of the romantic movement, Praz equates the "Romantic agony" with satanic eroticism, an equation that, in last analysis, fails to account for virtually all of the heroes central to the romantic movement.[23] Praz is but one of many scholars to emphasize satanic qualities in their study of romantic heroes; Sainte-Beuve had as early as 1870 attributed the ills of nineteenth-century French literature to its fascination with the satanic qualities of Byron and

21 Irving Babbitt, *Rousseau and Romanticism* (Boston, 1919); F. L. Lucas, "Prefatory Note," *The Decline and Fall of the Romantic Ideal* (rev. ed.; Cambridge, 1963), viii.
22 Cooke, *The Romantic Will*, 4.
23 Mario Praz, *The Romantic Agony*, trans. from Italian by Angus Davidson (rev. ed.; London, 1954).

de Sade.[24] Such emphasis underlies as well the early sections of Leslie Fiedler's popular *Love and Death in the American Novel* and helps to explain Lawrence Thompson's focus on Ahab as sympathetically portrayed hero of *Moby-Dick*.[25]

Perhaps the most important of those scholars in the Praz school is Peter Thorslev, who in two excellent articles and a book-length study of the Byronic hero makes a strong case for treating the romantic hero as satanic rebel.[26] In "The Romantic Mind Is Its Own Place," Thorslev argues that the romantic hero is a "renewed and refreshed" version of the Elizabethan satanic hero/villain. An especially important influence, according to Thorslev, is Milton's Satan, who "had reassumed his archangelic wings and had become intimately associated with romantic rebellion in the name of the new humanist self-assertion." Closely analyzing Satan's "the mind is its own place" speech (*Paradise Lost*, I, 251–59), Thorslev sees in it four points that relate directly to the hero in the romantic tradition: 1) that mental suffering is far worse than physical punishment, and that hell ultimately is a state of mind rather than a geographic location; 2) that a self-sufficient mind has the power to find inward happiness in even the most horrible surroundings; 3) that the independent mind can create without divine assistance; and 4) "that the individual mind has the ultimate freedom to create its own values, its own good and evil." Thorslev readily admits that the last two

24 Sainte-Beuve, *Portraits Contemporains* (rev. ed., 5 vols.; Paris, 1889), III, 430. Sainte-Beuve writes: "j'oserai affirmer, sans crainte d'être démenti, que Byron et De Sade (je demande pardon du rapprochement) ont peut-être été les deux plus grands inspirateurs de nos modernes, l'un affiché et visible, l'autre clandestin, —pas trop clandestin."

25 Leslie Fiedler, *Love and Death in the American Novel* (New York, 1960); Lawrence Thompson, *Melville's Quarrel with God* (Princeton, N.J., 1952); another example is Paul Zumthor, *Victor Hugo: Poète de Satan* (Paris, 1946).

26 Peter L. Thorslev, Jr., "The Romantic Mind Is Its Own Place," *Comparative Literature*, XV (1963), 250–68; "Incest as Romantic Symbol," *Comparative Literature Studies*, XI (1965), 41–58; *The Byronic Hero: Types and Prototypes* (Minneapolis, 1962).

points appear only implicitly in Satan's speech, and that Milton would probably deny them. And though Satan emerges as "the foremost romantic hero to 'will to be God,'" the four points made in his speech do not apply equally to all romantic heroes; in fact, the last one—which Thorslev terms the "existential sense"—suits only the "most 'advanced' romantics—such as Byron." Drawing most of his initial examples from the German *Sturm und Drang*, especially Schiller and Goethe, Thorslev focuses on Byron, "who carried the romantic Satanic tradition to its logical conclusion, and, in doing so, anticipated some of the pressing ethical and metaphysical problems which were to receive their philosophical formulations only with the advent of Nietzsche and modern existentialism."

Thorslev's article is a cogent one. As M. H. Abrams has shown, rebellion and revolution were crucial to romanticism,[27] and Thorslev is no doubt right to adopt them as central to an understanding of romantic heroism. But he is perhaps misguided to drape a satanic coloring over the rebellion characteristic of the period, and by his own admission he has considerable difficulty bringing all of the various types of heroes under his thematic umbrella. In *The Byronic Hero*, Thorslev censures Praz for his narrowness of vision, only to offer a conception of the Byronic hero which excludes Don Juan, who for Thorslev is not a Byronic hero because "he is, if anything, far more closely related to Tom Jones or to Candide than to any of the Romantic heroes . . . [H]e has no gothic coloring and little . . . metaphysical rebellion." Thorslev's definition would seem to exclude Werther, René, and Alastor as well, and applies only partially to Coleridge's Mariner, Lermontov's Pechorin, or Melville's Ishmael. And Thorslev's crucial insistence that it is in Byron's poetry that we find the quintessential romantic heroic personality would no doubt pose real problems for René Wellek, who denies that Byron is "ro-

---

27 M. H. Abrams, "English Romanticism: The Spirit of the Age," in Northrop Frye (ed.), *Romanticism Reconsidered: Selected Papers from the English Institute* (New York, 1963), 26–72.

mantic" at all, for Lilian R. Furst, who claims that he is somewhat of "an exception" among English romantics, or for Michael Cooke, who notes Byronic self-assertion as a "striking feature" of the romantic will but not "central."[28]

Thorslev and Praz are certainly not the only scholars to reach back into the English Renaissance for sources of romantic heroism. For both Clara McIntyre and Louis Bredvold the Elizabethan rational villain or Machiavel—in his intelligence, ambition, selfishness, and conscious disregard of social or moral norms—becomes a prototype for the later romantic hero.[29] Ultimately, however, McIntyre and Bredvold distort rather than clarify our understanding of romantic heroism. Shelley's Cenci might embody the qualities of the Renaissance Machiavel, but he is hardly heroic. The Elizabethan villain—an Edmund or Iago—operates from a Hobbesian perspective that is totally foreign to the romantic sensibility. The rational villain's universe is homocentric, devoid of any binding transcendental values; thus he claims the freedom to establish his own values drawn according to narrow self-interest, and views others as fair game for selfish, often sadistic, machinations. The romantic hero, on the other hand, indeed recognizes transcendent values, and his rebellion against social norms results generally from the painful incongruity between those norms and the divine ideals to which he has intuitive access. Cooke writes that romantics "opposed values that were merely hereditary and traditional, but only to the extent that these might prove a filigree of social accident, and always with an eye to the basic fabric of humanity, an eye to what is immemorial."[30]

---

28 René Wellek, "The Concept of Romanticism in Literary History," *Comparative Literature*, I (1949), 1–23; 147–72; Furst, *Romanticism in Perspective*, 64; Cooke, *The Romantic Will*, xiv. Abrams too labels Byron somewhat of an exception among romantic writers, and ignores him in *Natural Supernaturalism*—see p. 13.

29 Clara McIntyre, "The Later Career of the Elizabethan Villain-Hero," *PMLA*, XL (1925), 874–80; Louis Bredvold, *The Natural History of Sensibility* (Detroit, 1962), 81.

30 Cooke, *The Romantic Will*, x.

When Friedrich Schleiermacher asserts that "we have only understanding of God insofar as we are God ourselves, which means insofar as we have God within ourselves" (*Dialektik* 224), or Emerson sees each man as a finite god containing within a hieroglyphic to explain cosmic mysteries, they express the prevailing religious assumptions of the romantic movement: man is godlike, not so much in his power as in his nobility of spirit. Fairchild sees the romantic God as "authenticating the natural goodness of man and lending divine sanction to his expansive impulses," and with Douglas Bush would like to agree that the Romantic denies the fall of man, that he celebrates an Easter without Good Friday.[31] But here Fairchild is only partially accurate; man has fallen, but redemption is possible through man's heroic efforts. Surely Wordsworth in "Ode: Intimations of Immortality" acknowledges a fall: "Whither is fled the visionary gleam?/ Where is it now, the glory and the dream?" So too does Lamartine in "l'Homme," a poem dedicated to Byron:

> Limited in his nature, infinite in his longings,
> Man is a fallen god who remembers the heavens;
> He who has been disinherited of his former glory,
> Keeps the memory of his lost destiny.[32]

Even Emerson would not deny man's fallen state, as "Nature" opens with a devastating portrayal of man having fallen, having abdicated the divine potentiality within him; man is "a god in ruins." The Romantic differs from the Christian not in denying a fall but in

31 Ralph Waldo Emerson, "Nature," in Alfred R. Ferguson and Robert E. Spiller (eds.), *The Collected Works of Ralph Waldo Emerson* (12 vols. projected; Cambridge, Mass., 1971—), I, 7; Fairchild, *1780–1830, Romantic Faith*, 7; Douglas Bush, *Mythology and the Romantic Tradition in English Poetry* (Cambridge, Mass., 1937), 155.

32 Lamartine, *Oeuvres Poétiques Complètes*, ed. Marius-François Guyard (Paris, 1963), 6.

> Borné dans sa nature, infini dans ses voeux,
> L'homme est un dieu tombé qui se souvient des cieux;
> Soit que déshérité de son antique gloire,
> De ses destins perdus il garde la mémoire.

refusing to accept human limitation; every man can be a Joan of Arc, a Moses, a Christ, for by bringing himself in line with an intuitively glimpsed vision of divinity he can manage his own redemption. The divine vision resembles the Holy Spirit; access to it lies within the individual, but its source is an overall cosmic consciousness—what Hölderlin terms "Der Götter Gott"—to which the individual must submit. Thus the romantic hero differs fundamentally from the Elizabethan villain, for when he wants to transform society according to a personal, intuitive vision, it is because that vision is divine.

The most convincing attack on those who want to tie the romantic hero to the Machiavel comes from Frederick Garber. Contrasting the two brothers in Schiller's *Die Räuber*—Karl Moor as hero, Franz as villain—Garber points to a crucial difference: "Franz—or Iago, or any of the pure, Italianate Renaissance villains—feels no compunction about conventional lawlessness since his own desires are the only demands he will acknowledge. . . . On the other hand, the values of society do have meaning and importance for the romantic rebel, since he has a social feeling that prompts him to set himself up as antagonist."[33] Most of the romantic rebels resemble Byron's Corsair, the pirate who succumbs because he disrupts battle to save innocent women, then recoils horrified by the murder perpetrated by the women to save him. Corsair possesses "a single virtue and a thousand crimes," and it is the one virtue—human compassion—that leads to his demise. But ultimately Corsair is heroic precisely because he violates his own role as self-imposed moral arbiter, allows his "one virtue" to surface. Byron's Manfred, isolated in the privacy of self, is as the abbot says him, in a chaos of principles,

> . . . an awful chaos—light and darkness,
> And mind and dust, and passions and pure thoughts,
> Mix'd, and contending without end or order,—
> All dormant or destructive. (III, ii, 164–67)

33 Frederick Garber, "Self, Society, Value, and the Romantic Hero," *Comparative Literature*, XIX (1967), 325.

For Byron, man separated from God can only assert personal pride; but perhaps such assertion is less a matter of satanic defiance than of human psychological necessity. That which enables the hero to overcome "le néant" of Byron's Manfred is, Lamartine writes, "Noble instinct! conscience! ô vérité du coeur!" Seemingly self-generated, this "vérité du coeur" is in actuality part of a trinity—God, nature, man—which shares a common cosmic consciousness:

> I see infinity dawn and reflect itself
> All the way to the sunny seas which the night makes white;
> It diffuses its rays and there is nature;
> They are focused, and it is God . . .
> And life and death are without cease and without end
> The ebb and flow of the divine ocean![34]

Through adherence to this "vérité du coeur" the hero brings himself into harmony with "L'océan divin." As Coleridge reveals in his *Aids to Reflection*, the Romantic yearns always to be part of a greater harmony:

Will any reflecting man admit, that his own Will is the only and sufficient determinant of all he *is*, and all he does? Is nothing to be attributed to the harmony of the system to which he belongs, and to the pre-established Fitness of the Objects and Agents, known and unknown, that surround him, as acting *on* the will, though doubtless, *with* it likewise?

"For the hero, but never for the villain," Garber concludes, "one or another form of love—sex, friendship, or general human compassion—seem[s] always to get in the way" of his satanic tendencies.[35]

The problems arising from virtually any examination of the ro-

---

34 Lamartine, "Novissima verba," in *Oeuvres Poétiques Complètes*, 483, 484.

> . . . je vois l'infini poindre et se réfléchir
> Jusqu'aux mers de soleils que le nuit fait blanchir;
> Il répand ses rayons et voilà la nature;
> Les concentre, et c'est Dieu; . . .
> Et la vie et la mort sont sans cesse et sans fin
> Ce flux et ce reflux de l'océan divin!

35 Frederick Garber, "Self, Society, Value, and the Romantic Hero," 329.

mantic hero are implicit in Thorslev's studies; the nature of the hero is determined by those characters selected for analysis. Certainly the tradition of the satanic rebel developing out of the English Renaissance colored many of the gothic figures in late-eighteenth-century literature, and bears resemblance to certain later heroes as well—Manfred, for example, or Ahab, even Faust. But we must remember that every protagonist in romantic literature is not a hero; any theory of heroism which provides no basis for distinguishing a Cenci from a Prometheus, or a Schedoni from a Werther proves an inadequate explanation of the romantic heroic personality. Byron writes at the outset of *Don Juan*: "I want a hero: an uncommon want,/ When every year and month sends forth a new one"; indeed, the variety of heroes, the multiplicity of types and traditions involved, renders futile any attempt to locate a single prototypical hero. We are confronted instead with various, often contradictory, modes of romantic heroism.

To appreciate the contributions of romantic thought to our understanding of the heroic ideal it is necessary to review, at least briefly, the evolution of the concept of heroism in Western culture. In the twentieth century many scholars are prone to believe with W. H. Auden that the hero is simply the "exceptional individual . . . one who possesses authority over the average."[36] Sidney Hook agrees, arguing that "the hero in history is the individual to whom we can justifiably attribute preponderant influence in determining an issue or event whose consequence would have been profoundly different if he had not acted as he did."[37] But the theory of heroism offered by Auden and Hook renders irrelevant any consideration of the hero's moral character, or even of the moral quality of his contribution; indeed, Hook writes, "we must rule out as irrelevant the conception of the hero as a morally worthy man, not because ethical

---

36 W. H. Auden, *The Enchafèd Flood; or, The Romantic Iconography of the Sea* (New York, 1950), 93.
37 Sidney Hook, *The Hero in History: A Study in Limitation and Possibility* (Boston, 1969), 153–54.

judgments are illegitimate in history, but because so much of it has been made by the wicked" (154). For many of us, I suspect, the logical implications of Hook's premise prove distasteful: if the sole criterion for heroism is the extent to which the individual affects history or the course of civilization, then, regardless of political persuasion or moral beliefs, one would have to consider a man like Hitler heroic.

The process of enshrining heroes, however, demands some evaluation of the quality or nature of a man's effect upon history. We tend to consider heroic those individuals whose actions are not only grand but reflect our culture's shared values. W. B. Yeats writes, "When the imaginary saint or lover or hero moves us most deeply, it is the moment when he awakens within us for an instant our own heroism, our own sanctity, our own desire."[38] Emerson and Whitman would agree. For both, the hero personifies or makes tangible the ideals of a culture. Hence the true hero is never the individual but the mass of humanity he represents: "What is best written or done by genius in the world," Emerson writes, "was no man's work, but came by wide social labor, when a thousand wrought like one, sharing the same impulse."[39]

Auden, Hook, Yeats, Emerson, and Whitman share a firm conviction that the hero is irrevocably bound to his social order. No matter how great a man may be, his heroism traditionally has been conferred by a culture that recognizes his contribution and places positive value upon it. Even if the moral quality of the hero is irrelevant, the moral quality of his contribution is crucial. The hero of Virgil's *Aeneid*, G. R. Levy contends, establishes the precedent of the hero's inextricable tie to his social world: "The hero, no longer solicitous only to maintain the freedom of intact honor, where personal prestige was the sole source of integration, henceforth owed

38   W. B. Yeats, *Samhain*, No. 5 (Dublin, 1905), 11.
39   Ralph Waldo Emerson, *Representative Men*, vol. IV of E. W. Emerson (ed.), *The Complete Works of Ralph Waldo Emerson* (12 vols.; Boston, 1903), 199. On this subject see F. O. Matthiessen, *American Renaissance: Art and Expression in the Age of Emerson and Whitman* (New York, 1941), 632–34.

his primary allegiance to a cause. He was the subject, even if also the creator, of a temporal or spiritual dominion with which he had become in some measure identified."[40] Levy is certainly correct to emphasize the importance of social obligation to Virgil's concept of heroism, but her implication that "personal prestige was the sole source of integration" with earlier heroes is a bit misleading. Joseph Campbell points out that, as a rule, even the mythological hero functioned within a social sphere: "The full round, the norm of the monomyth, requires that the hero shall now begin the labor of bringing the runes of wisdom, the Golden Fleece, or his sleeping princess, back into the kingdom of humanity, where the boon may redound to the renewing of the community."[41]

Whereas Aeneas is indisputably the hero with a social mission and sense of civic responsibility, Achilles is frequently treated as the example of the early hero whose sole obligation is to the self. H. M. Chadwick, discussing *The Iliad*, writes:

It is essential to notice that the object so much prized is personal glory. . . . Occasionally we hear also of pride of family, but scarcely ever of any truly national feeling. Patroclos exhorts his men to bravery in order that they may earn glory not for the Achaean nation but for their own personal lord; and he adds further that by so doing they will bring shame upon the national leader. Achilles himself retires from the conflict owing to a personal wrong, and only returns to it in order to avenge his friend.[42]

But I think it is possible to overstate this aspect of Achilles' heroism to the extent that we misunderstand it. Achilles is not heroic because he pouts, withdrawing from his duty and destiny because of a personal affront to his honor; indeed, he is heroic in spite of his petulant behavior. Finally, Achilles' bravery and military prowess save the day for the Achaeans; he is remembered in Greek mythology and immortalized in Homer's poem because he wins a war that, without his participation, might well have been lost. Homer uses

---

40   G. R. Levy, *The Sword from the Rock: An Investigation into the Origins of Epic Literature and the Development of the Hero* (London, 1953), 215.

41   Joseph Campbell, *The Hero with a Thousand Faces* (New York, 1949), 193.

42   H. M. Chadwick, *The Heroic Age* (Cambridge, 1912), 329.

Hector—always conscious of his duty to Troy—as a contrast to highlight the folly of Achilles' self-indulgence. Regardless of his motives for doing so, Achilles does in fact return to battle; and it is the nature of his contribution, his effect on history so to speak, that earns him heroic stature. Hence I would argue that Virgil only gives full development to a crucial aspect of heroism already implicit in Homer.

In last analysis the romantic hero is far more traditional than he is modern. To fail to give full consideration to the profoundly moral quality of romantic thought is to misunderstand the movement. Cooke argues that romantic consciousness is "consciousness for" something, and "conveys the personal engagement and extension of the self into the object encountered and the shaping or becoming of the self that this entails. Thus, even if we see neoclassicism as teleological, and so biased toward conduct, and romanticism as etiological, or biased toward consciousness, the full implications of the latter really subsume some of the terms of the former position, to the extent that consciousness . . . implies a conduct of being."[43] The hero in romanticism appears peculiarly modern only when we strip away the moral premises that underlie him, when we are no longer able to see as clearly immoral Milton's Satan, Ahab, Cenci. Peter Thorslev's comment that the "pressing ethical and metaphysical problems" posed by the satanic romantic hero "receive their philosophical formulations only with the advent of Nietzsche and modern existentialism" points up this major obstacle confronting our understanding of the nature of romantic heroism. Modern scholars typically approach the romantics from a twentieth-century perspective, emphasizing in them those themes or motifs later developed by a Nietzsche, Buber, or Sartre, and ignoring crucial elements which seem implausible to the modern mind. I. A. Richards, for example, adopts Coleridge's poetic theory only after pruning it from its epistemological bases—which he terms "bogus entities";[44] but without

43 Cooke, *The Romantic Will*, 4.
44 I. A. Richards, *Principles of Literary Criticism* (1925; rpt. New York, 1968), 191–94. Later, in *Coleridge on Imagination* (Bloomington, Ind., 1934), Richards seems

17

the transcendental superstructure from which they organically develop, Coleridge's theories seem distinctly un-Coleridgean. Similarly, one might see the romantic hero, isolated in the self and cut off from any sustaining orthodoxy, as caught in the existential dilemma. Victor Brombert points out that "behind the impregnable solitude and compulsive self-centeredness of the [romantic hero] lurks the secret awareness that no relation can exist between man and man"; Wylie Sypher argues that "the romantic quest for freedom changed into the existentialist quest for an authentic self capable of being identified and sustained amid the average."[45] But such a dilemma seems at odds with Wordsworth's definition of the poet as "a man speaking to men,"[46] or Coleridge's Mariner, who must purge his guilt by telling his story to others about to embark on a wedding feast.

Although, as Lilian R. Furst has shown, the romantic hero "stands already well on the way to the modern anti-hero," he is not there yet.[47] The twentieth-century anti-hero is the product of artists who dug out "private caves, or air-raid shelters, of their own, and there they started to compose private satires, laments, fantasies and myths in the effort to fill the vacuum left by the death of the social Hero with a-social rebels, martyrs, misfits, minor prophets, or, in short, with aberrants and anti-heroes."[48] In a seriously fragmented culture that provides few shared moral values, the modern artist turns to a private, self-generated heroic code. Alex Zwerdling writes: "The qualities of heroism in the twentieth century have be-

---

more willing to compromise with Coleridge, adopting his transcendentalism as an appropriate "speculative instrument."

45   Brombert, "The Happy Prison," 78; Sypher, *Loss of Self in Modern Literature and Art*, 29.

46   William Wordsworth, "Preface to the Lyrical Ballads" (1800), in Thomas Hutchinson (ed.), *Wordsworth: Poetical Works*, rev. Ernest de Selincourt (London, 1969), 737.

47   Lilian R. Furst, *The Contours of European Romanticism* (London, 1979), 40.

48   Sean O'Faolain, *The Vanishing Hero: Studies in Novelists of the Twenties* (Boston, 1957), 14.

come almost totally unpredictable because they depend on the individual, private code of the writer."[49]

The crucial point thus far ignored in scholarly discussions of romantic heroism is that the concept of the hero requires a prior conception of a heroic ideal; it is the nature of this ideal, generated from the theoretical context of romanticism, that commands scrutiny. Admittedly it is difficult to locate a single figure who embodies the ideal, for by their mortality most romantic heroes are unable to sustain what is essentially a transcendental dimension. Many romantic artists have serious reservations about their heroes; in fact, René, Werther, Alastor, Ahab, Pechorin, Rappaccini, Dostoevsky's underground man all serve primarily as negative examples, demonstrating the human perversion of the heroic ideal. But taken as a group, understood within the theoretical context of romanticism, individual protagonists do provide a prescription for heroism even while demonstrating, at times, the impossibility of achieving it.

George Boas points out that the Romantic's quest, "whether for a woman or a blue flower, is a search for something beyond oneself,"[50] and the hero is not quite prepared to admit with the modern existentialist that the transcendental realm inhabited by the woman, the blue flower, nightingale, or skylark does not exist. The introspection characteristic of the romantic hero poses solipsistic dangers, as most artists were well aware. Novalis writes, "An absolute urge towards perfection and completeness is a kind of disease, as soon as it adopts a destructive and hostile attitude towards the imperfect, the incomplete," and Hamburger has shown that the German romantics, as a group, came to identify "evil with consciousness itself."[51] Yet to suggest that there exists no realm outside of the hero's heightened self-consciousness is to ignore the crucial fact of the romantic heroic quest: self-absorption is only a middle point in

49 Alex Zwerdling, *Yeats and the Heroic Ideal* (New York, 1965), 8.
50 George Boas, "The Romantic Self: An Historical Sketch," *Studies in Romanticism*, IV (Autumn, 1964), 14.
51 Hamburger, *Contraries*, 7. Hamburger translates the passage from Novalis cited in this sentence.

a larger passage, a purgatory so to speak, through which the hero must pass to gain access to a cosmic consciousness which brings true union with all mankind. As Geoffrey Hartman writes, "the Romantic poets do not exalt consciousness *per se*. They have recognized it as a kind of death-in-life. . . . Consciousness is only a middle-term, the strait through which everything must pass."[52]

Hartman's essay is immensely important as it calls attention to the vital romantic dialectic between self-consciousness and communal responsibility. Hölderlin writes: "There is only one quarrel in this world: which is more important, the whole or the individual part?" The artist and his heroic projection face the task of grasping an ideal vision that transcends the given empirical world. Access to the vision is available only through absorption into the self, which shares kinship with the vision's divine origin. "Inwards leads the mysterious way," writes Novalis; "within us, or nowhere, is eternity with all its worlds, the past and future." But the ultimate goal is union with an all-pervasive cosmic superstructure, for "the idea of the microcosm is the very highest to which man can attain."[53] Cooke briefly traces this tension as it develops in German idealistic philosophy, demonstrating that though the German transcendentalists celebrated the autonomous self they strove to place the self within a larger context:

Fichte himself, though given to what Coleridge calls a "crude egoismus," proves sus-

---

52 Geoffrey Hartman, "Romanticism and Anti-Self Consciousness," in Harold Bloom (ed.), *Romanticism and Consciousness*, 50–51. Alex Comfort offers something of a compromise position between George Boas or Geoffrey Hartman, and the more existential or nihilistic critics. For Comfort, romantic idealism is crucial to the movement, but the source and limit of such idealism lies in the hero's consciousness: "The distinguishing feature of the metaphysical theory which underlies romanticism is that it rejects the inevitable victory or inherence of these ideals without rejecting the ideals themselves. They exist only so long as man himself exists and fights for them." See Alex Comfort, *Art and Social Responsibility: Lectures on the Ideology of Romanticism* (London, 1946), 18.

53 Novalis, "Blütenstaub," in *Novalis Schriften*, II, 418. "Nach Innen geht der geheimniβvolle Weg. In uns, oder nirgends ist die Ewigkeit mit ihren Welten—die Vergangenheit und Zukunft."

ceptible to system, if not to "nature," and has come to seem a forerunner of totalitarian German philosophy; putting man in society, he sees perfect freedom in perfect obedience. In like manner, Schelling . . . leaves man autonomous in relation to "the objective world" only to lose him, qua individual, in . . . the idea of mankind as "a single consummate person" obeying the "law of freedom," and achieving "identity with the Absolute."[54]

"There is an oblivion of all existence, a silencing of all individual being, in which it seems as if we had found all things," Hölderlin writes in *Hyperion*; but also "there is a silencing, an oblivion of all existence, in which it seems as if we had lost all things, a night of the soul, in which not the faintest gleam of a star, not even the phosphorescence of rotten wood can reach us."[55] The first state that Hölderlin describes is the romantic ideal; the second is the tragic consequence befalling those unable to progress beyond solipsism. Union with cosmic consciousness requires an annihilation of self, a condition in which, as Emerson claims, "all mean egotism vanishes" and man becomes "part or particle of God."[56] Having transcended self through the self, the romantic poet or hero is prepared to assume his role as prophet, receiving then communicating his vision to mankind:

> Yet, fellow poets, us it behooves to stand
> Bare-headed beneath God's thunderstorms,
> To grasp the Father's ray, no less, with our own two hands
> And, wrapping in song the beautiful gift,
> To offer it to the people.
> For only if we are pure in heart,

---

54 Cooke, *The Romantic Will*, 81.

55 Hölderlin, *Sämtliche Werke*, ed. Friedrich Seebass (4 vols.; Berlin, 1943), II, 136.

Es giebt ein Vergessen alles Daseyns, ein Verstummen unsers Wesens, wo uns ist, als hätten wir alles gefunden.
Es giebt ein Verstummen, ein Vergessen alles Daseyns, wo uns ist, als hätten wir alles verloren, eine Nacht unsrer Seele, wo kein Schimmer eines Sterns, wo nicht einmal ein faules Hotz uns leuchtet.

56 Emerson, "Nature," *Collected Works*, I, 10.

Like children, and our hands are guiltless,
The Father's ray, the pure, will not sear our hearts. [57]

The romantic heroic ideal thus involves first an annihilation of self and assimilation of a transcendental consciousness, then a commitment to one's fellows that propels the hero into a prophetic, at times messianic, role. Poets are, Shelley asserts, "the hierophants of an unapprehended inspiration . . . the unacknowledged legislators of the world"; as Novalis confesses, "We are engaged on a mission: we are called to fashion a world." [58] Behind the genre of the *Universalgeschichte* in German romantic art and philosophy lies Pascal's claim that we might "consider the entire sequence of human beings, during the entire course of the Ages, as a single man who lives perpetually and learns something all the time." [59] In his essay entitled "Literary Ethics," Emerson insists that the poet achieves heroic stature only insofar as he participates in a monolithic "universal nature" that enables him to transcend self-consciousness:

The condition of our incarnation in a private self, seems to be, a perpetual tendency to prefer the private law, to obey the private impulse, to the exclusion of the law of universal being. The great man is great by means of the predominance of the universal nature; he has only to open his mouth, and it speaks; he has only to be forced to act, and it acts. (*Collected Works*, I, 104–105)

57 Hölderlin, "Wie wenn am Feiertage," in *Sämtliche Werke*, IV, 153.

> Doch uns gebührt es, unter Gottes Gewittern,
> Ihr Dichter! mit entblösstem Haupte zu stehen,
> Des Vaters Strahl, ihn selbst, mit eigner Hand
> Zu fassen und dem Volk ins Lied
> Gehüllt die himmlische gabe zu reichen.
> Denn sind nur reinen Herzens,
> Wie Kinder, wir, sind schuldlos unsere Hände,
> Des Vaters Stral, der reine versengt es nicht . . .

58 Percy Bysshe Shelley, "A Defense of Poetry," in David Lee Clark (ed.), *Shelley's Prose; or, The Trumpet of a Prophecy* (Albuquerque, N.M., 1954), 297; Novalis, "Blütenstaub," in *Novalis Schriften*, II, 426. "Wir sind auf einer *Mission*. Zur Bildung der Erde sind wir berufen."

59 See Abrams, *Natural Supernaturalism*, 201.

Most of the romantic artists embody what Hartman labels the major element of French romanticism, the attempt "to generate the communal from the individual, or to regenerate it from within self-consciousness."[60] Blake, Wordsworth, Shelley, Carlyle, Fichte, Schelling, Hegel, Hölderlin, and Novalis—Abrams writes—"conceived themselves as elected spokesmen for the western tradition at a time of profound cultural crises. They are represented in the traditional persona of the philosopher-seer or the poet-prophet . . . and they set out, in various yet recognizably parallel ways, to reconstitute the grounds of hope and to announce the certainty . . . of a rebirth in which renewed mankind will inhabit a renovated earth where he will find himself thoroughly at home."[61]

Influenced by Herder, the romantic artist comes to perceive "the whole man functioning as an integral part of an organic social whole," and in the figure of the hero explores the burdens and responsibilities of membership in a community, of what it means to belong "to a time, a place, and a group."[62] In his epic *La Chute d'un Ange*, Lamartine describes the transcendental vision that the poet-hero receives, an awareness of man's place in the cosmic order and a recognition of the humanistic moral obligations which that place thrusts upon him:

> The only divine book in which he writes
> His ever-expanding name, man, is your spirit!
> It is your reason, the mirror of supreme reason,
> Where there is presented in your darkness some shadow of itself.
> He speaks to us, O mortals, but it is in that one sense!
> All fleshly mouths alter God's words.
> The mind in us and the nature outside us,
> Here is the voice of God, the rest is imposture![63]

---

60 Geoffrey Hartman, "Reflections on Romanticism in France," in Thorburn and Hartman (eds.), *Romanticism: Vistas, Instances, Continuities*, 42.

61 Abrams, *Natural Supernaturalism*, 12.

62 *Ibid.*, 199–200.

63 Lamartine, "Huitième Vision," *Oeuvres Poétiques Complètes*, 942–43.

  Le seul livre divin dans lequel il écrit

For Hugo, "le poète est prêtre," a prophetic figure who must assume his messianic role within a decidedly social and political context:

It is above all to make reparations for the sophists' errors that we, today, should attach ourselves to the poet. He should walk before all people as a light and show them the way. He should restore to all the grand principles of order, morality and honor. And so that his power not overwhelm them, it is necessary that all the chords of the human heart vibrate under his fingers as the chords of a lyre. He will never echo a single word unless it originates from God. He will always remember what his predecessors have too often forgotten, that for him there is also one religion and one country.[64]

The romantic hero for Hugo prefigures a higher form of culture; the vision of such culture he receives intuitively, then tries to communicate it to mankind. He is, according to Ridge, "a prototype of the Messiah, whom the masses do not understand and rarely love but come to follow in time."[65] Wordsworth writes in his "Preface" to the 1802 edition of *Lyrical Ballads*: "The Poet binds together by passion and knowledge the vast empire of human society."

In this first chapter I have attempted to present the difficulties besetting any comprehensive examination of romantic heroism, to

---

Son nom toujours croissant, homme, c'est ton esprit!
C'est ta raison, miroir de la raison suprême,
Où se peint dans ta nuit quelque ombre de lui-même.
Il nous parle, ô mortels, mais c'est par ce seul sens!
Toute bouche de chair altère ses accents.
L'intelligence en nous, hors de nous la nature,
Voilà les voix de Dieu, le reste est imposture!

64 Victor Hugo, "William Shakespeare," *Philosophie II*, in *Oeuvres Complètes* (45 vols.; Paris, 1904–52), 42; "Préface" (1824) to "Odes et Ballades," in Bernard Leuilliot (ed.), *Victor Hugo: Poésie* (3 vols.; Paris, 1972), I, 84. "C'est surtout à réparer le mal fait par les sophistes que doit s'attacher aujourd'hui le poète. Il doit marcher devant les peuples comme une lumière et leur montrer le chemin. Il doit les ramener à tous les grands principes d'ordre, de morale et d'honneur; et, pour que sa puissance leur soit douce, il faut que toutes les fibres du coeur humain vibrent sous ses doigts comme les cordes d'une lyre. Il ne sera jamais l'écho d'aucune parole, si ce n'est de celle de Dieu. Il se rappellera toujours ce que ses prédécesseurs ont trop oublié, que lui aussi il a une religion et une patrie."

65 Ridge, *The Hero in French Romantic Literature*, 86. See also Zumthor, *Victor Hugo: Poète de Satan*, 121.

outline and to scrutinize the major scholarly approaches to the subject, and to move toward an understanding of the heroic ideal emerging from the period. Though my approach here, and throughout the book, is comparative, I make little attempt to distinguish among national movements; that has been done very well by Wellek, Wasserman, and Furst.[66] Implicit is that there is a definable romantic movement, international in scope, encompassing the historical period roughly established by Wellek and Frye,[67] though extending in America to include the writers of the mid-century renaissance. To stress the essential unity of the romantic movement as a whole, I have selected examples from English, German, French, and American literature to illustrate theses that apply, more or less, to all.

My analysis of romantic heroism is not, as most others have been, a study of types or traditions. Rather, its approach is thematic, examining a number of heroes representative of the various national movements in light of motifs that lie at the heart of romanticism in general: the hope of annihilation of self-consciousness through art (Chapter II); the quest for escape from egocentric self-absorption through various forms of religion as a focus of belief and aesthetic (Chapter III); the tension between the exercise of romantic will and submission to the demands of communal responsibility (Chapter IV); the self-destructive effects of narcissistic love, which debilitates both individual and community (Chapters V and VI); and the recognition of the inevitable failure of heroism which results in a peculiarly romantic concept of tragedy (Chapter VII). No attempt is made to be all-inclusive; though a large number of individual heroes receive extended analysis, many others do not. In my

---

66 Wellek, "The Concept of Romanticism in Literary History"; Earl Wasserman, "The English Romantics: The Grounds of Knowledge," *Studies in Romanticism*, III (1964), 17–34; Furst, *Romanticism in Perspective*.

67 Wellek, "The Concept of Romanticism in Literary History"; Frye assumes the period 1790–1830 as the "historical center" of romanticism—see Northrop Frye, "The Drunken Boat: The Revolutionary Element in Romanticism," in Northrop Frye (ed.), *Romanticism Reconsidered*, 1.

selection of examples I have tried to give full consideration to those heroes who proved most influential in the development of the romantic movement, but inevitably the reader will discover that I have overlooked or slighted heroes deserving more sustained consideration. Further, the thematic organizational principle of the book defies strict adherence to chronology. Though the study begins with the early hero of sensibility and gradually progresses toward the movement's climactic expression in the mid–nineteenth-century American Renaissance, several chapters trace a particular theme through several romantic literatures that span the period 1770–1860. Collectively, however, the essays that follow illustrate the nature of the romantic heroic ideal, as well as the many perversions of it; and the generalizations they offer should prove applicable to the vast range of romantic literature.

Louisiana State University Press is pleased to send this book to you for review.

Price $ 18.50
_____

Publication date 10/31/82
_____

Please note price and publication date in reviews and notices.

We request that your review be held until the above date and that two clippings be sent to

Louisiana State University Press
Baton Rouge, Louisiana 70803

Pamela Dear?

II

The Aesthetic Quest for Self-annihilation

Increasingly the dominant scholarly response to Goethe's *Die Leiden des jungen Werthers* (1774) has been to treat the novel as a kind of negative conduct book. By portraying an acutely sensitive character whose feverish pursuit of an ideal leads him from reality to wrestle with an insubstantial infinite, Goethe provides a model of action (or inaction) which the enlightened man of sensibility must avoid. The result, Hans Reiss contends, is that in *Werther* "all that we learn is that egocentric feeling is not a safe guide for living."[1] Echoing Reiss, Harry Steinhauer attacks the once prevalent scholarly response that Werther is an admirable man driven by noble passion to his demise in a radically imperfect world order,[2] because—Steinhauer argues—such an interpretation ignores the fact that Goethe's sympathies did not lie with his hero: "the documentary evidence, both within and outside the text, refutes this assumption beyond dispute."[3]

1   Hans Reiss, *Goethe's Novels* (Coral Gables, Fla., 1971), 43.
2   This position was argued by Herbert Schöffler, *Die Leiden des jungen Werther: Ihr geistesgeschichtlicher Hintergrund* (Frankfurt, 1938).
3   Harry Steinhauer, "Afterword," in Goethe, *The Sufferings of Young Werther*, trans. Harry Steinhauer (New York, 1970), 117.

Both Reiss and Steinhauer ground their reading of the novel in Goethe's belated disavowal of sympathy for his hero, a disavowal which sprang in large part from response to public reaction to the novel.[4] This public reaction included an outbreak of suicides (especially in France) among young men who—suffering from *mal du siècle*—found themselves mirrored in Werther; it also included the angry response of Johann Kestner (the model for Albert in the novel), who vehemently protested Goethe's portrayal of Albert and of Lotte's love for the hero. Goethe promised Kestner in an autumn 1774 letter that he would revise *Die Leiden des jungen Werthers* within a year, omitting those aspects which Kestner found distasteful.[5] And no doubt dismayed by the suicides, Goethe in his revision of the novel did undercut reader sympathy for the hero: Reiss contends that in the revised novel the hero's love for Lotte is unreturned and that Albert—Werther's antagonist—is more clearly noble.[6] Reading proofs of an 1824 reprint of the novel to commemorate the fiftieth anniversary of its publication, Goethe, Steinhauer informs us, "was strengthened in the aversion which he had expressed in conversation to different people over the years."[7] Though this revision brought the novel more in line with Goethe's mature (and increasingly conservative) sensibilities, the author perhaps noticed a certain tapering off in power and invention; conceivably speaking for Goethe, Werther writes to Wilhelm:

From this I've learned that an author must inevitably hurt his book by issuing a second, revised edition of his story, no matter how greatly it may be improved from the literary point of view. The first impression finds us receptive, and man is so constituted that he can be persuaded to believe the strangest things; but these impressions at once cling firmly to his memory, and woe to him who tries to erase and destroy them![8]

4 Gertrud Reiss, "Die beiden Fassungen von Goethes *Die Leiden des Werthers*" (Ph.D. dissertation, Breslau, 1924), 10.
5 See the letter in Hanna Fischer-Lamberg (ed.), *Der Junge Goethe* (6 vols.; Berlin, 1963–74), IV, 254–55.
6 Hans Reiss, *Goethe's Novels*, 41.
7 Steinhauer, "Afterword," *The Sufferings of Young Werther*, 124.
8 J. W. Goethe, *Die Leiden des jungen Werther*, vol. VI of Erich Trunz (ed.), *Goethes Werke* (14 vols.; Hamburg, 1949–60), 51. All references to *Werther* are to this

Because of the current scholarly fashion to undercut and vilify Werther, it is a necessary corrective to recall that the hero of *Die Leiden des jungen Werthers* emerged as a forlorn figure embodying all of the characteristics in vogue among readers of eighteenth-century sentimental fiction. Unable to find avenues for the expression of his idealism and sensitivity in civilized society, Werther nevertheless enjoys an affinity with nature that gives him spiritual resiliency. Werther rejects the cold, codified precepts of reason, and like Rousseau's Madame de Warens, takes moral guidance from the impulses of the heart. He condemns the neoclassical fondness for rules and established authority in art and reveres the heartfelt genius of Homer, Klopstock, and Ossian. The civilized town for Werther is "unerträglich," as he longs for a simple, pastoral existence among rural peasants with their abounding natural virtues of love, loyalty, and passion. Indeed, Goethe's brief prefatory remarks reflect a tacit anticipation of an audience that shares the hero's sentimental inclinations: "Whatever I have been able to discover about the story of poor Werther, I have collected with diligence, and I place it before you, and I know you will thank me for it. You cannot withold your admiration or your love from his spirit and character, nor your tears from his fate."[9]

Werther is the prototype of a series of melancholy, solipsistic romantic heroes ranging from Chateaubriand's René in France, Shelley's Visionary in *Alastor*, Keats's Endymion, and Byron's Harold—in England—to Melville's Ishmael and Mark Twain's Huck Finn in America. As such, he comes into clearer perspective when

---

edition. English translations that appear in the text are from *The Sufferings of Young Werther*, trans. Harry Steinhauer. "Ich habe daraus gelernt, wie ein Autor duch eine zweite, veränderte Ausgabe seiner Geschichte, und wenn sie poetisch noch so besser geworden wäre, notwendig seinem Buche schaden muß. Der erste Eindruck findet uns willig, und der Mensch ist gemacht, daß man ihn das Abenteuerlichste überreden kann; das haftet aber auch gleich so fest, und wehe dem, der es wieder auskratzen und austilgen will!"

9 "Was ich von der Geschichte des armen Werther nur habe auffinden können, habe ich mit Fleiß gesammelt und lege es euch hier vor, und weiß, daß ihr mir's danken werdet. Ihr könnt seinem Geist und seinem Charakter eure Bewunderung und Liebe, seinem Schicksale eure Tränen nicht versagen" (p. 7).

examined in light of subsequent developments in romantic ideology which he foreshadows and to a certain extent formulates. If one were a hard-headed rationalist one might treat Werther disdainfully—as do Reiss and Steinhauer—as a selfish, moody n'er-do-well who clearly portrays the inevitable, almost Darwinistic, demise of the individual who violates Pope's maxims in *An Essay on Man*: "And who but wishes to invert the laws/ Of order, sins against the Eternal Cause. . . . To reason right, is to submit." Or one might approach Werther more sympathetically as a foreshadowing of the Shelleyan or Keatsian hero who is doomed in his attempt to locate in the mortal world the vision of beauty emerging from his divine imagination and made tauntingly apparent in the guise of "la belle dame sans merci." Approached from the latter perspective, Werther's hopeless quest of Lotte becomes his militant struggle against the confining dimensions of pale mortality. The tragedy of Goethe's 1774 hero— and of romantic heroes generally—is his inability to experience unadulterated the blisses of "heaven's bourne."

A discernible pattern in the poetry of Shelley and Keats is the presentation of the agonized man of sensibility (usually the artist) who is granted a privileged insight into the nature of beauty and truth; but this insight is a double-edged sword, as the exquisite pleasure provided by the glimpses of immortality is counteracted by an unbearable sense of pain resulting from the mortal poet's awareness of his alienation from the realm he glimpses momentarily. In *Alastor* (1816), Shelley endows the hero's visions of perfection with female form; a "veiled maid," the envisioned ideal, spoke with a voice that "was like the voice of his own soul/ . . . / Knowledge and truth and virtue were her theme,/ And lofty hopes of divine liberty." [10] Enveloped in a dream vision, the poet is freed from self-consciousness, and in an erotic interlude surrenders "in her dissolving arms." Awakening from his dream, the poet finds himself in "the cold white light of morning"; the vision has evaporated, leaving behind only the conditions of mortality—an "empty scene" and "vacant woods":

10 Percy B. Shelley, *Shelley: Poetical Works*, ed. Thomas Hutchinson; rev. G. M. Matthews (London, 1970), 18, 11. 153–54. All subsequent references to Shelley's poetry are to this edition.

> Whither have fled
> The hues of heaven that canopied his bower
> Of yesternight? The sounds that soothed his sleep,
> The mystery and the majesty of Earth,
> The joy, the exultation? (11. 196–200)

Painfully aware that the "beautiful shape" is "Lost, lost, for ever lost,/ In the wide pathless desert of dim sleep" (11. 209–210), the poet is tragically removed from the vital forces of life, forever in quest of the forever elusive vision. "Thus driven/ By the bright shadow of that lovely dream," the Visionary is oblivious to the genuine human love offered by the Arab maiden and is, in effect, dead:

> Life, and the lustre that consumed it, shone
> As in a furnace burning secretly
> From his dark eyes alone. The cottagers,
> Who ministered with human charity
> His human wants, beheld with wondering awe
> Their fleeting visitant. (11. 252–57)

Earl Wasserman writes: "In the years after *Alastor*, Shelley repeatedly returned to the effect of the secret vision of perfection on the human spirit and to the frustrations of seeking to arrive in life at the unattainable point to which love tends."[11] "Lift Not the Painted Veil" portrays the dilemma of the individual who, driven by a desire for the ideal, pierces the veil of mortality, and returns to find "nor was there aught/ The world contains, the which he could approve."

The tension between the two opposing realms rending the poet receives substantial development in Shelley's tribute to Emilia Viviani, "Epipsychidion." Emilia is the poet's sister-soul, "a mortal shape indued/ With love and life and deity,/ And motion which may change but cannot die"; she is, in short, "An image of some bright Eternity" (11. 112–15). As such Emilia possesses a "glory" of being that "Stains the dead, blank, cold air with a warm shade/ Of unentangled intermixture, made/ By Love, of light and motion" (11. 91–94). She informs mortal life, giving it purpose and direction, as under her motion "life's dull billows move." But she is also unattainable

---

11 Earl Wasserman, *Shelley: A Critical Reading* (Baltimore, 1971), 417.

or insupportable in a mortal realm; hence the poet wails: "Ah, woe is me!/ What have I dared? where am I lifted? how/ Shall I descend, and perish not?" (11. 123–25). She does, however, provide the poet with glimpses of immortality necessary to raise his art above the mundane: She enables him to "blot from this sad song/ All of its much mortality and wrong" (11. 35–36), transforming his "sorrow" into "ecstasy." Wasserman contends that Emilia here reflects "the realization of his [Shelley's] own interior vision, the soul that had fled 'out of my soul.'"[12] Through the metaphor of incest, Shelley portrays the union of the poet with Emilia—his sister-soul—as the process through which man loses his self-conscious mortality and blends in harmony with the divine:

> Our breath shall intermix, our bosoms bound,
> And our veins beat together; and our lips
> With other eloquence than words, eclipse
> The soul that burns between them, and the wells
> Which boil under our being's inmost cells,
> The fountains of our deepest life, shall be
> Confused in Passion's golden purity.
> ....
> We shall become the same, we shall be one
> Spirit with two frames. . . . (11. 565–74)

This union of the poet with the divine—while preserved in art—vanishes in mortal life and renders the visionary a pathetic creature indeed:

> . . . Woe is me!
> The winged words on which my soul would pierce
> Into the height of Love's rare Universe,
> Are chains of lead around its flight of fire—
> I pant, I sink, I tremble, I expire! (11. 587–91)

John Keats differs a bit from his contemporary Shelley in that in his early poetry he portrays the union of mortal and divine as firmly rooted in concrete reality. M. H. Abrams contends that Keats "was too occupied with the solid world of concrete objects to find conge-

12 *Ibid*, 428.

nial any aesthetic philosophy of a reality beyond sense."[13] Abrams overstates the case, however, for Keats clearly looked to the visionary world as a means of self-transcendence. Endymion asks, "Wherein lies happiness? In that which becks/ Our ready minds to fellowship divine,/ A fellowship with essence; till we shine,/ Full alchemiz'd, and free of space."[14] Once we are "full alchemiz'd," freed from our mortality, "that moment have we stept/ Into a sort of oneness, and our state/ Is like a floating spirit's" (I, 11. 795–97). Like Shelley, Keats pictures this process of union as one which momentarily annihilates self-consciousness: "Melting into its radiance, we blend,/ Mingle, and so become a part of it" (I, 810–11). But for Keats in *Endymion*—which seems his response to *Alastor*—union with the vision is achieved only by accepting the beauty of the earth. Abandoning his pursuit of Cynthia, Endymion accepts the human love of Phoebe only to find her transformed into the ideal. Though one must make the inevitable journey back from heaven's bourne to "habitual self," he discovers that through the imagination he can transform cold mortality into the ideal. In a letter to Benjamin Bailey (November 22, 1817) Keats writes:

I am certain of nothing but of the holiness of the Heart's affections and the truth of Imagination—What the imagination seizes as Beauty must be truth—whether it existed before or not—for I have the same Idea of all our Passions as of Love. They are all in their sublime, creative of essential Beauty. . . . The Imagination may be compared to Adam's dream—he awoke and found it truth.[15]

Keats's optimistic belief in the power of the imagination to transform reality becomes tempered in his later poetry as increasingly the central theme becomes the tension between the vision of immortality and the conditions of human life. In his poem "God of the Meridian," Keats explores the consequences of the ecstatic state, an

13   M. H. Abrams, *The Mirror and the Lamp: Romantic Theory and the Critical Tradition* (New York, 1958), 314.

14   John Keats, *The Poems of John Keats*, ed. Jack Stillinger (Cambridge, Mass., 1978), 125. All subsequent quotations from Keats's poetry are from this edition.

15   John Keats, *The Letters of John Keats*, ed. Maurice Forman (rev. ed.; London, 1947), 67–68.

emphatic union with essence. Happiness results from the oxymoronic conditions of heaven's bourne and consequently it is experienced only through self-annihilation; yet, as Wasserman points out, "while man is mortal the projection of self cannot be complete because the spirit cannot wholly leave behind the sensory substance in which it is encased; the effort to nourish life's self by its proper pith must torment the sensory clay."[16] The knight in "La Belle Dame Sans Merci" can in a vision enter the "elfin grot" with the ideal maiden; but inevitably thoughts of mortality invade the temporary sanctuary and the grot becomes a "cold hill side" peopled by "pale kings, and princes too/ Pale warriors, death pale were they all" (11. 37–38).[17]

Typically for Keats one approaches the conditions of immortality through art. The poet in "Ode to a Nightingale" will blend with the immortal bird "Not charioted by Bacchus and his pards,/ But on the viewless wings of Poesy" (11. 32–33). Chained by his mortality to "The weariness, the fever, and the fret" of a world "where men sit and hear each other groan;/ Where palsy shakes a few, sad, last grey hairs,/ Where youth grows pale, and spectre-thin, and dies" (11. 23–26), the poet, in "embalmed darkness" can only "guess each sweet" gift from heaven's bourne. But these "guesses," which represent the imagination's attempt to capture the essence of immortality, give meaning to an otherwise painful world. Keats begins *The Fall of Hyperion* (1819) with the assertion: "Fanatics have their dreams, wherewith they weave/ A paradise for a sect; the savage, too/ From forth the loftiest fashion of his sleep/ Guesses at Heaven." Unfortunately, the savage's "guesses" are ephemeral, for they do not—as do Keats's "guesses"—receive embodiment in art:

> . . . pity these have not
> Trac'd upon vellum or wild Indian leaf
> The shadows of melodious utterance.

16 Earl Wasserman, *The Finer Tone: Keats' Major Poems* (Baltimore, 1967), 183.
17 For an excellent discussion of the process of ascent to and descent from immortality in "La Belle Dame Sans Merci," see Wasserman, *The Finer Tone*, 65–83.

But bare of laurel they live, dream, and die;
For Poesy alone can tell her dreams. (11. 4–8)

Imagination is rescued from "dumb enchantment" only by "the fine spell of words." Art lifts man above process, and in so doing strips him of self-consciousness. The "bold lover" on the Grecian urn may never kiss his maiden, but "She cannot fade . . . / For ever wilt thou love, and she be fair" (11. 19–20). In the immortal realm of art, love is "For ever warm and still to be enjoy'd,/ For ever panting, and for ever young" (11. 26–27). But the urn is a "Cold Pastoral" that, though "a friend to man" brings agony, since it makes mortal man painfully aware of his separation from a transcendent realm.

Listening to the nightingale "pouring forth thy soul abroad/ In such an ecstasy" (11. 58–59), Keats contemplates death as a release from the conditions of pale human life, an avenue to the immortal: "Now more than ever seems it rich to die,/ To cease upon the midnight with no pain." But he has doubts, fearing that death brings only oblivion: "Still wouldst thou sing, and I have ears in vain—/To thy high requiem become a sod" (11. 55–60). The bird is, in final analysis, a "deceiving elf," as its song lures the poet toward a realm he can never enter. Thoughts of his mortality intrude "like a bell/ To toll me back from thee to my sole self." Like the knight in "La Belle Dame Sans Merci," the poet in "Ode to a Nightingale" is left with only a memory of his imaginative glimpse of heaven: "Fled is that music—Do I wake or sleep?"

The imagination through art provides mortal man with his only experience of the conditions of heavenly bliss; such occurs only when the artist is able to surrender self-consciousness to his vision and be momentarily transformed. Central here is Keats's aesthetic of negative capability, the capacity of the artist to negate his identity and assume the qualities of the object contemplated. In a November, 1817 letter to Benjamin Bailey, Keats describes this process: "If a Sparrow come before my Window I take part in its existence [sic] and pic about the Gravel." [18] In a later letter to Richard Woodhouse

18   Forman (ed.), *The Letters of John Keats*, 69.

(October, 1818) Keats wrote: "A Poet is the most unpoetical of any thing in existence; because he has no Identity—he is continually in—and filling some other Body."[19] When his brother George left to voyage to America with his young bride, Keats asked that every evening at an appointed time they both read from *King Lear*. His hope was that by losing themselves in the realm of art they would achieve communion. Through negative capability, "the sense of Beauty overcomes every other consideration"; indeed, it "obliterates all consideration."[20] Art does provide escape—albeit temporary; this, however, is the most man can hope to achieve.

Considered against the background of Keats and Shelley, Werther emerges in clearer perspective. As the novel opens, Werther is in the "elfin grot," so to speak, transformed into a heavenly realm. He writes to Wilhelm: "I do not know whether deceptive spirits hover about this region or whether it is the warm, heavenly fantasies in my heart that transform everything about me into such a paradise."[21] In such a state Werther cannot execute his artistic inclinations; but because he is in a transcendent dimension he has no need of art, the conventional vehicle to that realm: "You ask whether you should send me my books—my dear friend, I beg you, in the name of Heaven, don't saddle me with them! I don't want to be guided, encouraged, inspired any more, for this heart is surging enough by itself."[22] Access to heaven's bourne has been granted Werther through the imagination; it is therefore a fictive structure, though possessing psychological reality. Just as Keats asserts "almost any

19 *Ibid.*, 228.

20 *Ibid.*, 72. James Engell examines in great detail the parallels between Keats and Goethe, emphasizing their related aesthetic concepts. As Engell notes, "Apparently, neither read anything the other wrote," but there exists, nonetheless, "an uncanny correspondence"—see *The Creative Imagination*, 277.

21 "Ich weß nicht, ob täuschende Geister um diese Gegend schweben, oder ob die warme, himmlische Phantasie in meinem Herzen ist, die mir alles rings umher so paradiesisch macht" (9).

22 "Du fragst, ob du mir meine Bücher schicken sollst? —Lieber, ich bitte dich um Gottes willen, laß mir sie vom Halse! Ich will nicht mehr geleitet, ermuntert, angefeuert sein, braust dieses Herz doch genug aus sich selbst" (10).

Man may like the spider spin from his own innards his own airy Citadel,"[23] so Werther confesses: "I turn back upon myself and find a world! But again, more in imagination and obscure desire than in actuality and living power. And so everything swims before my senses, and I smile my way dreamily through the world."[24]

In this charmed realm Werther first encounters his "belle dame," Lotte. She is his Emilia Viviani—his Cynthia or "sister soul"—who provides Werther with a glimpse of the conditions of immortality. Sharing his artistic and intellectual sympathies, she is also his doppelgänger—that "soul out of my soul" who exhibits characteristics which complement and complete his own. Just as the "sister season" spring completes and gives meaning to autumn in Shelley's "Ode to the West Wind," so Lotte's calm rationality balances Werther's tendency to emotional expansion. Significantly Werther receives warning from a female companion not to fall in love with Lotte, for she is engaged to "a very good man"; but experiencing the conditions of heaven, Werther asserts, "the information did not interest me much."[25]

Throughout *Die Leiden des jungen Werthers* there develops a pattern of ascent and descent corresponding to the similar rise to and descent from the conditions of immortality so common in Keats's poetry. And significantly Werther—like Keats's characters—makes his ascent to union with Lotte only through the medium of art. In the world of dance, music, or literature, Werther and Lotte become one; they seem momentarily to lose individual identity and merge into something larger than themselves. Shortly after meeting Lotte, Werther overhears her expressing literary preferences: "And the author I like best is the one in whose work I find my own world, the one who creates an environment like my own and whose story be-

---

23 Forman (ed.), *The Letters of John Keats*, 103.
24 "Ich kehre in mich selbst zurück, und finde eine Welt! Wieder mehr in Ahnung und dunkler Begier als in Darstellung und lebendiger Kraft. Und da schwimmt alles vor meinen Sinnen, und ich lächle dann so träumend weiter in die Welt" (13).
25 ". . . Die Nachricht war mir ziemlich gleichgültig" (20).

comes as interesting and sympathetic as my own domestic existence."[26] Werther intuitively knows that Lotte is referring to Goldsmith's *The Vicar of Wakefield* and responds: "I completely lost control of myself, told her everything that was on my mind."[27] He is transported from the finite world, and only after Lotte turns the conversation to others in the room does he notice "that they had been sitting there all this time."[28] In their discussion of literature, Werther flies like Keats's nightingale into the "forest dim":

How I feasted on those black eyes during the conversation, how those vivacious lips and those fresh, bright cheeks drew my whole being to her; how, completely absorbed in the delightful soul of her talk, I often did not hear the words in which she expressed herself! . . . In short, when we stopped in front of the pavilion, I got out of the carriage like a man in a dream and was so completely lost in dreams in the twilight world about me, that I scarcely heeded the music that echoed toward us from the brightly lit ballroom.[29]

Lotte too flees the agony of acute self-consciousness through art, informing Werther that whenever mortality weighs too heavily upon her, "I pound out a quadrille on my out-of-tune piano and everything immediately is alright again."[30] In Werther's description of Lotte dancing, the beautiful girl seems to lose self-consciousness as she is absorbed by the art form:

You should see her dance! Really, she is in it with all her heart and soul; her whole

26 "Und der Autor ist mir der liebste, in dem ich meine Welt wiederfinde, bei dem es zugeht wie um mich, und dessen Geschichte mir doch so interessant und herzlich wird als mein eigen häuslich Leben" (23).

27 "kam ich ganz außer mich, sagte ihr alles, was ich mußte."

28 "daß diese die Zeit über mit offenen Augen" (23).

29 "Wie ich mich unter dem Gespräche in den schwarzen Augen weidete—wie die lebendigen Lippen und die frischen, muntern Wangen meine ganze Seele anzogen—wie ich, in den herrlichen Sinn ihrer Rede ganz versunken, oft gar die Worte nicht hörte, mit denen sie sich ausdrückte— . . . Kurz, ich stieg aus dem Wagen wie ein Träumender, als wir vor dem Lusthause stille hielten, und war so in Träumen rings in her dämmernden Welt verloren, daß ich auf die Musik kaum achtete, die uns von dem erleuchteten Saal herunter entgegenschallte" (23–24).

30 "wenn ich was im Kopfe habe und mir auf meinem verstimmten Klavier einen Contretanz vortrommle, so ist alles wieder gut" (23).

body is one harmony, so carefree, so natural, as though there were nothing else in life, as though she thought of nothing else, felt nothing else; and I'm sure that in such moments everything vanishes before her.[31]

Like Porphyro admiring the dreaming Madeline in Keats's "Eve of St. Agnes," Werther wants desperately to enter the immortal realm with Lotte; hence he asks her to dance with him. She requests that he wait until the third dance, an allemande, for "It's the fashion here . . . that every couple belonging together remain together for the allemande."[32] As they begin dancing, Werther's ascent is complete; he is transported into the immortal realm of the gods:

I've never felt so light on my feet. I was no longer a mortal. To hold the most charming creature in my arms and to fly around with her like a whirlwind, so that everything around me faded away . . . I nevertheless took an oath that a girl that I loved, on whom I had any claim, would never waltz with anyone besides myself, even if it meant my end.[33]

Unlike Porphyro and Madeline, however, Werther and Lotte cannot flee into the storm via the magic of St. Agnes' Eve; rather they must descend to mortality. An "unbescheidenene Nachbarin" takes slices of an orange that Lotte slices, and Werther "felt a stab in my heart."[34] Then comes a woman who "wagged a threatening finger . . . and spoke the name 'Albert' twice, with much emphasis."[35]

31 "Tanzen muß man sie sehen! Siehst du, sie ist so mit ganzem Herzen und mit ganzer Seele dabei, ihr ganzer Körper eine Harmonie, so sorglos, so unbefangen, als wenn das eigentlich alles wäre, als wenn sie sonst nichts dächte, nichts empfände; und in dem Augenblicke gewiß schwindet alles andere vor ihr" (24).

32 "Es ist hier so Mode . . . daß jedes Paar, das zusammen gehört, beim Deutschen zusammenbleibt" (24).

33 "Nie ist mir's so leicht vom Flecke gegangen. Ich war kein Mensch mehr. Das liebenswürdigste Geschöpf in den Armen zu haben und mit ihr herumzufliegen wie Wetter, daß alles rings umher verging, und—Wilhelm, um ehrlich zu sein, tat ich aber doch den Schwur, daß ein Mädchen, das ich liebte, auf das ich Ansprüche hätte, mir nie mit einem andern walzen sollte als mit mir, und wenn ich drüber zugrunde gehen müßte. Du verstehst mich!" (25).

34 "daß mir . . . ein Stich durchs Herz ging."

35 "hebt einen drohenden Finger auf und nennt den Namen Albert zweimal im Vorbeifliegen mit viel Bedeutung."

The name operates on Werther like the word "forlorn" on Keats in "Ode to a Nightingale"; it "is like a bell/ To toll me back from thee to my sole self." Werther writes:

Enough—I became confused, lost my bearing, and got in with the wrong couple, so that everything was upside down, and it required all of Lotte's presence of mind, and some pulling and tugging, to put things quickly in order again.[36]

The storm outside—which Werther had explained away as heat lightning—grows more intense, "and the thunder drowned out the music."[37]

Werther and Lotte again ascend into "heaven's bourne" shortly after the dance, and, appropriately, the ascent is via the medium of art. Gazing out into the countryside, Lotte looks up at the sky, then at Werther; her eyes filling with tears, she lays her hand on his and murmurs, "Klopstock!" Werther recalls at once "the magnificent ode she had in mind and sank into the stream of emotions which she poured out over me with this password. I could not bear it, bent down over her hand and kissed it amid tears of deepest rapture. And I looked into her eyes again. —Noble man! If you had seen your apotheosis in those eyes!"[38] For a while after this moment, Werther is completely transported: "Sun, moon, and stars may calmly carry on their commerce, I don't know whether it is day or night, and the whole world around me is ceasing to exist."[39] Indeed, like Shelley with his epipsyche, Werther seems absorbed in "passion's golden purity":

I spend days as happy as those which God reserves for His saints; and whatever may

36 "Genug, ich verwirrte mich, vergaß mich und kam zwischen das unrechte Paar hinein, daß alles drunter und drüber ging und Lottens ganze Gegenwart und Zerren und Ziehen nötig war, um es schnell wieder in Ordnung zu bringen" (26).
37 "und der Donner die Musik überstimmte" (26).
38 "Ich erinnerte mich . . . der herrlichen Ode, die ihr in Gedanken lag, und versank in dem Strome von Empfindungen, den sie in dieser Losung über mich ausgoß. Ich ertrug's nicht, neigte mich auf ihre Hand und küßte sie unter den wonnevollsten Tränen. Und sah nach ihrem Auge wieder—Edler! hättest du deine Vergötterung in diesem Blicke gesehen" (27).
39 "seit der zeit können Sonne, Mond und Sterne geruhig ihre Wirtschaft treiben, ich weiß weder daß Tag noch daß Nacht ist, und die ganze Welt verliert sich um mich her" (28).

happen to me in the future, I cannot say that I have not experienced the joys, the purest joys, of life.[40]

Keats writes that heaven consists of life's moments of most intense pleasure "repeated in a finer tone";[41] by this he means that immortality duplicates blissful moments such as those experienced by Werther and Lotte stripped of the mortality that renders them ephemeral. United with Lotte in art, the hero transcends mortal despair.

She is sacred to me. All desire subsides in her presence. I never know what I feel when I am with her; it is as though my soul were whirling in every nerve. She has a tune which she plays on the piano with the touch of an angel, so simple and so spiritual. It is her favorite song and I am cured of all my anguish, confusion and despondency when she strikes the first note.

Not a word about the ancient magic power of music appears improbable to me. How the simple song moves me! And how she knows when to play it, often when I would like to put a bullet through my head. The confusion and darkness in my mind are dispelled and I breathe more freely again.[42]

Yet there still lurks Albert—the reminder of Werther's mortality, the ephemeral nature of his transcendence; when Lotte speaks of him, Werther writes, "I feel like a man who is stripped of all his honors and titles, and whose sword is taken from him."[43]

Like Keats, Werther becomes increasingly aware of the pain is-

40 "Ich lebe so glückliche Tage, wie sie Gott seinem Heiligen ausspart; und mit mir mag werden was will, so darf ich nicht sagen, daβ ich die Freuden, die reinsten Freuden des Lebens nicht genossen habe" (28).

41 Forman (ed.), *The Letters of John Keats*, 68.

42 "Sie ist mir heilig. Alle Begier schweigt in ihrer Gegenwart. Ich weiβ nie, wie mir ist, wenn ich bei ihr bin; es ist, als wenn die Seele sich mir in allen Nerven umkehrte. —Sie hat eine Melodie, die sie auf dem Klaviere spielet mit der Kraft eines Engels, so simpel und so geistvoll! Es ist ihr Leiblied, und mich stellt es von aller Pein, Verwirrung und Grillen her, wenn sie nur die erste Note davon greift.

Kein Wort von der Zauberkraft der alten Musik ist mir unwahrscheinlich. Wie mich der einfache Gesang angreift! Und wie sie ihn anzubringen weiβ, oft zur Zeit, wo ich mir eine Kugel vor den Kopf schieβen möchte! Die Irrung und Finsternis meiner Seele zerstreut sich, und ich atme wiederfreier" (39).

43 "da ist mir's wie einem, der aller seiner Ehren und Würden entsetzt und dem der Degen genommen wird" (38).

suing from the brief exposure to the conditions of immortality; he comes to understand "that which makes a man happy should also become the source of his misery."[44] While in the "elfin grot" Werther saw nature in its majestical splendour, and such exposure lifted him to divinity: "The shrubbery which grows down the arid sand hill opened up to me the inner, glowing, sacred life of nature—how I gathered all this into my warm heart, felt myself like a god in my overflowing abundance, and the glorious forms of the infinite world stirred my soul, giving life to everything."[45] Now banished from his "elfin grot," Werther discovers: "The full, warm feeling in my heart for living nature which flooded me with so much joy, which transformed the world about me into a paradise, is now becoming a source of unbearable torment for me, a torturing demon which pursues me everywhere."[46] The agonizing tension between the glimpse of immortality and the conditions of mortality leads Werther—as it does later for Keats—to long for death as an avenue to the divine; just as Keats longs to fly on the "viewless wings of poesy" with the nightingale into the "forest dim," so Werther writes: "Oh, how often did I then yearn to take the wings of a crane which flew overhead, and make for the shore of the boundless sea, to drink from the foaming cup of infinity that effervescent rapture of life, and to feel for only one moment, in my limited mental powers, a drop of the bliss of that Being who creates all things in and through Himself."[47]

44 "was des Menschen Glückseligkeit macht, wieder die Quelle seines Elendes würde" (51).

45 "wenn . . . das Geniste, das den dürren Sandhügel hinunter wächst, mir das innere, glühende, heilige Leben der Natur eröffnete: wie faβte ich das alles in mein warmes Herz, fühlte mich in der überflieβenden Fülle wie vergöttert, und die herrlichen Gestalten der unendlichen Welt bewegten sich allbelebend in meiner Seele."

46 "Das volle, warme Gefühl meines Herzens an der lebendigen Natur, das mich mit so vieler Wonne überströmte, das rings umher die Welt mir zu einem Paradiese schuf, wird mir jetzt zu einem unerträglichen Peiniger, zu einem quälenden Geist, der mich auf allen Wegen verfolgt" (51).

47 "Ach damals, wie oft habe ich mich mit Fittichen eines Kranichs, der über mich hin flog, zu dem Ufer des ungemessenen Meeres gesehnt, aus dem schäumenden

These inexpressible feelings make the hero more acutely aware of the wretchedness of his mortal condition: "A curtain has been drawn before my soul, so to speak, and the stage of infinite life is being transformed before my eyes into the abyss of an ever-open grave. Can you say 'this is,' when everything is transitory, when everything rolls by with the speed of a tempest and seldom lasts until its whole force is spent, but is swept along, alas, engulfed by the current and shattered on the rocks?"[48]

Werther's short letter of August 21 well expresses the intolerable split between the dream world of ideality and the waking world of mortality:

In vain I stretch out my arms toward her in the morning, when I wake from heavy dreams, in vain I seek her at night in my bed when a happy, innocent dream has deceived me into thinking that I was sitting beside her on that meadow, holding her hand and covering it with a thousand kisses. Oh, when I then grope for her, still half drunk with sleep, and then become fully awake through this act—a stream of tears breaks from my anguished heart, and I weep at the hopelessness of a dark future.[49]

Man's flights to immortality are always arrested by the nature of his mortality: "And when he soars in joy or sinks in suffering, is he not arrested in both, brought back to dull, cold consciousness at the

---

Becher des Unendlichen jene schwellende Lebenswonne zu trinken und nur einen Augenblick in der eingeschränkten Kraft meines Busens einen Tropfen der Seligkeit des Wesens zu fühlen, das alles in sich und durch sich hervorbringt" (52).

48 "Es hat sich vor meiner Seele wie ein Vorhang weggezogen, und der Schauplatz des unendlichen Lebens verwandelt sich vor mir in den Abgrund des ewig offenen Grabes. Kannst du sagen: Das ist! da alles vorübergeht? da alles mit der Wetterschnelle vorüberrollt, so selten die ganze Kraft seines Daseins ausdauert, ach, in den Strom fortgerissen, untergetaucht und an Felsen zerschmettert wird?" (52).

49 Umsonst strecke ich meine Arme nach ihr aus, morgens, wenn ich von schweren Träumen aufdämmere, vergebens suche ich sie nachts in meinem Bette, wenn mich ein glücklicher, unschuldiger Traum getäuscht hat, als säß' ich neben ihr auf der Wiese und hielt' ihre Hand und deckte sie mit tausend Küssen. Ach, wenn ich dann noch halb im Taumel des Schlafes nach ihr tappe und drüber mich ermuntere—ein Strom von Tränen bricht aus meinem gepreßten Herzen, und ich weine trostlos einer finstern Zukunft entgegen" (53).

very moment when he yearns to lose himself in the plenitude of the infinite?"[50] In such moments Werther can only wonder with Keats: "Was it a vision, or a waking dream,/ Fled is that music: —Do I wake or sleep?"

There are a number of parallels between *Die Leidens des jungen Werthers* and the biblical account of the crucifixion that suggest affinities between the plight of the agonized hero and the passion of Christ. These parallels have received considerable scholarly attention, so there is little need to rehearse them here; most are contained in the letter of November 15. Werther clearly sees himself as undergoing a martyrdom similar to that of Jesus. Steinhauer argues that Goethe employs the biblical analogy to suggest by contrast "the excrescence of [Werther's] disordered mind."[51] But the analogy serves a different purpose, and to a certain degree is an apt one. Like Jesus, Werther knows the ideal, for he embodies it; also like Jesus he must live in the mortal world and suffer from it. Central to Christology is the understanding that Jesus is not some hybrid creature who is half human, half divine; rather he is simultaneously wholly mortal and wholly God. So too is Werther—at least in his conception of things, a conception supported by the novel's language, which alternately describes him in language appropriate to divinity, then to the most dejected of men. The crucifixion becomes liberation for Christ, as it frees him of his mortality and grants him access to union with perfection—his source; likewise, Werther seeks death as the only avenue to freedom and fulfillment of his nature: "I have heard of a noble race of horses which, when they are terribly overheated and excited, instinctively bite into a vein to breathe more freely. So it is with me, I'd like to open a vein to gain eternal freedom."[52] The freedom which Werther seeks is a release from the

---

50 "Und wenn er in Freude sich aufschwingt oder im Leiden versinkt, wird er nicht in beiden eben da aufgehalten, eben da zu dem stumpfen, kalten Bewußtsein wieder zurückgebracht, da er sich in der Fülle des Unendlichen zu verlieren sehnte?" (92).

51 Steinhauer, "Afterword," *The Sufferings of Young Werther*, 111.

52 "Man erzählt von einer edlen Art Pferde, die, wenn sie schreklich erhitzt und aufgejagt sind, sich selbst aus Instinkt eine Ader aufbeißen um sich zum Atem

prison of his own self-destructive soul, which like the herd of horses, is overheated and run wild; suicide is thus an affirmation of the conditions of immortality, as it enables Werther to escape the suffocating restraints of time, social convention, and self, and to capture for eternity the embraces of Lotte.

Before Werther commits suicide, however, he must ascend once again to the "elfin grot." Hence he returns to Lotte for a last visit, and ascends with her to immortality through art, this time the poetry of Ossian. After reading awhile, Werther and Lotte begin to lose self-consciousness and merge in the domain of art: "They felt their own misery in the destiny of the heroes, felt it together and were united in their tears."[53] Lotte notices her senses numbing and begs the hero to continue reading; hers is now "the full voice of heaven."[54] Her senses confused, Lotte places Werther's hands against her breast and her cheek against his; at this moment "the world ceased to exist for them."[55] After casting a loving glance at the wretched man, Lotte hurries into the next room, leaving the pathetic Werther crying, "Farewell, Lotte! Farewell forever!"[56]

Werther is now prepared for death, as he wishes to capture forever the moment of transcendence he had experienced in Lotte's arms: "All this is transitory, but no eternity shall extinguish the glowing life which I savored yesterday in your lips, and which I feel within me now. She loves me! This arm has embraced her, these lips have trembled on hers. . . . She is mine! . . . Yes, Lotte, forever."[57] Though under the conditions of mortality Lotte belongs to

---

zu helfen. So ist mir's oft, ich möchte mir eine Ader öffnen, die mir die ewige Freiheit schaffte."

53 "Sie fühlten ihr eigenes Elend in dem Schicksale der Edlen, fühlten es zusammen, und ihre Tränen vereinigten sich" (114).

54 "der ganzen Stimme des Himmels!"

55 "Die Welt verging ihnen."

56 "Lebe wohl, Lotte! Auf ewig lebe wohl!" (115).

57 "Alles das ist vergänglich, aber keine Ewigkeit soll das glühende Leben auslöschen, das ich gestern auf deinen Lippen genoß, das ich in mir fühle! Sie liebt mich! Dieser Arm hat sie umfaßt, diese Lippen haben auf ihren Lippen gezittert. . . . Sie ist mein! . . . ja, Lotte, auf ewig" (117).

Albert, she is Werther's sister-soul and in heaven's bourne will be united with him forever. Thus Werther blots out mortality through suicide, asserting, "I am going ahead, going to my Father, to your Father. I will bring my plaint to Him and He will comfort me until you come, and I will fly to meet you, clasp you, and remain with you before the countenance of the Infinite in an eternal embrace."[58] Here his moments with Lotte will be "repeated in a finer tone."

Hans Reiss deemphasizes the love relationship of Lotte and Werther, asserting that their affair is nothing more than "the violent passion of a man for a woman"; death is the only alternative for Werther, Reiss contends, "because Werther does not find in love the fulfillment which he desires. His love thus becomes barren."[59] Such a reading distorts the validity of Werther's suicide. It is significant to remember that Werther and Lotte never physically consummate their love; it is always potential rather than actual. They come closest during their last evening together when Lotte, absorbed in the tales of Ossian, presses Werther's hands to her breast and rests her cheek on his. Here the young lovers resemble the "Bold Lover" and nymph in Keats's "Ode on a Grecian Urn," who "Though winning near the goal" never actually achieve union. Werther kills himself not because his love is barren but because it is so full of intensity that he cannot bear life without it; he is, in essence, too fulfilled, and death becomes the only means to experiencing that fulfillment unadulterated by the conditions of mortal existence. All love on earth is by its nature incomplete as it is ephemeral; love is sustainable only in the transcendent realm it foreshadows.

Ultimately *Die Leiden des jungen Werthers* is the tragic portrayal of the acutely sensitive individual who is unable to escape the devouring prison of solipsism save on those rare occasions when through the medium of art he ascends to the conditions of immortality. In a

58 "Ich gehe voran! gehe zu meinem Vater, zu deinem Vater. Dem will ich's klagen, und er wird mich trösten, bis du kommst, und ich fliege dir entgegen und fasse dich und bleibe bei dir vor dem Angesichte des Unendlichen in ewigen Umarmungen" (117).
59 Hans Reiss, *Goethe's Novels*, 41.

letter to Friedrich Schönborn (June 1, 1774) Goethe described Werther as an individual possessing a deep and pure sensibility and genuine lucidity of mind before losing himself in speculation.[60] The fourfold repetition of the verb form "I will" in the first sentences of the initial letter testifies to Werther's entrapment in self; the whole novel, Wolfgang Kayser contends, shows the influence of Leibniz's monadology and pietism, philosophical systems bestowing all authority on the individual soul, which emerges as a microcosm of the universe.[61] Werther is ill at ease in any institutional structure; he cannot find satisfactory employment, he has only contempt for the governmental system, and he insists on a private religious experience. For him the mores and moral obligations giving coherence to the lives of most men seem ridiculously inappropriate, as he is beyond good and evil; his love for Lotte may seem sinful to most men, but for Werther such terminology does not apply: "And what does it signify that Albert is your husband? Husband? That is something for this world—and for this world it is a sin that I love you. . . . Sin? Very well! . . . I have tasted this sin in all its heavenly rapture, I have sucked the balm of life and strength into my heart."[62]

But Werther desperately seeks self-annihilation, to become absorbed in transcendence. Art can purify his passions, release him from the prison of self. In the dance or while reading Ossian, Werther relinquishes his mortality. Lotte on these occasions resembles the Cynthia of Keats's *Endymion*; and she likewise becomes cruel or cold as she belongs to and can be possessed in an immortal realm which Werther cannot sustain. Always there is the inevitable descent, the "return to habitual self," as Werther lapses into solipsis-

60 Fischer-Lamberg (ed.), *Der Junge Goethe*, IV, 22.

61 Wolfgang Kayser, "Die Entstehung von Goethe's Werther," *Deutsche Viertel-jahrsschrift für Literaturwissenschaft und Geistesgeschichte*, XIX (1941), 430–57.

62 "Und was ist das, daß Albert dein Mann ist? Mann! Das wäre denn für diese Welt—und für diese Welt Sünde, daß ich dich liebe, daß ich dich aus seinem Armen in die meinigen reißen möchte? Sünde? Gut . . . ich habe sie in ihrer ganzen Himmelswonne geschmeckt, diese Sünde, habe Lebensbalsam und Kraft in mein Herz gesaugt" (117).

tic misery. While the art of others affords Werther temporary access to heaven's bourne, it is insufficient to sustain the conditions of immortality.

Unfortunately Werther is unable to create art himself. Like Keats's man of imagination he can "consecrate whate'er [he] look[s] upon";[63] but unlike Keats he cannot objectify his emotional state and so transcend it. In his second letter to Wilhelm, Werther laments his inability to execute his vision on canvas, for "I have never been a greater painter than I am in these moments."[64] But his vision is an interior one and so festers and torments him, begging for the release it never receives. E. M. Wilkinson and L. A. Willoughby point to the significance of the fact that *Emilia Galotti*—Gotthold Lessing's tragedy—receives mention at two crucial points in *Werther*. Reference to this play brings into relief Werther's dilemma as artist; for Lessing and for Goethe, the artist who cannot give form to his vision is merely a *Schwärmer*.[65]

This is where Goethe parts company with his hero. The novel is in large part autobiographical, of course, inspired by Goethe's own frustrated love for Charlotte Buff. There is a good deal of evidence to suggest that writing *Die Leiden des jungen Werthers* served as a purgation of sorts for Goethe, releasing him through art from his tormenting passion. Barker Fairley describes Goethe's state of mind just prior to writing the novel as "pathological."[66] Describing the conditions leading up to the novel, Goethe writes in his autobiography, *Dichtung und Wahrheit*:

In my collection of weapons, which was pretty considerable, I possessed a valuable and well-sharpened dagger. I always laid it next to my bed, and before I put out the

---

63 Forman (ed.), *The Letters of John Keats*, 112. Here Keats is quoting from Shelley's "Hymn to Intellectual Beauty."

64 "[ich] bin nie ein größerer Maler gewesen als in diesen Augenblicken" (9).

65 E. M. Wilkinson and L. A. Willoughby, "The Blind Man and the Poet: An Early Stage in Goethe's Quest for Form," *Studies in Honor of W. H. Bruford* (London, 1961), 44.

66 Barker Fairley, *A Study of Goethe* (Oxford, 1947), 12–59.

light I tried to see whether I could not sink the sharp point a few inches into my breast. As I was never able to do so, I finally laughed at myself, cast off all my hypochondriac caprices, and decided to continue living. In order to be able to do this calmly, however, I had to fulfill some poetic task, in which everything that I had felt, thought, and imagined about this important matter would find verbal expression.[67]

What was needed, Goethe writes, was a precipitating incident to give objective form to his suffering:

Suddenly I learned of the death of Jerusalem. Immediately after hearing a report of it, I received the most exact and detailed description of the occurrence—and at that moment the plan for *Werther* came into being. The whole thing crystallized from all sides and became a solid mass, like water in a container which is just at freezing-point and is immediately turned to hard ice by the slightest shake.[68]

Goethe quickly becomes a man possessed; he knows he must write to free himself of the Werther-like quality of his soul. Hence to Kestner—who was understandably upset over Goethe's portrayal of Albert and Lotte in the novel—Goethe responded in an autumn, 1774 letter:

Believe me, believe me; your worries, your *gravamina*, they will disappear like nocturnal phantoms if you are patient, and then—within one year I promise to cut out

67 "Unter einer ansehnlichen Waffensammlung besaß ich auch einen kostbaren wohlgeschiffenen Dolch. Diesen legte ich mir jederzeit neben das Bette, und ehe ich das Licht auslöschte, versuchte ich, ob es mir wohl gelingen möchte, die scharfe Spitze ein paar Zoll tief in die Brust zu senken. Da dieses aber niemals gelingen wollte, so lachte ich mich zuletzt selbst aus, warf alle hypochondrische Fratzen hinweg, und beschloß zu leben. Um dies aber mit Heiterkeit tun zu können, mußte ich eine dichterische Aufgabe zur Ausführung bringen, wo alles, was ich über diesen wichtigen Punkt empfunden, gedacht und gewähnt, zur Sprache kommen sollte." *Goethes Werke*, IX, 585. English translation is from Hans Reiss, *Goethe's Novels*, 10–11.

68 "Auf einmal erfahre ich die Nachricht von Jerusalems Tode, und, unmittelbar nach dem allgemeinen Gerüchte, sogleich die genauste und umständlichste Beschreibung des Vorgangs, und in diesem Augenblick war der Plan zu "Werther" gefunden, das Ganze schoß von allen Seiten zusammen und ward eine solide Masse, wie das Wasser im Gefäß, das eben auf dem Punkte des Gefrierens steht, durch die geringste Erschütterung sogleich in ein festes Eis verwandelt

everything that a public keen on gossip has retained of suspicion, misinterpretation, etc. I shall do this just as the north wind drives away mists and odours. . . . Werther must—must be. You do not feel *him*. You feel only me and yourselves.[69]

"Werther must—must be" in order for Goethe to find objective crystallization of his passion. He is then free of it and can move on to denounce his hero (or earlier self) in his mature years.

---

wird." *Goethes Werke*, IX, 585. English translation is from Hans Reiss, *Goethe's Novels*, 11.

69   "Bruder lieber Kestner! Wollt ihr warten so wird euch geholfen. Ich wollt um meines eignen Lebens Gefahr willen Werthern nicht züruck rufen, und glaub mir, glaub an mich, deine Besorgnisse deine Gravamina, schwinden wie Gespenster der Nacht wo du Geduld hast, und dann—binnen hier und einem Jahr versprech ich euch auf die lieblichste einzigste innigste Weise alles was noch übrig seyn mögte von Verdacht, Missdeutung pp im schwäzzenden Publikum! obgleich das eine Heerd Schwein ist, auszulöschen, wie ein reiner Nordwind, Nebel und Dufft. —Werther muss—muss seyn! —Ihr fühlt ihn nicht, ihr fühlt nur mich und euch." Fischer-Lamberg (ed.), *Der Junge Goethe*, IV, 254–55. English translation is from Hans Reiss, *Goethe's Novels*, 19.

III

The Romantic Communal Impulse: A
Search for Providential Order

The romantic hero seems to emerge from the tradition of sentimentality permeating late eighteenth-century fiction and drama. Buf-
feted by ill fortune, rejected and ignored by a callous and repressive
society suffering with the abuses of an *ancien régime*, the first romantic heroes are typically passive, introverted young men whose intense sensitivity and *belle âme* necessitate their own destruction.
"This man," Chateaubriand writes of René, "estranged on this
earth, sought in vain for a corner of the world where he could rest
his head: wherever he reposed, he had been created from miseries."[1]
Byron's Childe Harold is "as a weed,/ Flung from the rock, on
Ocean's foam to sail/ Where'er the surge may sweep, the tempest's
breath prevail," left to become "the wandering outlaw of his own
dark mind."[2] An alienated figure suffering from *Weltschmerz, mal du*

---

1 François René de Chateaubriand, *Les Natchez*, ed. Gilbert Chinard (Paris, 1932),
   367. "Cet homme, étranger sur ce globe, cherchoit en vain un coin de terre où il
   pût reposer sa tête: partout où il s'étoit montré, il avoit créé des misères."
2 Byron (George Gordon), *Childe Harold's Pilgrimage*, Canto III, ii, 16–18; III, iii,
   20. References to Byron's poetry are to E. H. Coleridge (ed.), *The Poetical Works
   of Lord Byron* (London, 1901).

51

siècle, or world-weariness, the hero of sensibility abandons ties with the outside world, turning inward upon his naked soul for solace and moral guidance: "I turn in upon myself," Werther tells Wilhelm, "and find a world there."[3] But unfortunately the world that Werther—and other such heroes—finds is not a particularly healthy one. Locked in a solipsistic prison, they discover late-eighteenth-century Europe barren soil in which to cultivate the whims of natural, heartfelt genius; unlike the milieu of Richardson's Pamela or Cumberland's Belcour, Werther's world is not one to reward an unwavering reliance on the virtues of the heart.

One might expect the sympathetic romantic artist to seize upon the plight of the melancholy hero as an opportunity to indict a social order that fails to provide avenues through which men like Werther could channel their enormous spiritual resources in constructive directions. Yet the primary impulse of *Die Leiden des jungen Werthers* or *René* is not toward social criticism; instead both become rather devastating portraits of the effects of uncontrolled solipsism. Neither is offered as a heroic ideal to be emulated by others, for both Goethe and Chateaubriand explicitly condemn their behavior. And though they retreat into solipsism, neither finds such retreat a satisfying haven from their despair: René admits, "Alas! I am only in search of some unknown good, whose intuition pursues me relentlessly,"[4] and Werther seeks in an ideal union with Lotte communion with an absolute love which transcends self. Though ineffectual and doomed, the hero of sensibility seems, finally, less a contemptible figure than a pitiful one. He offers early testimony to the fact that the romantic rebellion in literature is not simply a breakaway from conventions and traditions and a consequent turning inward to the individual soul, but it reflects as well an often desperate, at times unsuccessful, attempt to locate something outside the ego that transcends a deca-

3 J. W. Goethe, *Die Leiden des jungen Werther*, vol. VI of *Goethes Werke*, 13. "Ich kehre in mich selbst zurück, und finde eine Welt!"

4 François René de Chateaubriand, *René*, in Maurice Regard (ed.), *Oeuvres romanesques et voyages* (2 vols.; Paris, 1969), 128. "hélas! je cherche seulement un bien inconnu, dont l'instinct me poursuit."

dent culture—something that will provide meaning and order to chaotic existence.

The romantic artists seem keenly aware of the later criticism that Babbitt and others will hurl at them: individualism poses serious threats to the social order when it allows the hero's demand for self-determination to replace moral norms which are binding to all.[5] Admittedly most share the despair of a Novalis who writes, "We seek the infinite everywhere and always find only finite things,"[6] or of a Chateaubriand when he describes his youth:

> I retained only my youth and my illusions; I abandoned a world in which I had trampled the dust and counted the stars, for a world in which the earth and the heavens were unknown to me. What should happen to me if I should arrive at my voyage's end?[7]

But the romantic artist rarely rests content with the alternative posed by Fichtean solipsistic idealism, for such, carried to its logical extreme, results in the posture of the decadent dandy, "le culte de soi-même,"[8] or the satanic will to power characteristic of such romantic villains as Cenci, Rappaccini, or Ahab: both are perversions of the romantic mythic quest for self-transcendence, egotistical violations of the Kantian categorical imperative.

The bankruptcy of moral idealism implicit in total self-absorption is evident in Pechorin, central character of Lermontov's *A Hero of Our Time*. Absolutely dedicated to self-fulfillment, disdainful of conventional mores, Pechorin becomes a willing slave to an ego which pays little heed to the humanity of others. He approaches women as sacrificial offerings to his godlike ego, to be exploited,

---

5 Furst, *Romanticism in Perspective*, 55–56.

6 Novalis, "Blütenstraub," in *Novalis Schriften*, II, 412. "Wir *suchen* überall das Unbedingte, und *finden* immer nur Dinge."

7 François René de Chateaubriand, *Mémoires d'outre-tombe* (2 vols.; Paris, 1859), I, 328. "Je n'emportais que ma jeunesse et mes illusions; je désertais un monde dont j'avais foulé la poussière et compté les étoiles, pour un monde de qui la terre et le ciel m'étaient inconnus. Que devait-il m'arriver si j'atteignais le but de mon voyage?"

8 Elizabeth Creed, *Le Dandysme de Jules Barbey d'Aurevilly* (Paris, 1938), 4.

drained, then discarded: "And yet there's boundless pleasure to be had in taking possession of a young, fresh-blossomed heart. It's like a flower that breathes its sweetest scent to the first rays of the sun. You must pluck it at once, breathe in its scent and cast it on the roadway."[9] Toward the end of the novel, Pechorin comes to realize that his "love has brought no one happiness, for I've only tried to satisfy a strange inner need" (157). One might accuse Faust of a similar abuse of Gretchen's love, but Goethe's hero eventually transcends his egotism, accepts the burdens of cosmic consciousness; Pechorin never makes this crucial progression, though he does come to see the futility of his life:

I can't help wondering why I've lived, for what purpose I was born. There must have been some purpose, I must have had some high object in life, for I feel unbounded strength in me. But I never discovered it and was carried away by the allurements of empty, unrewarding passion. I was tempered in their flames and came out cold and hard as steel, but I'd lost forever the fire of noble endeavor, that finest flower of life. (156–57)

Hardly an embodiment of an heroic ideal, Pechorin simply reflects the perverted values of an age unable to cope with a self-consciousness that John Stuart Mill labels "that demon of the men of genius of our time, from Wordsworth to Byron, from Goethe to Chateaubriand."[10] As Lermontov writes: "Some readers might like to know my own opinion of Pechorin's character. My answer is given in the title of this book [*A Hero of Our Time*]. 'Malicious irony!' they'll retort. I don't know" (76).

Agonizingly aware of the psychological and social maladies potential in the solipsistic stage of the romantic quest, artists become all the more desperate in their search for final transcendence of self into a meaningful and ordered pattern of existence. Thomas Carlyle ends his *On Heroes, Hero-Worship, and the Heroic in History* (1840) with a chapter devoted to "The Hero as King"; focusing his discussion

9 Lermontov, *A Hero of Our Time*, trans. Paul Foote (Harmondsworth, England, 1966), 126. Subsequent references are to this edition.
10 See Wayne Shumaker, *English Autobiography* (Berkeley, Cal., 1954), 76.

on Cromwell and Napoleon, Carlyle argues that the ideal king is heroic in large measure because he is dedicated to meeting the needs of his constituents even at the expense of self-fulfillment. When Diogenes Teufelsdrockh, Carlyle's hero in *Sartor Resartus*, discovers that his individual will is compromised by obligations to those around him, he accepts the necessity of functioning within a social structure whose health depends upon individual self-annihilation; he commands himself to "Close thy *Byron*; open thy *Goethe*." Though Sypher sees Teufelsdrockh's dilemma as a postromantic *Weltschmerz* resembling the existentialist position of Martin Buber,[11] other scholars have located in Carlyle's hero the prototypical progression crucial to the romantic heroic ideal.[12] Another Carlylian hero, Jocelin of Brakelond in *Past and Present*, finds spiritual health and transcendence as part of the tightly ordered existence characteristic of medieval life. Unified in dedication to the glory of God, medieval society is offered by Carlyle as the ideal antithesis to the moral and psychological chaos of nineteenth-century Europe; as Alfred Cobban asks, "was not feudal society supremely distinguished from modern by its recognition both in theory and practice of the value and significance of communal life, of the natural interdependence of individuals and of classes, and of the beauty of self-devotion to a corporate ideal?"[13]

Carlyle's celebration of medieval life is part of an overall cult of the Middle Ages that permeated the romantic movement. The author of a long work on Joan of Arc, Robert Southey argues that "bad as the feudal times were, they were far less injurious than these commercial ones to the kindly and generous feelings of human nature, and far, far more favorable to the principles of honour and integrity." The Middle Ages offered to the Romantic, uncomfortable

---

11 Sypher, *Loss of Self in Modern Literature and Art*, 30–31.

12 Hartman, "Romanticism and Anti-Self Consciousness," 47; Morse Peckham, "Toward a Theory of Romanticism," 16–23.

13 Alfred Cobban, *Edmund Burke and the Revolt Against the Eighteenth Century; a study of the political and social thinking of Burke, Wordsworth, Coleridge and Southey* (London, 1960), 265–66.

with the sterile intellectualism of the Enlightenment, a religious conception of society, grounded in authority verifiable not through reason but through faith; but, most of all, it was cohesive: "What appeal more suitable, then, than from an Age of unbelief to the Ages of Faith, from an age of rebellion and self-assertion to the age of subordination and caste, from an age of the breaking of all bonds and loosening of all ties—social, moral and religious—to the age of fixed feudal hierarchy and unalterable law?"[14] Novalis begins his essay "Die Christenheit oder Europa" with praise of medieval Christendom, indicting the Reformation and secular philosophy as responsible for current moral and spiritual chaos:

> Hatred of religion . . . turns the unending creative music of the cosmos into the monotonous rattling of a monstrous great mill, driven by the current of chance and itself drifting on this current, a mill per se, without builder or miller, in truth a genuine perpetuum mobile, a mill that grinds itself.[15]

As a means of transcending the despair characteristic of a chaotic age, Novalis suggests a return to the ideal of a unified Christian Europe, centered upon the Cult of the Virgin. Heinrich Kleist too is torn by the contradictory ideals of the period, between what Hamburger calls "the Protestant's reliance on his own conscience and the Prussian officer's unquestioning loyalty to secular authority"; though *Michael Kohlhaas* celebrates defiance of established authority by a man sure of his personal moral vision, *Die Hermannsschlacht* calls for subordination of the individual's conscience to a national cause. Though at one stage of his life vehemently anti-Catholic, objecting particularly to the Roman emphasis on ritual and ceremony, Kleist eventually became a Catholic convert. And in a late short story, "Die heilige Cäcilie oder die Gewalt der Musik,"

14 *Ibid.*, 265.
15 Novalis, "Die Christenheit oder Europa 1799," in Gerhard Schulz (ed.), *Novalis Werke* (Munich, 1969), 508. "Noch mehr—der Religions— . . . machte die unendliche schöpferische Musik des Weltalls zum einförmigen Klappern einer ungeheuren Mühle, die vom Strom des Zufalls getrieben und auf ihm schwimmend, eine Mühle an sich, ohne Baumeister und Müller und eigentlich ein echtes Perpetuum mobile, eine sich selbst mahlende Mühle sie."

Kleist presents four fanatical anti-Papists who rush into a church intent upon disrupting the service; however, all four are in the process converted to Catholicism by music and leave the service in a state of religious mania after hearing the *gloria in excelsis*.[16]

Absorption into a structured religious perspective thus offers for a significant number of romantic poets a viable means of transcending spiritual despair. Noted for its theological blasphemies and "free thought,"[17] the age curiously offers a large number of artists marked by intense religious fervor: Novalis, Kleist, Coleridge, Chateaubriand, Lamartine—to mention but a few. Shortly after Byron's death, Lamartine provides in *Le Dernier Chant du pèlerinage d'Harold* (1825) a fifth canto to *Childe Harold's Pilgrimage* in which the dying and aged Harold longs for a sign that will furnish him religious faith: "Oh that I might hear a single word! . . . merely a sigh/ a sigh would suffice to clear my doubt."[18] In a foreword, Lamartine writes that his purpose in *Le Dernier Chant du pèlerinage d'Harold* is to demonstrate "the necessity of faith coming from above";[19] and if Lamartine's vision of Harold achieving self-transcendence by surrendering to the glory of God seems inappropriate for Byron, it nevertheless accurately mirrors the romantic hope for union with "der Götter Gott." For Lamartine and, indeed, most romantics, Byron had become the prototypical autonomous rebel laboring under *la mal du siècle*, "the Ossian of a most civilized society, and nearly corrupted by the same excess of his civilization: the poetry of satiety, of disenchantment and of the decay of the age."[20] Thus in bringing Har-

16 Hamburger, *Contraries*, 67; 107–12.
17 Fairchild, in *1780–1830, Romantic Faith*, calls romantic religion "a tissue of heresies."
18 Lamartine, *Oeuvres Poétiques Complètes*, 235. "Que j'entende un seul mot! . . . un soupir seulement! / Un soupir suffirait pour éclaircir mon doute!"
19 Edmond Estève, *Byron et le romantisme français*, 350n. "la nécessité d'une foi venue d'en haut."
20 Lamartine, "Commentaires," in Jean des Cognets (ed.), *Méditations Poétiques* (Paris, 1956), 225. "l'Ossian d'une société plus civilisée et presque corrompue par l'excès même de sa civilisation: la poésie de la satiété, du désenchantement et de la caducité de l'âge."

old—the hero by whom Byron was best known throughout Europe—within the framework of religious redemption, Lamartine offers a prescription that both cures the characteristic malady of the age and leads to fulfillment of the heroic mission.

Embellished with Christian symbols and biblical allusions, Coleridge's "Rime of the Ancient Mariner" portrays man's progression from sin—through punishment and repentance—to reconciliation with God and community. Though the poem's ultimate concern may be, as Maud Bodkin argues, the ideal progression characteristic of everyman,[21] it focuses on the trial, responsibilities, and triumphs of a specific man: the poet. In perhaps the best single study of the poem, Robert Penn Warren demonstrates that the central subject of the "Rime" is the poetic imagination;[22] yet understood within the framework of Christian symbols permeating the poem, the "Rime" makes a powerful statement regarding the poet-hero's responsibilities both to God and to his fellows.

Providentially selected by God to receive revelation of His divine mysteries, the poet-prophet of Coleridge's poem bears striking resemblance to such biblical prophets as Jonah and Zacharias. Like the Old Testament prophets who "spake as they were moved by the Holy Ghost" (II Peter 1: 21), the Mariner accepts his responsibility to bring his divine message within a human community. He is driven by a deep-seated compulsion to relate his experience to others, for not only must he speak as part of a private penance but, convinced that his message is of divine origin, he believes that his revelations are crucial to the salvation of the audience.

Thus the Mariner seems to rest firmly in the tradition of the poet-prophet as outlined by C. M. Bowra: "In the dawn of the world the poet sings in the belief that his words come to him from some divine power which chooses him as its intermediary and speaks, as it were, through him."[23] Although the link of what Max

---

21 Maud Bodkin, *Archetypal Patterns in Poetry* (London, 1934), 26–30.
22 Robert Penn Warren, "A Poem of Pure Imagination: An Experiment in Reading," *Selected Essays* (New York, 1958), 239.
23 C. M. Bowra, *Inspiration and Poetry* (London, 1956), 1.

Schultz calls "the impassioned outburst of the prophet with the prophetic utterance of the poet" is well within an ancient tradition,[24] Coleridge's Mariner reflects the romantic intensification of that tradition. Murry Roston argues that with romanticism "poetry had . . . become a holy service," and that in so thoroughly a prophetic poet as Blake, poetry could have no "function other than that of conveying a divine message."[25] But Blake is not alone among romantics committed to the prophetic nature of art; M. H. Abrams contends that virtually all of the English romantics "represented themselves in the traditional persona of the . . . poet-prophet."[26] In a prefatory letter to "Ode on the Departing Year, 1796," Coleridge places himself squarely in this romantic revival of the Hebraic concept of the poet-prophet: "You, I am sure, will not fail to recollect that among the Ancients, the Bard and the Prophet were one and the same character; and you know that although I prophesy curses, I pray fervently for blessings."[27]

Wordsworth describes the process involved in the poet's progression to prophet in the thirteenth book of *The Prelude* (1850 edition):

> and I remember well
> That in life's every-day appearances
> I seemed about this time to gain clear sight
> Of a new world—a world, too, that was fit
> To be transmitted, and to other eyes
> Made visible. . . .[28]

Like Wordsworth, Coleridge's Mariner is both passive receiver and active transmitter. Constantly acted upon by natural elements, distressed men, and supernatural forces, the Mariner is at first the

---

24 Max Schultz, *The Poetic Voices of Coleridge: A Study of His Desire for Spontaneity and Passion for Order* (Detroit, 1963), 27.

25 Murray Roston, *Prophet and Poet: The Bible and the Growth of Romanticism* (Evanston, Ill., 1965), chapter 8.

26 Abrams, *Natural Supernaturalism*, 12.

27 See Max Schultz, *The Poetic Voices of Coleridge*, 26.

28 William Wordsworth, "The Prelude," in *Wordsworth: Poetical Works*, Book XIII, ll. 367–72.

receiver, seemingly passive in a cosmic drama beyond his comprehension. But as he moves back into human community from the "painted ship upon a painted ocean," the Mariner becomes an active transmitter—or prophet—who with "glittering eye" hypnotizes the Hermit, the wedding guest, and the reader.

Focus in the poem falls upon the three days and nights of trial when, after initially slaying the albatross, the Mariner becomes a passive pawn in God's providential scheme. The Mariner's suffering culminates in the blessing of the water snakes, symbolic of his recognition of the kinship he shares with God's marvellous creation. This is the one supreme moment of illumination; suddenly the worthless becomes priceless, the cursed becomes blessed, the passive pawn emerges as active proclaimer.

Poets, Wordsworth writes in *The Prelude*, as "Prophets of Nature" bring to the desolate "A lasting inspiration, sanctified/ By reason, blest by faith: what we have loved,/ Others will love, and we will teach them how" (XIV, 444–47). "Sanctified by reason" and "blest by faith," the poet-prophet assumes his primary function: to love and to teach others to love, hence becoming "joint labourers in the work/ . . . / Of [the people's] deliverance" (XIV, 441–43). Such too is the function of Coleridge's Mariner, as through love he achieves redemption; further, the gospel of love becomes the essence of the Mariner's prophetic message, the substance of the poet's song:

> He prayeth best, who loveth best
> All things both great and small;
> For the dear God who loveth us,
> He made and loveth all. (ll. 614–17)[29]

The source of the message that the Mariner (or poet) receives is God. Coleridge's early poem "The Eolian Harp" compares the mind of the poet to a lute gently caressed by divine breeze:

> And what if all animated nature

29 Samuel Taylor Coleridge, "The Rime of the Ancient Mariner," in Ernest Hartley Coleridge (ed.), *Coleridge: Poetical Works* (London, 1973), 186–209.

Be but organic Harps diversely fram'd
That tremble into thought, as o'er them sweeps
Plastic and vast, one intellectual breeze,
At once the Soul of each, and God of all? (11. 44–48)

J. Robert Barth notes that the wind for Coleridge acts as the Holy Spirit,[30] animating the poet and furnishing his voice. The analogy of the wind/harp to the Holy Spirit/Poet illuminates the Mariner and his experience on the "painted ocean." He is passive until "breathed" upon by God and assisted by "my kind saint"; at this moment he assumes an active role as transmitter of sacred mysteries in a providential plan. Like Zacharias, the Mariner is struck dumb after his violation of God's trust and achieves prophetic voice only in acknowledging the beauty of God's plan. Like Jonah, the Mariner is spared the terrible consequences of willful disobedience because he is commissioned to perform a specific task: going forth "like one that hath been stunned," the Mariner returns to his homeland "a sadder and a wiser man" bearing a painful but enlightened message to redeem all.

As often noted, Coleridge's Mariner follows in the tradition of the Wandering Jew—a metaphor of the poet common in romantic literature. The legend of the Wandering Jew has its origin in the story of Cain: "Behold, thou hast driven me out this day from the face of the earth; and from thy face shall I be hid; and I shall be a fugitive and a vagabond in the earth; and it shall come to pass, that every one that findeth me shall slay me" (Genesis 4:14). From John L. Lowes we learn that Coleridge turned from work on a fragment, "The Wanderings of Cain," to write "The Rime," and that many of the qualities of the hero in the former found their way into the Mariner.[31] O. Bryan Fulmer, Edward Gibbons, and Robert Penn Warren all make strong cases for striking resemblances between the

---

30 J. Robert Barth, *Coleridge and Christian Doctrine* (Cambridge, Mass., 1969), 91.
31 John Livingstone Lowes, *The Road to Xanadu: A Study in the Ways of the Imagination* (rev. ed.; Boston, 1959), 235.

Mariner and the tradition of the Wandering Jew of which Cain is the prototype.[32] But the Mariner breaks from the tradition in a significant way, for in the course of the poem he ceases to be the wanderer and assumes the role of pilgrim. This distinction is crucial to the poem and deserves sustained consideration: a wanderer is on a purposeless journey without end; the pilgrim anxiously departs upon a previously charted course, looking forward to ultimate fulfillment of a sanctified purpose. The wanderer surrenders his will and becomes a passive pawn; the pilgrim is always the active agent.

The initial part of the "Rime" concerns what Warren has called "crime and punishment." The crime is, of course, the Mariner's killing of the albatross, and as in Cain's murder of his brother, the punishment that ensues clearly results from the crime: "And the albatross begins to be avenged" (Marginal note, 1. 119). With the albatross hung around his neck, the Mariner stands branded with the mark of Cain—a visible symbol of his ostracism from human community.[33] He is the wanderer, the outcast: "Alone, alone, all, all alone,/ Alone on a wide wide sea!/ And never a saint took pity on/ My soul in agony" (11. 232–35). Crucial here is the element of moral responsibility: the Mariner deserves the calamities that befall him, or otherwise the necessity of prayer and penance seems absurd. As J. R. Ebbatson writes, "to trivialize the crime makes the punishment Draconian and the poem nonsensical."[34]

Robert W. Graves, in an unpublished M.A. thesis, shows that Coleridge very skillfully links the Mariner's transformation to the process of Christian conversion in the New Testament.[35] The climax

---

32 O. Bryan Fulmer, "The Ancient Mariner and the Wandering Jew," *Studies in Philology*, LXVI (1969), 797; Edward Gibbons, "Point of View and Moral in 'The Rime of the Ancient Mariner,'" *University Review*, XXXV (1969), 259; Warren, "A Poem of Pure Imagination," 256.

33 Paul Magnuson, *Coleridge's Nightmare Poetry* (Charlottesville, Va., 1974), 72.

34 J. R. Ebbatson, "Coleridge's Mariner and the Rights of Man," *Studies in Romanticism*, II (1962), 180.

35 The parallel between the "Rime" and Acts 2:2–4 was first brought to my attention in a seminar paper prepared by one of my former graduate students at Georgia State University, Mr. Robert W. Graves.

of the poem comes at the precise moment when the Mariner changes from wanderer to pilgrim, a moment effected by the Mariner's sincere prayer of repentance: "The self-same moment I could pray;/ And from my neck so free/ The albatross fell off" (11. 288–90). Not only does the Mariner repent but he undergoes a symbolic process that equates with the baptism by water ("my garments all were dank" [302]) and reception of the Holy Spirit as described in the Book of Acts, 2: 2–4: "Suddenly there came a sound from heaven as a rushing mighty wind. . . . And there appeared unto them cloven tongues like as fire; And they were all filled with the Holy Spirit, and began to speak with other tongues as the Spirit gave them utterance." The corresponding process in Coleridge's poem is described as follows: "And soon I heard a roaring wind" (309); "The upper air burst into life!/ And a hundred fire-flags sheen" (313–14); "Sweet sounds rose slowly through their mouths" (352). The significance of the biblical parallels to the poem lies in the symbolic nature of the Mariner: He is Coleridge's projection of the poet as prophet. After repenting, the Mariner surrenders his imagination to the shaping of the Holy Spirit; he then becomes the pilgrim on a specific mission: to bring human society the message of God's love.

In accepting his role as prophet, Coleridge's Mariner recognizes his place in a divinely sanctioned destiny. Behind the "Rime of the Ancient Mariner" and, indeed, many of the central works of the romantic period, lies an acceptance of what Alexander Pope's contemporary Thomas Rymer had described as "that constant order, that harmony and beauty of Providence, that necessary relation and chain, whereby the causes and effects, the vertues and rewards, the vices and their punishments are proportion'd and link'd together."[36] Although certain romantic villains—Shelley's Cenci, Hawthorne's Chillingworth, Melville's Ahab, for instance—see providence as a "dark necessity" that relieves them of moral responsibility, most romantic artists cheerfully accept their role as prophets, enlightened

---

36 Thomas Rymer, "The Tragedies of the Last Age," in C. A. Zimansky (ed.), *The Critical Works of Thomas Rymer* (New Haven, Conn., 1956), 75.

individuals possessed of insight into a providentially ordained future who are called upon to move mankind toward its destiny. In his preface to *La Chute d'un Ange*, Lamartine writes: "I want to reveal the transmigration of the spirit; the stages that the human soul travels through in order to fulfill its perfected destinies and to arrive at its ends by means of Providence and the trials of the earth."[37] For Carlyle and Tennyson the heroic personality prefigures man's unilateral progression toward even higher forms of cultural and spiritual development. Those heroes who come closest to the romantic heroic ideal—Faust, Prometheus, Joan of Arc—transcend "les épreuves sur la terre" and the existential despair commonly resulting from them, as they are assimilated into a divinely orchestrated historical process.[38]

Schiller's *Wilhelm Tell* (1804) offers an excellent example of the fusion of human and divine purposes. As the play opens, a respected citizen—Baumgarten—has murdered an Austrian tax collector intent upon a sexual liaison with his wife. Though his action may seem private revenge for a personal wrong, Baumgarten becomes for Schiller a noble rebel against illicit repression, part of a divinely sanctioned process aimed at overthrowing debased authority: "That he did not fulfill his foul desire/ Is due to God and to my trusty axe" (I, i).[39] Baumgarten foreshadows Tell, who while awaiting his victim claims to be an executioner appointed by God, the instrument of divine justice: "There is a God to punish and avenge" (IV, iii); after

37 Lamartine, "Avertissement de la nouvelle édition," *La Chute d'un Ange*, vol. XVI of *Oeuvres Complètes de Lamartine* (41 vols.; Paris, 1860–66), 8. "Ce sujet, ai-je dit, c'est l'âme humaine, je veux exposer ce sont les phases que l'esprit humain parcourt pour accomplir ses destinées perfectibles et arriver à ses fins les voies de la Providence et par les épreuves sur la terre."

38 Abrams, *Natural Supernaturalism*, 47–57; 200.

39 Friedrich Schiller, *Wilhelm Tell*, in F. Schiller, *Sämtliche Werke*, ed. Gerhard Fricke and Herbert G. Göpfert (5 vols.; Munich, 1960), II, 920. "Daß er sein bös Gelüsten nicht vollbracht,/ Hat Gott und meine gute Axt verhütet." The English translation given in the text is from Friedrich Schiller, *Historical Dramas*, trans. Samuel Taylor Coleridge and E. A. Aytoun (5 vols.; London, 1882), III, 10.

the deed Tell asserts: "God has helped" (V, ii).[40] To modern readers Baumgarten and Tell might seem self-appointed murderers, conveniently inventing God's favor to justify brutal slaughter; but the providential scheme that assimilates them raises Tell and Baumgarten to a mythic dimension, at least for Schiller and his romantic audience. As François Jost asserts, Tell embodies the ideals of freedom current in the aftermath of the French Revolution, becoming the "prototype *par excellence* of an oppressed people's liberator."[41]

The fusion of personal, social, and divine purposes in Schiller's play suggests the communal responsibility that gradually comes to govern romantic art. Disillusioned with the outcome of the French Revolution, wary of uncontrolled solipsism, and desperately seeking a sense of permanence that would provide coherence to their fragmented world, many of the romantics longed for the emergence of a heroic figure to lead civilization to a new birth. Carlyle's vision of the monastic community of Jocelyn in *Past and Present* typifies the order the artist seeks: a harmonious society grounded in simple religious faith and espousing the sacred virtues of hard work and submission to properly constituted authority. The passionate Christianity of Coleridge, Chateaubriand, and Kleist, the fondness for classical Greece characteristic of Goethe and Byron, the lament over the passing of the Arthurian chivalric order in Tennyson's *Idylls of the King*, the abolitionist fervor, enthusiasm for John Brown and experiments in utopian living of the American Transcendentalists—these illustrate the tendency of some romantics to escape solipsism through the restoration or creation of a coherent, humane social order. The true hero is neither the melancholy, maladjusted introvert with the "belle âme" nor the satanic, monomaniacal figure of prodigious intellectual powers; rather, the ideal hero of the age emerges as a titanic individual who, after rejecting and overthrowing a cor-

---

40 Friedrich Schiller, *Sämtliche Werke*, II, 1004; 1023; Coleridge and Aytoun (trans.), *Historical Dramas*, III, 92. "Es lebt ein Gott, zu strafen und zu rächen"; "Gott hat geholfen."

41 François Jost, "A Mythic Type: William Tell," *Introduction to Comparative Literature* (Indianapolis, 1974), 223.

rupt social order, struggles on behalf of his fellows to inaugurate a new culture. Faust and Prometheus are the prototypical romantic heroes; submitting to a providential destiny that calls them to heroic action, both become agents of social and cultural redemption.

As Goethe's play opens, Faust labors under an egotistical absorption in an academic quest for knowledge that alienates him from the community once honorably served by his father. Unlike his servant Wagner, Goethe's hero recognizes the sterility of his intellect and attacks learning—even reason itself—as a parasite that saps the soul's vitality. Faust's study has become a metaphoric prison, cutting him off from the transcendental truth he so desperately seeks:

> Woe! stuck within this dungeon yet?
> Curse this dank frowsty cabinet,
> Where even Heaven's dear ray can pass
> But murkily through tinted glass![42]

Significantly Faust does not, like the modern existential hero, emerge as the solitary individual confronting a metaphysical void; rather, he becomes to the age "le symbole du mal du siècle"[43] because he perceives a transcendental, potentially redeeming vision from which he seems forever alienated. The Sign of the Makrokosmus furnishes the hero with a momentary glimpse into the order celebrated by the three archangels at the play's outset:

> How all one common weft contrives,

42 ll. 398–401. All references to *Faust* are to the edition in *Goethes Werke*, ed. Erich Trunz, vol. III. English translations—unless noted otherwise—are from J. W. Goethe, *Faust: A Tragedy*, ed. Cyrus Hamlin; trans. Walter Arndt (New York, 1976).

> Weh! steck' ich in dem Kerker noch?
> Verfluchtes dumpfes Mauerloch,
> Wo selbst das liebe Himmelslicht
> Trüb durch gemalte Scheiben bricht!

43 Charles Dédéyan, *Le Thème de Faust dans la Littérature Européenne* (2 vols.; Paris, 1959), II, 285.

Each in the other works and thrives!
How heavenly forces rising and descending,
Pass golden ewers in exchange unending,
On wings with blessing fragrant
From Heaven the earth pervading,
Fill all the world with harmonies vagrant![44]

Tragically the vision serves only to remind Faust of his alienation from the cosmic harmony he perceives:

How, boundless Nature, seize you in my clasp?
You breasts where, all life's sources twain,
Both heaven and earth are pressed,
Where thrusts itself my shriveled breast,
You brim, you quench, yet I must thirst in vain?[45]

The ideal offered by Goethe's drama involves Faust's—and man's—assimilation into the cosmic harmony which seems, at times, remote indeed. This assimilation requires that man struggle continuously against the limitations imposed by his mortality, and at the outset Faust relinquishes that struggle. In contemplating suicide the hero ceases to strive, hence denying God's vision of man as a perpetually

---

44 *Faust*, ll. 447–53.

> Wie alles sich zum Ganzen webt,
> Eins in dem andern wirkt und lebt!
> Wie Himmelskräfte auf und nieder steigen
> Und sich die goldnen Eimer reichen!
> Mit segenduftenden Schwingen
> Vom Himmel durch die Erde dringen,
> Harmonisch all das All durchklingen!

45 *Faust*, ll. 455–59.

> Wo fass' ich dich, unendliche Natur?
> Euch Brüste, wo? Ihr Quellen alles Lebens,
> An denen Himmel und Erde hängt,
> Dahin die welke Brust sich drängt—
> Ihr quellt, ihr tränkt, und schmacht'
>   ich so vergebens?

dynamic figure; ironically, Faust languishes in the state of resignation to which Mephistopheles later hopes to lead him via black magic and sensual pleasure.

But the hero's despair is part of a larger providential scheme, governed by an omniscient Lord who knows that with divine assistance Faust will transcend his melancholy to fulfill his destiny:

> Though now he serve me but in clouded ways,
> Soon I shall guide him so his spirit clears,
> The gardener knows by the young tree's green haze
> That bloom and fruit will grace it down the years.[46]

The organic metaphor here suggests that Faust's eventual redemption is part of a divinely orchestrated process. The catalyst is to be Mephistopheles: "He soon prefers uninterrupted rest;/ To give him this companion hence seems best/ Who roils and must as Devil help create."[47] Mephistopheles serves well in part because he is, as Madame de Staël calls him, the "expression de l'ironie et de l'incrédulité,"[48] unable to comprehend the glorious destiny which uses him as a pawn; and too he functions as an effective catalyst because the Lord knows Faust's true desire for transcendence, his yearning for assimilation into the vision provided by the Sign of the Makrokosmus: "A worthy soul through the dark urge within it/ Is well aware

46 *Faust*, ll. 308–11.

> Wenn er mir jetzt auch nur verworren dient,
> So werd' ich ihn bald in die Klarheit führen.
> Weiß doch der Gärtner, wenn das Bäumchen grünt,
> Daß Blüt' und Frucht die künft' gen Jahre zieren.

47 English translation is from J. W. Goethe, *Faust*, trans. Walter Kaufmann (Garden City, N.Y., 1961), ll. 341–43.

> Er [Faust] liebt sich bald die unbedingte Ruh;
> Drum geb' ich gern ihm den Gesellen zu,
> Der reizt und wirkt und muß als Teufel schaffen.

48 Cited by Charles Dédéyan, *Le Thème de Faust*, II, 285.

of the appointed course."[49] In the songs celebrating Easter—which save Faust from suicide—the choir of angels foreshadows the hero's final transcendence of solipsistic despair:

> Christ is arisen
> Out of corruption's womb.
> Leave behind prison,
> Fetters and gloom!
> Those who proceed for him,
> Lovingly bleed for him,
> Brotherly feed for him,
> Travel and plead for him,
> And to bliss lead for him,
> For you the Master is near,
> For you he is here.[50]

The love of Christ—typifying surrender rather than affirmation of self—is at this point in the drama foreign to Faust. In arranging a rendezvous with Gretchen and with Helen, in bringing Faust into sustained contact with peasant humanity, Mephistopheles unwittingly makes the hero aware of its rejuvenating power. Rather than providing the one supreme and self-sufficient moment as Mephistopheles expects, love launches Faust's soul from its debased state to a condition of perpetual striving for the Absolute. Thus the devil becomes, as he uncomprehendingly admits, "Part of that force which would/ Do ever evil, and does ever good."[51]

Though he may be as Heinrich Heine labels him, "ein 'subtiler Geist,'"[52] Mephistopheles is by nature impervious to the transcen-

---

49 *Faust*, ll. 328–29. "Ein guter Mensch in seinem dunklen Drange/ Ist sich de rechten Weges wohl bewußt."

50 English translation is from Kaufmann, ll. 797–807.

"Christ ist erstanden,/ Aus der Verwesung Schoß;/ Reißet von Banden/ Freudig euch los!/ Tätig ihn Preisenden,/ Liebe Beweisenden,/ Brüderlich Speisenden,/ Predigend Reisenden,/ Wonne Verheißenden/ Euch ist der Meister nah,/ Euch ist er da!"

51 *Faust*, ll. 1335–36. "Ein Teil von jener Kraft,/ Die stets das Böse will und stets das Gute schafft."

dental dimension that informs the hero's quest. To the Archangels' praise of divine creation and providence, Goethe's devil can respond only with a discordant denial: "on suns and worlds I can shed little light,/ I see but humans, and their piteous plight."[53] The Lord censures the devil for his limited vision, prompting from Mephistopheles a response which suggests a latent humanitarian, though homocentric, impulse: "I feel for mankind in their wretchedness,/ It almost makes me want to plague them less."[54] Though there are aspects of Mephistopheles that render him an interesting, even likable character—his humor, wit, and earthy realism, for example— his calloused sacrifice of Gretchen, her child, and mother belies the noble humanity readers like Heine want to thrust upon him. Mephistopheles would be villainous indeed were it not for the fact that his limited vision reduces him to a pawn in God's providential plan and Faust's ultimate destiny.

Mephistopheles' inability to comprehend the nature of the love which Faust seeks provides an element of irony crucial to Goethe's drama. To Faust's first glimpse of Gretchen, a vision he equates with ideal Beauty, Mephistopheles replies in sensual, debunking terms:

> That paragon of women, sirrah,
> Shall soon confront you in the flesh.
> No fear—with this behind your shirt
> You'll soon see Helen of Troy in every skirt![55]

For Mephistopheles, Faust's sexual consummation with Gretchen culminates her usefulness; she has provided sensual pleasure and hence can be destroyed. But for Faust the sexual union becomes

52 Heinrich Heine, *Sämtliche Werke* (7 vols.; Philadelphia, 1867), VI, 510.

53 *Faust* ll. 279–80. "Von Sonn' und Welten weiß ich nichts zu sagen,/ Ich sehe nur, wie sich die Menschen plagen."

54 *Faust*, ll. 297–98. "Die Menschen dauern mich in ihren Jammertagen, Ich mag sogar die armen selbst nicht plagen."

55 *Faust*, ll. 2601–2604. "Du sollst das Muster aller Frauen/ Nun bald leibhaftig vor dir sehn./ Du siehst, mit diesem Trank im Leibe,/ Bald Helenen in jedem Weibe."

irrelevant. His love for Gretchen grants him reprieve from self-absorption, and sets him on an eternal quest for meaningful self-surrender: "To give one's whole self, and to feel/ An ecstasy that must endure forever!/ Forever! —For its end would be despair,/ No, without end! No end!"[56] Though Gretchen's death plunges Faust into temporary despair—leading him to lament, "That I had never been born!"[57]—he has through her religious faith and profound love become aware of the sublime side of God's mysterious creation. Eventually this awareness enables him to transcend remorse and to exhibit new optimistic resolve:

> Enlivened once again, life's pulses waken
> To greet the kindly dawn's ethereal vision;
> You, earth, outlasted this night, too, unshaken,
> And at my feet you breathe, renewed Elysian,
> Surrounding me with pleasure-scented flowers,
> And deep within you prompt a stern decision;
> To strive for highest life with all my powers.[58]

The private love that Faust shares with Gretchen seems unable to satisfy Faust's longing, for he is driven by a Promethean desire to exhibit his love for all mankind within a social sphere. During the verbal exchange over the conditions of their pact, Faust tells Mephistopheles that he is willing to surrender his soul in afterlife because

---

56 *Faust*, ll. 3191–94. "Sich hinzugeben ganz und eine Wonne/ Zu fühlen, die ewig sein muß!/ Ewig! —Ihr Ende würde Verzweiflung sein./ Nein, kein Ende! Kein Ende!"

57 English translation by Kaufmann, l. 4596. "O wär' ich nie geboren!"

58 English translation by Kaufmann, ll. 4679–85.

> Des Lebens Pulse schlagen frisch lebendig,
> Ätherische Dämmerung milde zu begrüßen;
> Du, Erde, warst auch diese Nacht beständig
> Und atmest neu erquickt zu meinen Füßen,
> Beginnest schon, mit Lust mich zu umgeben,
> Du regst und rührst ein kräftiges Beschließen,
> Zum höchsten Dasein immerfort zu streben.—

"Beyond to me makes little matter;/ If once this earthly world you shatter,/ The next may rise when this has passed."[59] The new world that the hero hopes to initiate will sweep away the abuses hampering the peasant humanity to whom he feels drawn. Faust knows that the common man labors under an antiquated and debilitating social order, that he finds temporary release only on special occasions like Easter when his spontaneous zest for life breaks through social and political barriers. No doubt Faust's discontent with the established order contributes to his reluctance to embrace Gretchen's orthodox Christianity, thrust upon him during the "catechism scene"; yet Faust is hardly agnostic, for he voices a religious faith grounded in a pantheistic affirmation of God's presence in the human heart and natural order:

> The All-comprising,
> The All-sustaining,
> Does he comprise, sustain not
> You, me, himself?[60]

In the second part of *Faust* Goethe's hero embarks upon his quest to improve the social order. He preserves an empire, saves a state from bankruptcy by instituting paper currency, and achieves fame and wealth. But in the process Faust becomes corrupted and fascinated by the forces of evil that serve him. Blindly assuming that his quest for personal power will benefit others, Faust in his pride falls back into his solipsistic prison. He destroys Baucis and Philemon because their piety seems a petty but annoying hindrance to his power. Soon after this action, however, an old woman—Care—strikes him blind. Like Milton's Samson Agonistes, Faust in his blindness sees himself properly for the first time since the Gretchen disaster, and he denounces the forces of black magic which had assisted him in his rise to power: "Could I but clear my path at every

---

59 *Faust*, 1660–63. "Das Drüben kann mich wenig kümmern;/ Schlägst du erst diese Welt zu Trümmern,/ Die andre mag darnach entstehn."

60 *Faust*, ll. 3438–41. "Der Allumfasser,/ Der Allerhalter,/ Faßt und erhält er nicht/ Dich, mich, sich selbst?"

turning/ Of spells, all magic utterly unlearning."[61] The repudiation of magic frees Faust again from his ego and prepares him for eventual salvation. His vision of a land reclamation project, transforming pestiferous swamps into fertile land from which a republic of free men might develop, serves for Faust as an intimation of the moment for which he would be willing to surrender his soul:

> This is the highest wisdom that I own,
> The best that mankind ever knew:
> Freedom and life are earned by those alone
> Who conquer them each day anew,
> Surrounded by such danger, each one thrives,
> Childhood, manhood, and age lead active lives.
> At such a throng I would fain stare,
> With free men on free ground their freedom share.
> Then, to the moment I might say:
> Abide, you are so fair![62]

Mephistopheles, still unable to comprehend the ideal of self-surrender, thinks he has provided Faust the supreme moment, and hence has won the hero's soul. But by offering his soul for the welfare of others, Faust makes his final escape from acute self-consciousness, from the tormenting hell plaguing him at the play's outset. Faust finds ultimate fulfillment in life not, as Mephistopheles expects, because he is sated with egotistical pleasures, but because

---

61 *Faust*, ll. 11404–05. "Könnt' ich Magie von meinem Pfad entfernen,/ Die Zaubersprüche ganz und gar verlernen."

62 *Faust*, ll. 11573–82.

> Ja! diesem Sinne bin ich ganz ergeben,
> Das ist der Weisheit letzter Schluß;
> Nur der verdient sich Freiheit wie das Leben,
> Der täglich sie erobern muß.
> Und so verbringt, umrungen von Gefahr,
> Hier Kindheit, Mann und Greis sein tüchtig Jahr.
> Solch ein Gewimmel möcht' ich sehn,
> Auf freiem Grund mit freiem Volke stehn.
> Zum Augenblicke dürft' ich sagen:
> Verweile doch, du bist so schön!

73

he repudiates entirely the selfishness to which Mephistopheles caters.

Erich Heller argues that the devil does indeed have legal claim to the hero's soul, which he loses only because of "the intervention of the inscrutable grace of God."[63] But, significantly, Faust uses the conditional tense in relaying his vision: he says not that he *is* satisfied but only that he "might" be supremely content if his vision were to be realized. Hence one might well argue that the hero continues to strive at the play's close and that, consequently, Mephistopheles has not yet won the wager. The implication is that Faust will remain dissatisfied until the fusion of his ideal, transcendental vision and mortal reality is accomplished. At that point, one assumes, the evolutionary progression of man toward divinity would have run its destined course. For God, and for Goethe, the Promethean figure who sacrifices his soul for the improvement of mankind becomes truly heroic, ready to move on to even greater planes of experience.

Finally Goethe's play is not so much about a particular hero as it is a celebration of a divinely ordained process culminating in man's triumph over the limits seemingly imposed by mortality and self-interest. Eugène Lerminier writes that Faust is "le drame du panthéisme moderne, de ce panthéisme idéal qui met la pensée à l'origine et au dénouement des choses."[64] Lamartine admires the play for its "drame le plus miraculeux, le plus naturel et le plus surnaturel de tous les drames conçus par le génie religieux de l'humanité."[65] For Carlyle, as cited by Dedéyan, "Faust montre que cet effort peut être consacré et béni du Ciel."[66] Cosmic in scope, *Faust* offers the prototype of the romantic individual who transcends a purgatorial existence to achieve heroic stature; but he does so only by his active engagement in a providentially sanctioned mission.

---

63 Erich Heller, "On Goethe's Faust," in Victor Lange (ed.), *Goethe: A Collection of Critical Essays* (Englewood Cliffs, N.J., 1968), 142.

64 Eugène Lerminier, *Au delà du Rhin, ou tableau politique et philosophique de l'Allemagne depuis Mme de Staël à nos jours* (2 vols.; Paris, 1846), II, 206.

65 Lamartine, *Cours familier de littérature* (Paris, 1866), XXI, 262.

66 Charles Dédéyan, *Le Thème de Faust*, II, 495.

Shelley shares with Goethe a firm belief that man and the human community are evolving toward a higher, purer order of existence. Throughout the English poet's work there develops an awareness of the gradual destruction of civilization. But convinced that "The soul of man, like unextinguished fire,/ Yet burns toward heaven,"[67] Shelley as poet trusts that from the decay can emerge an humanitarian order approximating a Platonic ideal community of free men. The necessary ingredient in such transformation of civilization is a revolution of the human spirit, a process whereby man comes to realize that "the great secret of morals is love, or a going out of our own nature and an identification of ourselves with the beautiful which exists in thought, action, or person, not our own."[68] Shelley offers a mythic rendering of this process in *Prometheus Unbound* (1820), a symbolic closet drama whose hero is no mere man but an embodiment of human nature as it should be, "the type of the highest perfection of moral and intellectual nature, impelled by the purest and truest motives to the best and noblest ends."[69] Shelley's apocalyptic vision of humanity's eventual deliverance from tyranny offers the consummate heroic ideal: the one hero and the community he represents fuse into a single force with the moral strength required to transform the world. Through love and acceptance of a redemptive and providential destiny, the human spirit realizes its heroic potential.

As Shelley's drama opens, Prometheus is defiant, "eyeless in hate" (I, i, 9) and a declared foe of Jupiter, the principle of evil in the universe who represents the powers of blackness devouring the human soul. Not only is Jupiter's dominion linked to social manifestations of evil such as war and cruelty but it also extends to human malignity: "self-love or self-contempt" and "self-mistrust." He embodies all that "makes the Heart deny the yes it breathes." Chained

---

67 Act III, i, 5–6. All references to *Prometheus Unbound* are to Thomas Hutchinson (ed.), *Shelley: Poetical Works*, and are cited parenthetically.

68 Percy Bysshe Shelley, "Defense of Poetry," in David Lee Clark (ed.), *Shelley's Prose*, 282–83.

69 Shelley, "Preface," *Prometheus Unbound*, in *Shelley: Poetical Works*, 205.

to a rock and tormented by furies who are "foul desire round" his "astonished heart," Prometheus symbolizes "the human soul when instead of escaping from itself through love . . . is shackled and tormented by its own hostility."[70] When Demogorgon asserts in Act III that "All spirits are enslaved which serve things evil," he refers back to Prometheus as we see him in Act I: In his calm hatred, Shelley's hero becomes Jupiter's servant.

But through his suffering Prometheus gains wisdom, realizes the power of love, and relinquishes his hatred of Jupiter:

> I speak in grief,
> Not exaltation, for I hate no more,
> As then ere misery made me wise. The curse
> Once breathed on thee I would recall. (I, i, 56–59)

Chained to the rock, Prometheus is subjected to the tormenting vision of idealism corrupted, most notably the perversion of Christianity and the bloody aftermath of the French Revolution. He realizes that human idealism fails because men seem unable to escape selfish desires, because all, like himself, pursue courses marred by hatred and vengeance. But gradually for Prometheus good triumphs over evil; with a simple yet forceful exercise of will, Shelley's hero expels evil from his heart: "It doth repent me: words are quick and vain;/ Grief for awhile is blind, and so was mind./ I wish no living thing to suffer pain" (I, i, 303–305). His renunciation of personal revenge—an act of unselfish love—culminates the hero's spiritual regeneration. The forces of Demogorgon (*i.e.*, cosmic necessity) spring into action, tumbling Jupiter from his throne and freeing Prometheus (or mankind) from hatred's tyranny. Prometheus is clearly transformed: "his pale wound-worn limbs/ Fell from him" and "the overpowering light/ Of that immortal shape was shadowed o'er/ By love . . . " (II, i, 71–73).

Through his reformation of heart Prometheus achieves union

70 David Perkins, *The Quest for Permanence: The Symbolism of Wordsworth, Shelley, and Keats* (Cambridge, Mass., 1959), 159.

with Asia—a symbol of the transcendent power of Beauty and Love which provides the permanence the Shelleyan hero seeks. The two retire to a cave "all overgrown with trailing odorous plants,/ Which curtain out the day" (III, iii, 11–12), where Prometheus hopes to escape the flux and decay permeating human life: "we will sit and talk of time and change,/ As the world ebbs and flows, ourselves unchanged" (III, iii, 23–24). Unlike Faust, who sacrifices himself for a utopian vision of an ideal society that continues in time, Prometheus seems to withdraw from his fellows, to achieve a salvation that at first glance seems only personal.

Yet Shelley's hero embodies the human spirit, and his personal salvation triggers a process eventually redeeming all mankind. Even the earth mirrors the hero's regeneration. While Prometheus is chained to the rock only "blue thistles," "toads," and "poisonous weeds" grace the earth's surface; but after love transforms the hero's soul, "toads, and snakes, and efts" become beautiful. As in the "Ancient Mariner," "all things had put their evil nature off" (III, iv, 77). Through the hero's suffering and love, a new, humane social order begins its evolutionary process:

> The loathesome mask has fallen, the man remains
> Sceptreless, free, uncircumscribed, but man
> Equal, unclassed, tribeless, and nationless,
> Exempt from awe, worship, degree, the king
> Over himself; just, gentle, wise. . . . (III, iv, 193–97)

Bravely opposing the malevolent forces operative in the universe, cleansing his heart of its malignity, and assuming responsibility for his fellows, man fulfills the heroic ideal. Shelley, as romantic poet, is both seer and moralist, fulfilling his obligation to humanity by making tangible his private, prophetic vision of what is possible and how it is to be achieved.

The Ancient Mariner, Faust, and Prometheus reflect the romantic search for a hero who transcends personal despair and alienation to accept his role in a providential order. His role requires that the hero escape the morbid self-absorption so often characteristic of the romantic protagonist and become active in a social arena, leading his fellows in their quest for a new culture based upon enduring values. The heroic ideal thus involves the fusion of personal, social, and divine purposes; in his acceptance of communal responsibility the hero fulfills God's providential plan, rejuvenates a decadent culture, and transforms his despair into a personal fulfillment granting serenity and hope.

IV

The Failure of the Heroic Ideal: American Questioning of the Perfectionist Premise

The element of communal responsibility in the romantic heroic ideal becomes especially pertinent in American literature because of what Lewis P. Simpson calls "the remarkable congruence of history and fiction" in American culture.[1] From its beginnings America has always seemed more a concept of mind—an idea—than a specific geographical locale. In their attempt to make sense of their role in the process of history, the architects of the American political experience saw their work as a grand experiment, an attempt to realize the vision of the eighteenth-century *philosophes*. For John Adams and his generation, "The Revolution was effected before the war commenced."[2] Adams understood that "the nation created by the Revolution exists not in blood but in mind," and that its central document, the Declaration of Independence, was as Thomas Jefferson

---

1 Lewis P. Simpson, "John Adams and Hawthorne: The Fiction of the Real American Revolution," *Studies in the Literary Imagination*, IX (Fall, 1976), 1.
2 John Q. Adams, Letter to H. Niles, February 13, 1818, in Adrienne Koch (ed.), *The American Enlightenment* (New York, 1965), 228.

conceived it, the logical culmination of the European Enlightenment, "the climax of the Great Critique."[3] Thus from the outset the American faced the difficult task of self-definition, of locating and justifying himself within an intellectual context of European origin. Many of the central works of American romanticism reflect this quest for self-definition and, as Simpson shows, in the process they illuminate the pervasive tendency of the American to internalize history, to link self-consciousness to the larger problem of national identity.

If Americans, as George Washington writes, "are . . . to be considered as the actors on a most conspicuous theatre, which seems to be peculiarly designated by Providence for the display of human greatness and felicity,"[4] then the representative heroes of our early national literature assume major symbolic importance. For romantic historians such as George Bancroft and William Hickling Prescott, the hero loses individual qualities to become, as David Levin writes, the "idealization of American motives," emblematic of "all that is most noble in the American character."[5] Emerson writes in the mid–nineteenth century that Boston has been "appointed in the destiny of nations to lead . . . civilization" and is "continuing [its] holy errand into the wilderness."[6] To lead the providential mission, there develops in our literature from Edwards to Emerson, Sacvan Bercovitch writes, the prototypical "American self as the embodiment of a prophetic universal design."[7] In its understanding of its providential role, and in accepting the challenge posed by a Europe looking to a new world for fulfillment of an idealized vision of perfected human society, America becomes, in a sense, the supreme romantic

3 Simpson, "John Adams and Hawthorne," 6.
4 Worthington Chauncey Ford (ed.), *The Writings of George Washington* (14 vols.; New York, 1889–93), X, 225.
5 David Levin, *History as Romantic Art: Bancroft, Prescott, Motley, and Parkman* (Palo Alto, Cal., 1959), 50–51; 71.
6 Emerson, "Boston," in E. W. Emerson (ed.), *Complete Works*, XII, 188–89.
7 Sacvan Bercovitch, *The Puritan Origins of the American Self* (New Haven, Conn., 1975), 136.

hero. Hence in dramatizing the heroic individual's search for identity and fulfillment, the American romantic artist gives expression to the nation's understanding of its role in historical process.

In his attempt to embody the heroic ideal, the romantic artist confronts a fundamental tension introduced but never reconciled by the political theorists giving birth to the nation. The American experiment was perhaps most revolutionary in its premise that the state exists to serve the individual, a premise reflected in the fact that the amended Constitution devotes far more attention to the individual's rights and freedoms than to his responsibilities to the emerging nation. For Jefferson, "that government is best which governs least"; but the central question remains: what amount of liberty must the individual forfeit in order for the state to function effectively in defense of liberty at all? Behind the Jeffersonian dream lies the assumption that the community of individuals that was to become the nation was a collection of responsible selves who understood the necessity of sacrifice for communal welfare; otherwise democracy becomes chaotic disaster, giving rise to the nightmarish vision of the mob scenes in Hawthorne's "My Kinsman, Major Molineux."

A major facet of the American romantic movement—transcendentalism—derives its force from a commitment to individual fulfillment, even if it means abrogating governmentally imposed responsibilities. In an 1831 address, William Ellery Channing asserted that "all moral and religious truth may be reduced to one great cultural thought, perfection of mind."[8] Developing from a union of "Unitarianism—whose characteristic dogma was trust in individual reason as correlative to Supreme Wisdom" and "German Idealism, as taught . . . by Kant and Jacobi, Fichte and Novalis, Schelling and Hegel, Schleiermacher and De Wette, by Madame de Staël, Cousin, Coleridge and Carlyle," American transcendentalism epitomized the emphasis on romantic individualism implicit in the Dec-

8 W. E. Channing, *The Works of William Ellery Channing, D. D.* (Boston, 1877), 127.

laration of Independence: it "was an assertion of the inalienable integrity of man . . . [his] birthright to universal good."[9] Emerson expresses well the crucial dichotomy in romantic thought in his analysis of American intellectual history between 1820 and 1840:

> The former generations acted under the belief that a shining social prosperity was the beatitude of man, and sacrificed uniformly the citizen to the State. The modern mind believed that the nation existed for the individual, for the guardianship and education of every man. This idea, roughly written in revolutions and national movements, in the mind of the philosopher had far more precision; the individual is the world.[10]

But Emerson's idealistic emphasis on self-fulfillment functions effectively within a social context only if one grants his premise that the self celebrated "was not only his but America's."[11]

Though Emerson, Channing, Thoreau, and Whitman articulate the premise of "perfectible realm of mind" embodied in the Declaration,[12] certain other American romantics—notably Hawthorne and Melville—question the premise of perfectibility, exposing in their fiction the personal and social dangers inherent in the individual's doomed quest for passionate self-fulfillment at any cost. George Santayana, in his 1911 address "The Genteel Tradition in American Philosophy," argued that during the course of the early nineteenth century Calvinism "lost its basis in American life"; with Emerson and the Transcendentalists, "the sense of sin totally evaporated. . . . How strange to the American now that saying of Jonathan Edwards, that men are naturally God's enemies!"[13] But with Hawthorne and Melville the lingering remnants of Calvinism remained. Santayana's description of Calvinism as "an expression of the agonized conscience" presenting "a view of the world which an

9   W. E. Channing, "A Participant's Definition," in Perry Miller (ed.), *The American Transcendentalists: Their Prose and Poetry* (Garden City, N. Y., 1957), 36–37.

10 Emerson, "Historic Notes of Life and Letters in New England," in E. W. Emerson (ed.), *Complete Works*, X, 326.

11 Bercovitch, *Puritan Origins*, 165.

12 Simpson, "John Adams and Hawthorne," 4.

13 George Santayana, *The Genteel Tradition: Nine Essays by George Santayana*, ed. Douglas L. Wilson (Cambridge, Mass., 1967), 42–43.

agonized conscience readily embraces" illuminates much of the best fiction of both Hawthorne and Melville—a man who, according to Hawthorne, "can neither believe, nor be comfortable in his unbelief."[14] Both may be said to be "divided between tragic concern at his own miserable condition, and tragic exultation about the universe at large," and each "oscillates between a profound abasement and a paradoxical elation of the spirit."[15] Hawthorne writes, "There is evil in every human heart, which may remain latent, perhaps, through the whole of life; but circumstances may rouse it to activity."[16] Yet his concept of the human soul, while agonizingly aware of human depravity, remains a curiously optimistic affirmation of its essential beauty:

The human Heart to be allegorized as a cavern; at the entrance there is sunshine, and flowers growing about it. You step within, but a short distance, and begin to find yourself surrounded with a terrible gloom, and monsters of divers kinds; it seems like Hell itself. You are bewildered, and wander long without hope. At last a light strikes upon you. You press towards it yon, and find yourself in a region that seems, in some sort, to reproduce the flowers and sunny beauty of the entrance, but all perfect. These are the depths of the heart, or of human nature, bright and peaceful; the gloom and terror may lie deep; but deeper still is the eternal beauty.[17]

As "dark" romantics, both Hawthorne and Melville write novels which serve as parodies of transcendentalist social experiments and assessments of human nature (*The Blithedale Romance*, *The Celestial Railroad* by Hawthorne, *Pierre* by Melville).[18] Furthermore, Hol-

---

14   Nathaniel Hawthorne, *The English Notebooks*, ed. Randall Stewart (New York, 1962), 433.

15   The quoted passages are from Santayana's discussion of Calvinism in *The Genteel Tradition*, 41.

16   Hawthorne, *The American Notebooks*, ed. Claude M. Simpson, vol. VIII of *The Centenary Edition of the Works of Nathaniel Hawthorne*, 29.

17   *Ibid.*, VIII, 237.

18   Michael J. Hoffman argues that in *Moby-Dick* "Melville dramatizes the fallacy of the Transcendentalistic position," and Hoffman quotes a letter from Melville to Hawthorne in which the author of *Moby-Dick* reveals his central reservation about Emerson: "I could readily see in Emerson, not withstanding his merit, a gaping flaw. It was, the insinuation that had he lived in those days when the world was

lingsworth in *The Blithedale Romance* and Ahab in *Moby-Dick* are Emersonian heroes of self-reliance *in extremis*; though they both exhibit heroic qualities, each becomes villainous and defeated in a quest for self-realization which dwarfs his humanity and severs all ties binding him to the communal order. From the work of Hawthorne and Melville develops the awareness that, as Robert Penn Warren writes, "the prime example of individualism, the man of will who says, 'I please myself,' is the victim of the last illusion: he can have no self. Why? Because the true self, among the many varieties of fictive selves, can develop only in a vital relation between the unitary person and the group. That is, the self is possible only in a community." [19]

Hawthorne and Melville manifest an essentially Calvinistic awareness of man's innate depravity which would seem to call into question any expectation of human or social perfectibility. Indeed, one might well wonder how puritan America could have ever expected success from the idealistic vision underlying the Declaration. The hope sprang from faith in providence, a firm conviction that the grace of God would inform their quest and ensure its successful completion. Bercovitch points out that for the American puritan there were two kinds of providence: one was essentially individual, guiding the otherwise doomed soul to a predestined salvation; the second was basically secular—the providence of history—intervening in social and political affairs to guide a nation toward its destiny. Crucial to both is explicit faith in God's direct presence in human affairs. For the homocentric idealism of the Renaissance humanist or the secular self-assertion of the Rousseauistic romantic, the American puritan harbored contempt and distrust; he "required a higher authority, an external absolute." [20]

---

made, he might have offered some valuable suggestions." See Michael J. Hoffman, "The Anti-Transcendentalism of *Moby-Dick*," *Georgia Review*, XXIII (1969), 3–16.

19 Robert Penn Warren, *Democracy and Poetry* (Cambridge, Mass., 1975), 25.

20 Bercovitch, *Puritan Origins*, 40; 10–11.

Like Shelley's Prometheus and Goethe's Faust, the puritan hero manifests the fusion of both providences—individual and historical—for his private progression toward redemption coincides with the nation's fulfillment of its destiny. In his *Magnalia Christi Americana*, Cotton Mather presents such a hero in John Winthrop, the first governor of New England. Overcoming personal faults and moving toward personal faith in God's providence, Winthrop gains significance not as an individual but as prototypical embodiment of the soul's journey to God. The *Magnalia Christi Americana* "transmutes history itself into a drama of the soul," though, as Bercovitch elaborates:

> To transmute history does not in this case mean to reject or submerge historical details. It does mean that the "real facts" become a means to a higher end, a vehicle for laying bare the soul—or more accurately, the essential landmarks in the soul's journey to God. And the journey thus abstracted provides a guide for every man . . . in the choices he must face, the war he must engage in between the forces of evil and good in his heart. . . . Secular realism tells us what is different, unique, about the individual; Mather uses detail to convert *historia* into *allegoria*. He makes the particular events of Winthrop's life an index to the hero's universality.[21]

But Winthrop is heroic not only because in his personal progression to God he provides a model for others but because his individual salvation is inextricably bound to the nation's realization of its providential destiny. Mather labels his hero "Nehemias Americanus," identifying the American with the biblical figure who first governed the Israelites' restored theocracy after their captivity in Babylon, inspiring God's people to accept once again the burden of their holy covenant. Rekindling the Israelites' sense of destiny, protecting them from heathen neighbors, and reforming both civil and religious abuses, Nehemiah revitalized what had become a stagnant, despairing community. For the puritan, the heroic self discovers its identity only in relation to the providence which directs it and the community which commands its service. The many biographies of Washington written in the early nineteenth century reflect the same

21 *Ibid.*, 8.

heroic concept; they "are portraits of the saint as the *figura* of a communal errand."[22]

For Hawthorne—the "unchurched Puritan" or "secular calvinist"[23]—the two distinct forms of providence rarely merge. Several scholars have pointed out that "My Kinsman, Major Molineux" suggests two related levels of interpretation: a Freudian, individual search for a viable father figure which provides the hero self-definition and a promising future; and a nation's quest for identity after severing ties to the fatherland in its deposition of the scapegoat king.[24] But as Daniel Hoffman contends, while Robin seems successful in his acquisition of a viable identity, the outlook for the nation is not so hopeful; fueled by the "double-visaged" principle of anarchic rebellion, the community is left bereft of an ordering principle. A similar pattern operates in *The Scarlet Letter*: the Faustian Dimmesdale achieves personal salvation through the ironic assistance of the satanic Chillingworth, though his maturity and spiritual deliverance have no effect upon the community's sterility and decay.

As a variation of the Faust motif, *The Scarlet Letter* deserves scrutiny, for it demonstrates that without the fusion of the two providential realms heroism proves impossible. So many Faustian elements permeate Hawthorne's 1850 novel that scholars have some difficulty deciding which of the three central characters is Hawthorne's Faust; Leslie Fiedler seemingly solves the dilemma by concluding that "all three . . . make the Faustian commitment, but they are providentially tricked into Grace."[25] Many of the elements of Goethe's *Faust*

---

22 *Ibid.*, 150. See also Richard Hankins, "Puritans, Patriots, and Panegyric: The Beginnings of American Biography," *Studies in the Literary Imagination*, IX (Fall, 1976), 95–109.

23 Fiedler, *Love and Death in the American Novel*, 421; Peter L. Thorslev, Jr., "Hawthorne's Determinism: An Analysis," *Nineteenth-Century Fiction*, XIX (1964), 141–57.

24 Roy Male, *Hawthorne's Tragic Vision* (New York, 1964), 48–53; Daniel Hoffman, *Form and Fable in American Fiction* (New York, 1961), 117.

25 Fiedler, *Love and Death in the American Novel*, 514–19; others who have noted the Faustian elements of *The Scarlet Letter* include Daniel Hoffman, *Form and Fable*, 185; and Charles Dédéyan, *Le Thème de Faust*, II, 543–45. Jane Lundblad surveys

are indeed present: the intellectual, respected, and alienated man of sensibility who desperately seeks love but proves too weak to achieve it; the "saint-like" woman victimized by the hero's passion but who, in accepting the consequences of her sin, receives the grace of God; and the Mephistopheles-like demon who probes the Faustian hero "like a treasure-seeker in a dark cavern"[26] in an attempt to damn his soul, only to become the providential agent spurring the hero toward his redemption.

Chillingworth in many ways seems the perfect Mephistopheles to Dimmesdale's Faust. His "entry on the scene . . . out of the sky, or starting from the nether earth, had an aspect of mystery, which was easily heightened to the miraculous" (121); and his demonic purpose is clear, for with "a smile of dark and self-relying intelligence" Chillingworth tries to coax Hester to reveal her lover's identity, vowing "Sooner or later, he must needs be mine!" (75). The community at large, prone to accept divine intervention in their daily lives, sees "a providential hand in Roger Chillingworth's so opportune arrival" (121); even the most sensible think "that Heaven had wrought an absolute miracle, by transporting an eminent Doctor of Physic, from a German University, bodily through the air, and setting him down at the door of Mr. Dimmesdale's study" (121). At first glance the diabolical physician's conception of himself as an agent of "dark necessity" (174) intent upon Dimmesdale's spiritual destruction renders the community's faith in providence ironic. Ultimately, however, it is Chillingworth rather than the community who misunderstands his role:

It grew to be a widely diffused opinion, that the Reverend Arthur Dimmesdale, like many other personages of especial sanctity, in all ages of the Christian world, was haunted either by Satan himself, or Satan's emissary, in the guise of old Roger Chil-

---

the qualities and conventions of the gothic romance tradition and documents Hawthorne's indebtedness. See Jane Lundblad, *Nathaniel Hawthorne and European Literary Tradition* (New York, 1965), 81–149.

26 Nathaniel Hawthorne, *The Scarlet Letter*, vol. I of *The Centenary Edition of the Works of Nathaniel Hawthorne*, 124. Subsequent references are to this edition and are cited parenthetically.

lingworth. This diabolical agent had the Divine permission, for a season, to burrow into the clergyman's intimacy, and plot against his soul. . . . The people looked, with an unshaken hope, to see the minister come forth out of the conflict, transfigured with the glory which he would unquestionably win. (178)

Dimmesdale's final confession and transformation prove the community's expectations to be accurate. Unwittingly Chillingworth, in his attempt to destroy Dimmesdale, becomes the necessary agent of the minister's redemption; thus, like his German counterpart, Hawthorne's Mephistopheles seems *"Ein Teil von jener Kraft,/ Die stets das Böse will und stets das Gute schafft."* [27]

But the illuminating parallels between *The Scarlet Letter* and *Faust* serve to highlight significant thematic differences. Whereas Faust becomes godlike in transcending human limitations, Dimmesdale becomes human in accepting his frailty. Indeed, Fiedler is probably accurate when he claims that for Hawthorne there can be no hero; the American author demonstrates throughout his work "the illusion of heroism, the dream of transcending one's humanity, is the last diabolic temptation." [28] Another fundamental difference: unlike Faust's redemption, which involves the improvement of mankind and realization of a communal destiny, Dimmesdale's salvation is solely personal. Though his soul-searching and purgatorial progression toward transfiguration might serve as a prototype of the individual soul's "journey to God," Dimmesdale is in no sense like Washington, "the *figura* of a communal errand." The community remains sterile, still unwilling to admit into its society the procreative principle of femininity embodied and vilified in the *A* on Hester's breast.

Melville's *Moby-Dick* (1851) presents a sustained exploration of the nature of romantic heroism, and of the vital relationship between the heroic personality and the community which he serves. Alan Heimert has argued persuasively that Melville presents in *Moby-Dick* a metaphor for nineteenth-century America's political situation; like the *Pequod*, the nation is a loose collection of "isola-

27 *Faust*, ll. 1336–37.
28 Fiedler, *Love and Death in the American Novel*, 516–19.

toes" of disparate national origin in search of communal purpose.[29] A great deal of scholarly controversy has developed regarding the novel's central focus: whose novel is *Moby-Dick*, Ishmael's or Ahab's? Though often criticized, the novel's divided focus is appropriate, for *Moby-Dick* relates the interrelated stories of both Ahab and Ishmael. Each belongs to a distinct tradition of romantic heroism, and in Melville's novel these two traditions are set against one another in an attempt to call attention to the hero's responsibilities within both a cosmic and social context.

Without question Ahab—the "grand, ungodly, god-like man"[30]—has heroic qualities. Stanley Geist argues that such qualities result from Ahab's suffering, an "ennobling" experience that lifts him to the level of Promethean titan: "For if the greatness of the individual, residing wholly within his own vision of the world, was contingent upon no one and nothing outside himself, what distinction remained on the timeless and bodiless spiritual plane between human and superhuman?"[31] Yet, in leading the crew of the *Pequod* to its destruction in his monomaniac quest for personal revenge, Ahab takes his place in the tradition of demoniac heroism fostered by Manfred and Ethan Brand.[32] Equating "all his intellectual and spiritual exasperations" with the white whale, Ahab is prompted by a satanic drive to discover the inscrutable, to slash away the veil hiding intellectual certainty. "That inscrutable thing is chiefly what I hate," Ahab tells Starbuck. "And be the white whale agent, or be the white whale principal, I will wreak that hate upon him" (144). In his search for

---

29 Alan Heimert, "*Moby-Dick* and American Political Symbolism," *American Quarterly*, XV (Winter, 1963), 498–534.

30 Herman Melville, *Moby-Dick; or, The Whale*, ed. Harrison Hayford and Hershel Parker (New York, 1967), 76. Subsequent references are to this edition and appear parenthetically.

31 Stanley Geist, *Herman Melville: The Tragic Vision and the Heroic Ideal* (Cambridge, Mass., 1939), 43–44.

32 F. O. Matthiessen contends that Melville modeled Ahab on Hawthorne's Ethan Brand, "whom Melville regarded as typifying the man whose inordinate development of will and brain 'eats out the heart.'" See Matthiessen, *The American Renaissance*, 450.

certainty, his quest to transcend human limitations, other mortals become mere tools to serve the captain's demonic purpose: those forming his crew, Ahab cries, "are not other men, but my arms and my legs" (465); Queequeg with his tattoos becomes for Ahab a "devilish tantalization of the gods" (399); little Pip, the cabin boy who fell overboard and saw "God's foot upon the treadle of the loom" (347), receives Ahab's aid because, the captain tells him, "I do suck most wondrous philosophies from thee! Some unknown conduits from the unknown worlds must empty into thee" (433). Though defiant in his alienation, Ahab is not without his humanity; during one quite moving dialogue with Starbuck, Ahab pleads, "Close! stand close to me, Starbuck; let me look into a human eye; it is better than to gaze into sea or sky; better than to gaze upon God" (444). Yet such recognition serves only to remind Ahab that his satanic quest had led him from human fellowship, that he is completely the slave of the demonic forces represented by the Zoroastrian fire-worshipper, Fedallah: "So far gone am I in the dark side of earth, that its other side, the theoretic bright one, seems but uncertain twilight" (433).

John Parke suggests that one level of meaning in *Moby-Dick* involves Ahab's tragic confrontation with a world devoid of providence, a "physical, ethical, metaphysical chaos."[33] But Parke, like Lawrence Thompson, makes the mistake of identifying the novel's overall thematic pattern with Ahab's quest. Because it is through Ishmael's eyes that the voyage of the *Pequod* becomes a spiritual journey, Ahab's importance in the novel rests largely on his role as a projection of the narrator's intellectual and spiritual restlessness. Considering the structure of the book—which begins and ends with focus on Ishmael—and the overt parallels to the biblical myths of Job and Jonah, David Hirsch's assertion that the novel is most fruitfully approached as an epic in the biblical tradition with Ishmael as the center of consciousness seems more plausible than the readings

---

33 John Parke, "Seven *Moby-Dicks*," *New England Quarterly*, XXVIII (1955), 331.

offered by Geist, Parke, and Thompson.[34] Indeed, through the effects of the *Pequod*'s voyage on Ishmael's developing spiritual and moral identity the divine providence which Ahab denies becomes apparent.

Tied by his choice of name—"Call me Ishmael"—to the biblical wanderer, the narrator of *Moby-Dick* bears direct affinities to heroes in the romantic *mal du siècle* tradition: the Mariner, Harold, René, Werther. Passive throughout the voyage, Ishmael goes to sea in search of an allusive identity: "And still deeper the meaning of that story of Narcissus, who because he could not grasp the tormenting, mild image he saw in the fountain, plunged into it and was drowned. But that same image, we ourselves see in all rivers and oceans" (14). At first the "damp, drizzly November" in Ishmael's soul leads the melancholy narrator, fascinated with death, to identify his purpose in life with Ahab's quest. Like his captain, Ishmael early reveals that he is in search of "the ungraspable phantom of life" which is "the key to it all" (14); indeed, he is conscious of a certain affinity to Ahab from the outset:

> I felt a sympathy and a sorrow for him, but for I don't know what, unless it was the cruel loss of his leg. And yet I also felt a strange awe of him; but that sort of awe, which I cannot at all describe, was not exactly awe; I do not know what it was. But I felt it; and it did not disincline me towards him. (77)

This sympathetic awe finally leads Ishmael to confess that "because of the dread in my soul . . . Ahab's quenchless feud seemed mine" (155).

The word *seemed* is all important here. Melville merges the reader's sympathies with Ishmael's so that we respond as he does to events around him. Like Ishmael, we hear so much about the "ungodly, god-like" Ahab before he first appears that we await anxiously the emergence of a superhuman, almost mythical, creature of grand stature; and with Ishmael we are prone to agree: "Reality out-

---

34 David Hirsch, "The Dilemma of the Liberal Intellectual: Melville's Ishmael," *Texas Studies in Literature and Language*, V (Summer, 1963), 169–70.

ran apprehension; Captain Ahab stood upon his quarter-deck" (109). The novel's shift of focus from Ishmael to Ahab reflects the narrator's temporary absorption into the identity of the monomaniacal captain, whose quest both fascinates and appalls him. But the central thematic focus of the novel involves Ishmael's—and the reader's—gradual disengagement from Ahab, a final escape from the irredeemably selfish and nihilistic alienation of the defiant captain. The escape is effected through Ishmael's relationship to the cannibal-prince Queequeg. Possessing at all times engraved into his body "a complete theory of the heavens and the earth, and a mystical treatise on the art of attaining truth," Queequeg embodies and eventually passes on to Ishmael via his coffin the complete Christian teaching of love and religious faith denied by the anti-Christ, Ahab.

The Christlike qualities of the cannibal Queequeg present an interesting antithesis to the satanic antichristian madness of Ahab.[35] Whereas Ahab is baptized in fire "in nomine diaboli" by Fedallah, rejects the Christian admonition of the *Rachel* ("Do to me as you would have me to do to you in the like case"), and dies vowing eternal hatred of the forces represented by the white whale, Queequeg acts instinctively from a divine law of love, assuming, at the risk of his life, responsibility for his fellows. He leaves home to wander on the dangerous seas not on a mission of selfish revenge but in a sincere effort "to learn among the Christians, the arts whereby to make his people still happier than they were; and more than that, still better than they were" (57). When an impudent bumpkin who insults Queequeg falls overboard and almost drowns, the savage in what seems "madness" jumps overboard to save the boy's life. Not only does this action illustrate the Christian doctrines of love and forgiveness but it serves as the first in a series of incidents in which Queequeg, like Christ, becomes in his love an agent of rebirth: when Tashtego falls overboard the *Pequod* Queequeg again risks his life to draw another from the threshold of death; he offers the coffin pre-

---

35 For discussion of Ahab as anti-Christ see Henry A. Murray, "In Nomine Diaboli," *New England Quarterly*, XXIV (1951), 439.

pared during his sickness as a life preserver with thirty life lines, enough for the entire crew; and finally Queequeg's coffin saves Ishmael's life at the novel's close.

Queequeg's coffin assumes major symbolic importance for it becomes the cohesive metaphor into which the novel's metaphysical paradoxes converge. Specifically, as William Rosenfeld points out, the coffin embodies the cannibal's intense religious faith.[36] Introduced to Ishmael at the Spouter Inn by the proprietor Peter Coffin, Queequeg initially impresses the hero with his extreme religious devotion during Ramadan. His tattoos engraved into his body, Queequeg surrenders completely to his faith, never once attempting to comprehend the inscrutable symbols. During his illness, Queequeg carefully engraves his tattoos into his coffin, and after recovering his health converts the coffin into a life buoy. Even Ahab notices the significance of Queequeg's symbolic act: "Here now's the very dreaded symbol of grim death, by a mere hap, made the expressive sign of the help and hope of most endangered life. A life-buoy of a coffin! Does it go further? Can it be that in some spiritual sense the coffin is, after all, but an immortality-preserver!" (433). The engraved coffin which Ishmael embraces at the novel's close embodies the antithesis to Ahab's satanic isolation.

From the beginning of their relationship it is obvious that Ishmael sees in Queequeg qualities which he finds soothing to the melancholy stemming from his early spiritual alienation. "I began to be sensible of strange feelings," Ishmael admits shortly after meeting Queequeg. "I felt a melting in me. No more my splintered heart and maddened hand were turned against the wolfish world. This soothing savage had redeemed it" (53). Later, thinking "metaphysically" of his situation on the monkey-rope with Queequeg, Ishmael remarks: "I seemed distinctly to perceive that my own individuality was now merged in a joint stock company of two; that my free will had received a mortal wound; and that another's mistake or misfor-

36 William Rosenfeld, "Uncertain Faith: Queequeg's Coffin and Melville's Use of the Bible," *Texas Studies in Literature and Language*, VII (Winter, 1966), 317–27.

tune might plunge innocent me into unmerited disaster and death" (271). Despite his apparent reluctance to welcome human interdependence, Ishmael here recognizes its necessity, as well as its virtual universality: "I saw that this situation of mine was the precise situation of every mortal that breathes" (271). This recognition is a most significant step in his break from the bonds linking him to Ahab's satanism.

Ishmael's recognition of the necessity of human interdependence moves into an appreciation of its beauty in the chapter "A Squeeze of the Hand." Sitting "cross-legged on the deck . . . under a blue tranquil sky," Ishmael squeezes the "gentle globules" of whale sperm, joyously exclaiming: "Squeeze! squeeze! squeeze! all the morning long; I squeezed that sperm till I myself almost melted into it; I squeezed that sperm till a strange sort of insanity came over me; and I found myself unwittingly squeezing my co-laborers' hands in it. . . . Come; let us squeeze hands all round; nay, let us all squeeze ourselves . . . universally into the very milk and sperm of kindness" (348–49). In the sperm Ishmael washes himself clean of the pledge to destroy and pursue, of his involvement in Ahab's blasphemous quest. "I forgot all about our horrible oath," he confesses. "In that inexpressible sperm, I washed my hands and my heart of it. . . . I felt divinely free of all ill-will, or petulance, or malice, of any sort whatsoever" (348). Realizing that man must place "his conceit of attainable felicity" not "anywhere in the intellect," but "in the heart" (349), Ishmael comes to the acceptance of the beauty of human love and brotherhood which washes away the sin of his implication in Ahab's quest and qualifies him for physical and spiritual salvation at the end of the novel.

The cycle of Queequeg's thematic relationship to Ishmael's developing spiritual identity is completed in the hero's resurrection in the Epilogue. Freed at least enough from his isolating Faustian drive for power and knowledge in his baptism of sperm to allow his desire for human interdependence to emerge, Ishmael is carried from the brink of death by embracing the coffin engraved with Queequeg's "mystical treatise"—whose message is faith and love. Melville quite appropriately ends his novel with a note from Job, for like Job, Ishmael is on a troubled passage to faith, forced to subdue his isolating desire for intellectual certainty in order to embrace the saving ideals of faith and love.

Moby-Dick is a most significant novel in romantic literature because it gives us both the descendant of the *mal du siècle* tradition—Ishmael—and the epitome of the demoniac hero—Ahab, and then explores the tension created between them. In virtually all the literary works containing romantic heroes we find a portrayal of the utter failure of solipsism; Werther, René, Childe Harold, Faust, Manfred, Ahab all discover the individual soul incapable of providing the sense of permanence they desperately seek. Melville, in the relationship of Ishmael to Queequeg, provides a tentative solution for the introverted romantic hero's dilemma. The hero cannot, as Pope, Dryden, or Molière would suggest, commit himself to the civilized world of Catherine the Great, a decadent Greece, Albert, or the selfish, hypocritical ship owners in *Moby-Dick*; nor can he, like Ethan Brand or Ahab, turn into his own soul, cutting himself off from his fellows. Instead, the hero must, after rejecting a debased, impersonal social and religious order, affirm the ideals of love and religious faith through a selfless interaction with other individual men.

V

The Romantic Love Object: The Woman as Narcissistic Projection

> . . . she was one
> Fit for the model of a statuary
> (a race of mere imposters, when all's done—
> I've seen much finer women, ripe and real,
> Than all the nonsense of their stone ideal).
> Byron, *Don Juan*, II. cxviii

A crucial element of the romantic heroic quest involves the hero's often desperate attempt to secure a meaningful love relationship. Typically in romantic literature the woman to whom the hero commits himself appears as the "earthly analogue" of a transcendental ideal;[1] however, in line with romantic epistemology, this ideal is self-generated, taking its identity from the artist's intuitive conception of Truth and Beauty and "Veiling beneath that radiant form of Woman" (*Epipsychidion*). As Marius Bewley explains Shelleyan romantic love, the male hero "finds in the loved person a reflection or objectification of his own hidden perfection, a means of defining his own loveliness to himself, a kind of sexually attractive *Doppelgänger*."[2] This ideal projection of self usually becomes an unattainable, disembodied, Cybele-like goddess who consumes her lover, requiring from him a religious asceticism which saps the male's virility. In most instances, the ultimate result is a loss of feminine identity and a sterile, narcissistic love relationship which proves self-destructive.

1 Perkins, *The Quest for Permanence*, 170.
2 Marius Bewley, *The English Romantic Poets* (New York, 1970), 738.

As the narcissistic projection of the romantic hero, the ideal woman emerges as the fitting counterpart to the masculine ego; she is the male hero's mirror image, his "soul out of my soul"—the one "belle âme" with the sensitivity and intelligence to respond sympathetically to the melancholy hero's plight. Peter Thorslev maintains that "there is a very real sense in which the only love possible for the Romantic hero—for Chateaubriand's René, for the Byronic hero as epitomized in Manfred, for Shelley's poet-hero in *Alastor, Laon and Cythna* or *Epipsychidion*—is an incestuous love."[3] The incestuous attachment highlights the fact that the ideal woman is the male's mirror image, that she depends entirely for her identity upon the narcissistic male. Just as God created man in his own image, so the romantic poet fashions his ideal mate from a Platonic conception of self. René wishes that God had given him, as he had furnished Adam, a mate drawn from his side—an extension of his body and soul: "O Lord, if only Thou hadst given me a woman after my heart's desire, if Thou hadst drawn from my side an Eve, as Thou didst once for our first father, and brought her to me by the hand . . . Heavenly beauty!"[4] Wordsworth's sister is dear to him in "Tintern Abbey" primarily because she provides a channel through which he can recapture an idealized personal past: "in thy voice I catch/ The language of my former heart, and read/ My former pleasures in the shooting lights/ Of thy wild eyes . . . / May I behold in thee what I was once" (11. 116–20). For Shelley the epipsyche or "sister soul" must be "a miniature as it were of our entire self . . . the portrait of our external being . . . an assemblage of the minutest particles of which our nature is composed."[5] Astarte, the deceased beloved of Byron's Manfred, mirrors not only the hero's eyes, hair, features, and voice but also shares "the same lone thoughts and wanderings,/ The quest of hidden knowledge, and a mind/ To compre-

---

3 Thorslev, "Incest as Romantic Symbol," 43.
4 Chateaubriand, *René*, 130. "O Dieu! si tu m'avais donné une femme selon mes désirs; si, comme à notre première père, tu m'eusses amené par la main une Ève tirée de moi-même . . . Beauté céleste!"
5 Clark (ed.), *Shelley's Prose*, 170.

hend the universe" (II, ii, 109–11). Though the arrival of the female Faust might give cause for celebration, one wonders if Astarte is not rather the male Faust in petticoats.[6]

The incestuous relationship between hero and heroine illustrates the intricate tie between the romantic concept of women and romantic epistemology. When Novalis writes in *Heinrich von Oftendingen*, "I am the central point, the blessed source,"[7] he gives expression to a central strain of romantic epistemology: the poet or hero locates within himself the source of all knowledge. As Emerson writes in "Nature" (1836): "Every man's condition is a solution in hiero-glyphic to those inquiries he would put"; man "is himself the creator in the finite," a "transparent eyeball" through whom "the currents of the Universal Being circulate." For Wordsworth, the poet's task is to recapture the essence of his youth, a time when he was "unable to think of external things as having external existence, and [he] communed with all that [he] saw as something not apart from, but inherent in, [his] own immaterial nature."[8] For most romantics, however, self-knowledge is but a preliminary step toward affinity with a transcendental realm; thus it is not an egotistical enterprise—Emerson claims that "all mean egotism vanishes." As Georges Pou-

6 Jerome McGann writes: "The female counterparts of Byron's heroes . . . corre-spond exactly to the state of the hero's soul which they inhabit. They objectify the passionate impulses in the man whose imagination made them what they are. This is as much to say that none of them are truly 'persons.'" Jerome McGann, *Fiery Dust: Byron's Poetic Development* (Chicago, 1968), 189.

7 Kluckhohn and Samuel (eds.), *Novalis Schriften*, I, 317. "Ich bin der Mittelpunkt, der heilge Quell,/ Aus welchem jede Sehnsucht stürmisch fließt/ Wohin sich jede Sehnsucht, mannichfach/ Gebrochen wieder still zusammen zieht."

8 Quoted by Earl Wasserman, "The English Romantics: The Grounds of Knowl-edge," 26. Wasserman cautions against attributing to all English romantics a single, fixed epistemology. If my necessarily brief discussion does not seem ap-plicable to each romantic poet, it does, I trust, accurately reflect basic epistemo-logical assumptions from which the bulk of romantic art develops. Georges Pou-let writes: "For the Romantic, man first of all is a self-generative force. . . . His expansion is therefore not simply psychological. It is really ontological. To ex-pand, is to realize one's being." See Georges Poulet, *The Metamorphoses of the Circle*, trans. Carley Dawson and Elliott Coleman (Baltimore, 1966), 97.

let explains, for the Romantic "to withdraw to the center [of the circle, or the self] is not to renounce the plenary life, to condemn oneself to a diminished life; it is . . . to return to the original forces, to go to the fountainhead."[9] Intuitively the Romantic recognizes the reality that lies outside the self, and his dilemma, according to Poulet, is to bring the center of the circle, or the self, into harmony with the "peripheral universe," or the circumference; or, in Coleridgean terms, to bring about a union of subject and object, to create a condition in which perceiver and perceived "are identical, each involving, and supposing the other."[10] As the poet confesses in *Epipsychidion*, "In many mortal forms I rashly sought/ The shadow of that idol of my thought" (11. 267–68). Emily ("a mortal shape indued/ With love and life and light and deity"), the veiled maiden of *Alastor*, Cynthia (the "completed form of all completeness" in Keats's *Endymion*), and Hawthorne's Priscilla (endowed "with many of the privileges of a disembodied spirit") thus become narcissistic projections of intuitive apprehensions of the Divine.

An earthly embodiment of divine truth, the romantic heroine often and appropriately assumes the qualities of a goddess; she transcends mortality, becoming inaccessible to her would-be lover and demanding from him saint-like adoration and, ultimately, self-annihilation. Friedrich Schlegel's *Lucinde* (1799) portrays the romantic love relationship in religious terms, as love for Julius and Lucinde becomes a transforming force liberating the lovers from mortal restraints and ennobling sexual attraction; Oskar Walzel writes that such "romantic conception of love made it possible to combine the exalted and the vulgar, the spiritual and the sensual. . . . This, anticipating Schelling, is the metaphysical prerequisite of the idea of a cultural morality, which through the spirit ennobles sensuousness, fancy, and passion."[11] The poet in *Epipsychidion* seeks sexual union with Emily which will become "Confused in Passion's golden purity," absorbing the two of them into "One passion in twin-hearts"

9   Poulet, *The Metamorphoses of the Circle*, 95.
10   See Wasserman, "The English Romantics," 25.
11   Oskar Walzel, *German Romanticism*, trans. A. E. Lussky (New York, 1965), 82.

pointing "to Heaven" and leading to "one annihilation" (11. 571–87). Happiness for Keats's Endymion is "that which becks/ Our ready minds to fellowship divine,/ A fellowship with essence; till we shine,/ Full alchemiz'd, and free of space"; this fellowship leads to "Richer entanglements, enthralments far/ More self-destroying" (I, 777–99).

Keats's "The Eve of St. Agnes" presents an excellent example of the romantic heroine as goddess who commands from her mortal lover a religious dedication which lifts him to a transcendent dimension. Carefully observing the rituals of St. Agnes' Eve, Madeline kneels "for heaven's grace and boon," becoming "a splendid angel, newly drest,/ Save wings, for heaven: —Porphyro grew faint: / She knelt, so pure a thing, so free from mortal taint" (11. 223–25). Profoundly affected by his consecrated vision, Porphyro asks if he might not become Madeline's "vassal blest":

> Thy beauty's shield, heart-shap'd and vermeil dyed?
> Ah, silver shrine, here will I take my rest
> After so many hours of toil and quest,
> A famish'd pilgrim, —saved by a miracle. (11. 336–40)

The imagery of ice and coldness in the poem suggests that the realm inhabited by Madeline corresponds to the frozen and timeless dimension of the would-be lovers on Keats's "Cold Pastoral," the Grecian urn; "trembling in her soft and chilly nest," Madeline dreams of an ideal love which was "a midnight charm/ Impossible to melt as iced stream" (11. 282–83). Upon awakening to discover the mortal Porphyro, Madeline shrinks from disappointment with the "pallid, chill, and dread" admirer. But Porphyro has undergone a rather elaborate, ritualistic preparation himself, moving from "a little moonlight room,/ Pale, lattic'd, chill, and silent as a tomb" to Madeline's enchanted chamber, where "Beyond a mortal man impassion'd far/ . . . [he] arose,/ Ethereal, flush'd, and like a throbbing star/ Seen mid the sapphire heaven's deep repose;/ Into her dream he melted" (11. 316–19). Porphyro brings to Madeline's "iced" dream the warmth of "flush'd . . . throbbing" passion; it is this, Earl

Wasserman argues, that complements and completes Madeline's dream, as the dream "is only lifeless and chill unless it is animated by the color of passion, the roseate sensuousness that at length is born in Porphyro."[12] But significantly Porphyro's heat does not melt Madeline's "iced" dream; rather, "Into her dream he melted." The poem ends after the two lovers have fled "ages long ago" into the eternal "bitter chill" of the storm, through the "frozen grass" and away from the destructive warmth of the castle. The warmth of human passion is made eternal, consumed by, though complementing, the dream of the transcendent ideal. Behind in the mortal heat of the castle the lovers leave "Angela the old," who "Died palsy-twitch'd, with meagre face deform," and the Beadsman, who "after thousand aves told/ . . . slept among his ashes cold" (11. 375–78).[13]

Thoreau points out in *Walden* that "a bucket of water soon becomes putrid, but frozen remains sweet forever."[14] This metaphor of ice as the eternal, transcendental realm permeates romantic literature, illuminating the nature of the ideal woman and her relationship to the mortal lover. Separated by fate and circumstance from a mortal union with his beloved Catherine, Heathcliff in Emily Brontë's *Wuthering Heights* yearns for death, access to a transcendental dimension where his cheek can be "frozen against hers." Keats's Knight engages in his erotic interlude with "la belle dame" on "the cold hillside." Lamia, whose beauty is veiled "To keep it unaffronted, unassail'd/ By the love-glances of unlovely eyes," is united with Hermes "in a long immortal dream." With "the God fostering her chilled hand," Lamia surrenders to her lover, who is "Full of

12 Wasserman, *The Finer Tone*, 111.
13 In an earlier draft of the poem, Keats drew an even more emphatic contrast between the lovers, who "alchemize" the heat of mortal passion into celestial radiance, and the two old people left behind, who are destroyed by the unalchemized, time-bound warmth of mortal existence: "Angela went off/ Twitch'd with Palsy; and the face deform/ The beadsman stiffen'd, 'twixt a sigh and laugh,/ Ta'en sudden from his beads by a weak little cough." See M. Allott (ed.), *The Poems of John Keats* (New York, 1970), 479, n. 375–77.
14 Henry David Thoreau, *Walden*, ed. J. Lyndon Shanley (Princeton, N.J., 1971), 297.

adoring tears and blandishment"; together, "Into the green-recessed woods they flew;/ Nor grew they pale, as mortal lovers do" (see I, 101–45). The poet in *Epipsychidion*, seeking "this soul out of my soul," thinks he locates "the veiled Divinity" in a woman "whose voice was venomed melody," whose "breath . . . was like faint flowers," and whose "touch was as electric poison"; her looks issue a "flame . . . into [the poet's] vitals . . . / And from her living cheeks and bosom flew/ A killing air, which pierced like honey-dew/ Into the core of my green heart" (11. 256–63). The heat of this woman's love proves false and destructive. More in line with the poet's quest is the "glorious shape" who seems like "the cold chaste Moon, the Queen of Heaven's bright isle,/ Who makes all beautiful on which she smiles"; this woman is the "wandering shrine of soft yet icy flame" (11. 281–83). Unfortunately, as the poet lies "within a chaste cold bed," the woman rejects the mortal lover, crying "Away, he is not of our crew." The poet surrenders "The moving billows of [his] being . . . / Into a death of ice, immovable" (1. 315); he is then prepared for "the Vision veiled from me/ So many years— . . . Emily." She brings forth in him a "wild odour" which "is felt/ Beyond the sense, like fiery dews that melt/ Into the bosom of a frozen bud" (11. 110–11).

The romantic poet/hero usually prefers the "frozen maiden"— the embodiment of his intuitive understanding of divine truth—to the living, warm, and fertile woman. *Alastor*'s Visionary ignores the loving entreaties of the Arab girl to pursue the veiled maiden whose "voice was like the voice of his own soul," and whose theme was "Knowledge and truth and virtue." Emerson, in his poem "Each and All," laments the passing of a young girl to sexually experienced woman; in entering her husband's "hermitage" she moves "like the bird from the woodlands to the cage," losing her "gay enchantment" as she becomes "a gentle wife, but fairy none." Coverdale and Hollingsworth in Hawthorne's *The Blithedale Romance* both ultimately reject the "high spirited" and sexually vibrant, experienced Zenobia, instead falling in love with Priscilla, "the weakly maiden" who is "enshrouded within the misty drapery of the veil," and whose tenure in "a human dwelling," Coverdale fears, will not be of sufficient duration to "melt the icicles out of her hair."

The Blithedale Romance is only one of several nineteenth-century works which present the poet/hero with a choice between the mortal, sexually alluring woman and the disembodied, faintly discernible Platonic counterpart to the hero's soul. Shelley's *Alastor*, Hardy's *Jude the Obscure*, and Poe's "Ligeia" afford additional examples of the tendency in nineteenth-century literature to portray the ideal woman as an embodiment of the male hero, taking the form of the "sister soul." In all instances the "sister soul" is juxtaposed to a dramatic foil who more clearly corresponds to the conventional woman, and in each case the hero finds the conventional woman unsatisfying. A disturbing undercurrent emerges as the infatuation with the narcissistic projection spells doom for the hero and for the woman as well. Such a perception of woman proves debilitating and ultimately self-destructive; the woman loses feminine identity or individuality as she becomes undifferentiated from the male, and the social order potentially suffers from the ensuing sterility.

Shelley's *Alastor* (1816) presents a sustained exploration of the narcissistic infatuation with the mirror image of self, thereby becoming a paradigm of the male-female relationship dominating romantic literature. Two works read by Shelley in 1811 exerted considerable influence on the composition of *Alastor* and afford insight into its basic theme. The first, C. M. Wieland's *Agathon*—which Shelley reread with Mary in 1814—portrays the plight of an extreme idealist whose commitment to Psyche, a clear personification of Platonic love, leads him beyond the limits of rational behavior; the purification of the flesh resulting from Agathon's monomaniacal pursuit of the ideal accords with Shelley's affinity to the tradition of Platonic love most succinctly expressed in *The Symposium*. The second, Miss Sydney Owenson's *The Missionary*—which Shelley read "with especial enthusiasm and admiration" in May, 1811—presents the plight of a priest who abandons a life of cloistered idealism to pursue ideal Beauty embodied in an alluring but unattainable priest-ess; the quest results in the male's ruin.[15] In a letter written in the same month during which Shelley read *The Missionary*, the poet re-veals his fear of "the horror, the evil, which comes to the self in solitude."

This same "horror" and "evil" resulting from solipsistic behavior becomes the central theme of *Alastor*. "A youth of uncorrupted feel-ings and adventurous genius led forth by an imagination inflamed and purified through familiarity with all that is excellent and majes-tic" (Preface), Shelley's Visionary becomes infatuated with "a veiled maiden," the "prototype of his conception," who is in fact a projec-tion of the poet/hero's solipsistic instincts taking the shape of his doppelgänger. "Obedient to the light/ That shone within his soul" (11. 492–93), the hero's pursuit of the visionary maiden leads him away from the outside world into a natural landscape which be-comes a metaphor for the recesses of self: "A spirit seemed to stand beside him . . . held commune with him as if he and it/ Were all that was" (11. 479–97). By the journey's end, the ever-expanding self totally consumes the natural landscape, as it too is replete with narcissistic imagery: "The beams of sunset hung their rainbow hues/ High 'mid the shifting domes of sheeted spray/ That canopied his path o'er the waste deep" (11. 334–36); "the crags closed round with black and jaggèd arms;/ The shattered mountain overhung the sea" (11. 359–60); ". . . the cove/ Is closed by meeting banks, whose yel-low flowers/ For ever gaze on their own drooping eyes,/ Reflected in the crystal calm" (11. 405–407).

The Preface to *Alastor* provides a perspective on the tragic poet/ hero which Shelley might well have deemed necessary to temper the reader's sympathy with just rebuke. Shelley informs us that the poem portrays an idealistic youth who, though initially content with the ineffable nature of the universe, eventually seeks a perfect Being with whom he may unite. Although he has a glimpse of this Being to whom he attributes an ideal synthesis of the intellect, the imagi-

15   Newman Ivey White, *Shelley* (2 vols.; New York, 1947), I, 700–701.

nation, and the senses, the Visionary's failure to realize its embodiment destroys him. Thus the poet's demise serves as a warning to mankind: "The picture is not barren of instruction to actual men. The Poet's self-centered seclusion was avenged by the furies of an irresistible passion pursuing him to speedy ruin." Shelley recognizes in his Preface that the solipsistic quest is a perilous one, for "among those who attempt to exist without human sympathy, the pure and tender-hearted perish through the intensity and passion of their search after its communion, when the vacancy of their spirit suddenly makes itself felt." As Richard Holmes points out, Shelley's Preface to *Alastor* reinforces the conclusion of his earlier essay "On Love": "Satisfactory love can only be found within the context of a human community of responsible relationships";[16] it also recalls the censure of Shelley's mother-in-law, Mary Wollstonecraft, who dismissed the grand passion as "panting after an unattainable perfection."[17]

The "veiled maiden" of the poem has a dramatic foil in the Arab maiden, who offers the Visionary conventional love but to whom the hero seems impervious. Holmes makes the point that the Arab girl occupies a "slavish role," and thus is not a satisfactory alternative to the "veiled maiden"; later, in fact, Shelley insists that a sexual relationship could be satisfying only "when the woman was herself completely liberated from social and intellectual servitude."[18] Holmes's point may or may not be valid; love, on occasion, makes willing slaves of us all. But what is clear in the relationship of the Arab girl to the poet is that the latter rejects the human love offered by the former to pursue the tantalizing though sterile projection of his inherent narcissism.

To punish the egotism which leads the poet to repudiate human love, "the spirit of sweet human love" sends "A vision to the sleep of him who spurned/ Her choicest gifts" (11. 203–204). With appro-

16 Richard Holmes, *Shelley: The Pursuit* (New York, 1975), 301.
17 Mary Wollstonecraft, *A Vindication of the Rights of Women: Strictures on Political and Moral Subjects* (London, 1792), 162.
18 Holmes, *Shelley*, 303.

priate justice, the vision is the embodiment of his narcissistic dream: "Her voice was like the voice of his own soul/ Heard in the calm of thought." Unable to resist the alluring vision, the poet "eagerly pursues/ Beyond the realms of dream that fleeting shade;/ He overleaps the bounds" (11. 206–207). In a later fragment, "Prince Athanase," a sage tells another visionary youth ("a hopeless wanderer, through mankind") that "The mind becomes that which it contemplates" (1. 139); the implication here is that contemplation in itself is not evil, but depends for its value upon its object. For Shelley's hero, contemplation has become solipsistic, causing divorce from reality, suppression of social instincts, and, finally, a celibacy which channels sexuality into enervating autoerotic fantasies.[19]

The veiled maiden receives from her would-be lover a devotion bearing striking resemblance to that of the introverted ascetic to his divine ideal; like Porphyro, the poet is a "famished pilgrim." A suggestion of this parallel emerges from the epigraph to the poem, drawn from *The Confessions* of Saint Augustine: "*Nondum amabam, et amare amabam, quaerebam quid amarem, amans amare.*" Earl Wasserman sees these lines as analogous to the poet's condition: "Like St. Augustine, the Visionary is compelled by a desire that, by virtue of its infinitude, can have no immediately attainable object; and just as Augustine's love could be satisfied only by the infinite and perfect God, so the Visionary seeks an Absolute which will match his mind's perfect conceptions and ideals."[20] Yet Wasserman's parallel is misleading, for in discussing Augustine's lines out of context he fails to point out that Augustine is reviewing, confessing, and condemning a youthful sexual exuberance which he has since rigidly suppressed. The appropriate passage from *The Confessions* describes a yearning for human love which might have saved the poet of *Alastor*:

---

19 Ellsworth Barnard in *Shelley's Religion* (New York, 1964) groups *Alastor* with "Prince Athanase," "Epipsychidion," and "Adonais" as poems in which "the actual earthly life of humanity is either completely forgotten, or is felt as an obstacle that hinders the individual soul from attaining its appointed end."

20 Wasserman, *Shelley: A Critical Reading*, 18.

To Carthage I came, and a hissing cauldron of shameful love seethed around me on all sides. I was not in love, yet I loved to love and, in the hidden depths of unsated desire, I hated myself for my partial lack of desire. I sought some object that I might love, loving the very act of love; I hated peace of mind and a path unbeset by pitfalls. For, though I was hungry within me with the inner food which is Thyself, my God, I experienced no longing as a result of that hunger. Rather, I lacked the desire for incorruptible nourishment, not because I was filled with it, but the more empty I was, the greater my loathing became. And that is why my soul was unhealthy and, in its ulcerated condition, projected itself into the open, wretchedly desirous of being scraped in friction with sensible things. . . . To love and to be loved was far sweeter to me if I also succeeded in enjoying my beloved in the flesh.[21]

Augustine's later rejection of *amans amare* and human passion parallels the Visionary's oblivious attitude towards the Arab maiden; thus the epigraph to the poem expresses a sexual norm from which both deviate. Shelley, the advocate of "sweet human love," harbors little sympathy for either. Shelley's visionary hero comes to share with Augustine the Confessor an essentially ascetic perspective that demands absolute withdrawal from a world contaminated by satanic influences. To a certain extent, the narrator of *Alastor* serves as Shelley's corrective voice in the poem, as he assumes the perspective suggested by the Augustinian epigraph. The narrator offers an ideal medium between the world of spirit and the world of flesh, blending the "murmurs of the air,/ And motions of the forests and the sea" with the "voice of living beings" and uniting the "woven hymns/ Of night and day" with "the deep heart of man" (11. 45–49). Yet, though he condemns the poet's solipsistic excesses, the narrator acknowledges that the Visionary's "light adorned the world around it" and left "Nature's vast frame, and the web of human things/ . . . not as they were" (11. 715–20). The tragedy, for Shelley, is that the poet's vision could have proved redemptive had it not ensnared the Visionary in its solipsistic web.

Shelley's *Alastor* repeats a pattern established earlier in Chateaubriand's *René* (1803). The hero in the French novella, like Shelley's

---

21 Augustine, *Confessions*, trans. Vernon J. Bourke (Washington, D.C., 1966), Book III, opening paragraph.

Visionary, is "a young man infatuated with illusions, satisfied with nothing, withdrawn from the burdens of society, and wrapped up in idle dreams."[22] Unable to establish lasting human relationships, René lives essentially an ascetic existence; he is "une grande âme" for whom "la terre n'offre rien." The sole axis of René's existence becomes his sister, Amélie, an ideal unattainable phantom who confesses, "I have always had a penchant for the religious life," and who abandons René to enter a convent because "now is the time to heed Heaven's call."[23]

But Amélie's relationship to René is at best a mixed blessing. Returning to the hero just as he "finds himself at times overwhelmed by the burden of his own corruption and incapable of doing anything great or noble or just,"[24] Amélie furnishes René an inspiring vision which momentarily lifts him from solipsistic despair; in this sense she resembles the song of Keats's nightingale or the vision of Emily in Shelley's *Epipsychidion*. But as with most romantic visions, Amélie proves unattainable. Admitting that Amélie is sent by God "to save me and to punish me,"[25] René discovers that their inevitable separation reduces him to an ineffectual supplicant, unable to function in human society. René thus labors under the typical romantic tragic curse: possessed of sufficient sensitivity and genius to perceive the transcendental ideal generated from within and embodied in feminine guise, he is unable either to embrace the ideal or to live in a mortal world toxic to it: "My soul, which no passion had yet wasted, sought an object to which I could attach myself."[26]

Amélie serves a vital thematic function in the novel in that her

22 Chateaubriand, *René*, 144. "un jeune homme entêté de chimères, à qui tout déplaît, et qui s'est soustrait aux charges de la société pour se livrer à d'inutiles rêveries."
23 *Ibid.*, 134. "il est temps que je mette à profit les avertissements du Ciel."
24 *Ibid.*, 127. "ne se trouve quelquefois accablé du fardeau de sa propre corruption, et incapable de rien faire de grand, de noble, de juste."
25 *Ibid.*, 141. "me sauver et pour me punir."
26 *Ibid.*, 126. "mon âme, qu'aucune passion n'avait encore usée, cherchait un objet qui pût l'attacher."

behavior forms an illuminating counterpoint to the hero's solipsistic despair. René's "other self," Amélie sympathizes with René's impatience with mortal existence, his desire for permanence. Likewise, she shares his burden of corruption (that is, his incestuous attachment), for she enters the convent in part to chastise the illicit sexual desires with which René is unable to cope. But in her Christian commitment, Amélie realizes her brother's desire to surrender to a larger power, and in so doing becomes purified:

Her earthly ornaments were replaced by a long muslin robe, which sacrificed none of her appeal. The cares of her brow vanished under a linen head-band, and the mysterious veil, the two-fold symbol of virginity and religion, was placed on her shorn head. Never had she appeared so beautiful. The penitent's eye was fixed on the dust of the world, while her soul was already in heaven.[27]

Freed from her "forbidden passion" and serene in Christian community, Amélie serves as a painful reminder to the hero of his own inability to transcend his solipsism.

Père Souël, the respectable Catholic priest who at the novella's close provides René with an appropriate, though unheeded, corrective vision, makes clear that Amélie's surrender to the disciplining power of the Church is the preferred alternative to the hero's self-centered despair:

Solitude is bad for the man who does not live with God. It increases the soul's power while simultaneously robbing it of every opportunity to find expression. Whoever has been endowed with talent must devote it to serving his fellow man, for if he does not make use of it, he is first punished by an inner misery, and sooner or later Heaven visits on him a fearful retribution.[28]

27 Ibid., 139. "une longue robe d'étamine remplace pour elle les ornements du siècle, sans la rendre moins touchante; les ennuis de son front se cachent sous un bandeau de lin; et le voile mystérieux, double symbole de la virginité et de la religion, accompagne sa tête dépouillée. Jamais elle n'avait paru si belle. L'oeil de la pénitente était attaché sur la poussière du monde, et son âme était dans le ceil."
28 Ibid., 145. "La solitude est mauvaise à celui qui n'y vit pas avec Dieu; elle redouble les puissances de l'âme, et même temps qu'elle leur ôte tout sujet pour s'exercer. Quiconque a reçu des forces doit les consacrer au service des ses semblables; s'il les laisse inutiles, il en est d'abord puni par une secrète misère, et tôt ou tard le ciel lui envoie un châtiment effroyable."

Père Souël's censure is significant not only because it expresses the theme of Chateaubriand's novella but also because it serves as a necessary comment on what I would call the romantic perversion of Christian asceticism. Both René and the Visionary of *Alastor* adopt the lifestyle of the medieval Christian ascetic, as outlined by Violet MacDermot in *The Cult of the Seer in the Ancient Middle East*:

> The ascetic saw in Christianity the means of entry into the divine world in this life. The ascetic life was essentially a witness to the experience that there existed a non-material dimension, the entry to which was a form of death. The themes of 'The Ascetic Way of Life' illustrate the extent to which the saint approached the condition of death. In relation to the physical world, the ascetic was a dead man; he left the society of man, abandoning all his possessions. His habitation was the desert, the traditional Egyptian burial place. In so far as he was able, he aimed to live as if he were deprived of a physical body.[29]

The resemblances which both René and Shelley's Visionary bear to this tradition are strikingly obvious; both withdraw from the world to pursue their uncompromising dedication to a visionary embodiment of divine perfection. But there is a significant disparity between the ascetic lives of René and the Visionary and those characteristic of the Christian, and it is this disparity which Père Souël highlights in his censure of Chateaubriand's hero. Essentially both René and the Visionary devote themselves to narcissistic visions; their asceticism lacks the redeeming, disciplining figure of Christ. Without the real, objective presence of Christ in his life, the ascetic becomes blasphemous, as his is a human attempt to imitate the divine without heavenly sanction; this is the essence of Père Souël's counsel.

The perverted nature of romantic asceticism becomes readily apparent viewed in light of Thomas à Kempis' *Imitation of Christ*. René and Shelley's Visionary share with "the greatest Saints" what Thomas labeled an attempt "to avoid the company of men whenever they were able" and to strive "with all their might to mortify in

29   Violet MacDermot, *The Cult of the Seer in the Ancient Middle East: A Contribution to Current Research on Hallucinations Drawn from Coptic and Other Texts* (Berkeley, Calif., 1971), 27.

themselves all worldly desires"; but they fail to realize that "the sole road to God is through the power and teaching of Jesus Christ, true God and true Man; by the subordination of nature to divine grace; by self-discipline; and by devout use of the Sacraments of the Catholic Church, in particular that of the Holy Eucharist."[30] While the romantic ascetic devotes his attention to the realization of a self-generated ideal, the Christian ascetic "strives to preserve himself free from all self-seeking . . . to conquer self, and by daily growing stronger than self, to advance in holiness." Thomas writes that "those who follow only their natural inclinations defile their conscience, and lose the grace of God."

Though perverted or misdirected, the asceticism of the romantic hero mimics in significant ways the lifestyle of the Christian saint. For one thing, the dedication requires celibacy: the Visionary rejects the overtures of the Arab maiden and René fails to consummate his marriage to the Indian girl in Louisiana. Even the sexually alluring vision of the veiled maiden which haunts Alastor at night, coming "Like the fierce fiend of a distempered dream,/ And shook him from his rest, and led him forth/ Into the darkness" (11. 225–27), has its origin in the voluptuous disguises which Satan or his minions assumed in order to tempt the early Christian ascetics. Saint Anthony, according to Athanasius, was nightly tempted by the devil in the shape of a woman, and instances of similar demonic seductions are common in hagiographical literature. Such nocturnal visionary visitations, however, were often recognized as characteristic of those who had dedicated their lives to phantoms of their own imaginations. The authors of the gnostic text *Pistis Sophia* "described the 'postmortem' life of men who had subjected themselves to 'images' of their own creation," and MacDermot points to the older monks of another ascetic group who recognized "certain ill-effects on the mind arising in consequence of the solitary life. A number of ac-

---

30 Thomas à Kempis, *The Imitation of Christ*, trans. Leo Sherley-Price (London, 1952), Book I, ch. 20, p. 50; ch. 2, pp. 37–38; Sherley-Price's "Introduction," 12–13.

counts show that the ascetics were subject to hallucinations which, with proper training, they were able to recognize and reject. Those monks who accepted the illusory appearances as divine revelations were treated by the elders as suffering from delusions of grandeur."[31]

The relationship of Shelley's Poet to the "veiled maiden" resembles the relationship of Jude Fawley and Sue Bridehead in Thomas Hardy's 1895 novel, *Jude the Obscure*. Cousins, Jude and Sue share a love which Sue's husband, Phillotson, labels "Shelleyan": an "extraordinary sympathy . . . exists between the pair. . . . They seem to be one person split in two!"[32] Called by several scholars a prototype of the modern woman, Sue is every bit the equal of Jude—a man of no mean intellectual development: "She was once," Jude tells Mrs. Edlin toward the end of the novel, "a woman whose intellect was to mine like a star to a benzoline lamp" (318). Sue is a woman who resists all attempts to mold her life in a traditional pattern, adopting as her motto John Stuart Mill's words, "She, or he, 'who lets the world, or his own portion of it, choose his plan of life for him, has no need of any other faculty than the ape-like one of imitation'" (177).

Yet the modern woman, the seemingly ideal complement for the nineteenth-century man, is frigid. The sexual act to Sue is like "the amputation of a limb," and she wishes "that Eve had not fallen, so that (as the primitive Christians believed) some harmless mode of vegetation might have peopled Paradise" (178). In many ways Sue seems modeled on the Cybele of antiquity, who required of her devotees their vitality if not their manhood as a sacrifice necessary in sustaining the realm of birth and decay over which she ruled; in one common version of the legend, Cybele castrates her lover Attis to prevent his marriage to another.[33] Sue's mates—the undergradu-

31 Violet MacDermot, *The Cult of the Seer*, 155ff.

32 Thomas Hardy, *Jude the Obscure*, ed. Irving Howe (Boston, 1965), 182. Subsequent references are to this Riverside edition, and are noted parenthetically.

33 N. G. L. Hammond and D. H. H. Scullard (eds.), *The Oxford Classical Dictionary* (rev. ed.; Oxford, 1970), 146.

ate at Cambridge, Phillotson, Jude—likewise must become celibate to please her.

Sue, like Alastor, also adopts a lifestyle which mimics that of the medieval Christian ascetic. When defeated by the deaths of her adopted and natural children, Sue returns to the sexual embraces of Phillotson as a flagellant, telling Jude, "Our life has been a vain attempt at self-delight. But self-abnegation is the higher road. We should mortify the flesh—the terrible flesh—the curse of Adam" (272–73). But Sue's "self-abnegation" is an ironic reversal of that practiced by the Christian ascetic, for whereas the latter punished the flesh because of his natural attraction to it, Sue indulges in the flesh as a means of chastizing what is an essentially spiritual—though illicit—love.

Sue places the blame for her frigidity on the social system, namely the archaic institution of marriage, which in her eyes amounts to slavery: her frigidity results from "the necessity of being responsive to this man whenever he wishes" (168). This Sue claims despite the fact that she dominates all of her personal relationships; one could hardly expect a less demanding mate than Phillotson. Jude concurs with Sue's appraisal, saying to Mrs. Edlin at the novel's close: "Strange difference of sex, that time and circumstance, which enlarge the views of most men, narrow the views of women almost invariably. . . . Our ideas were fifty years too soon to be any good to us. And so the resistance they met with brought reaction in her, and recklessness and ruin in me" (318). Ultimately Jude and Sue are deluding themselves. While an antiquated and repressive social structure aggravates their problem, the problem is one which transcends nineteenth-century England. D. H. Lawrence writes that Sue "is the production of the long selection by man of the woman in whom the female is subordinate to the male principle."[34] Sue's repression of the principle of femininity results in sterility and consequent self-destruction.

34 D. H. Lawrence, *Lawrence on Hardy and Painting: Study of Thomas Hardy and to These Paintings*, ed. J. V. Davies (London, 1973), 108.

Like the "veiled maiden" of *Alastor*, Sue too has a dramatic foil—the animal-like Arabella. First capturing Jude's attention by pelting him with "the characteristic part of a barrow-pig," Arabella is "a complete and substantial female animal—no more, no less" (32–33). Though she is Sue's antithesis, Arabella is hardly a more satisfying embodiment of the principle of femininity. She, like the trollop in Victorian pornography, engages in sexual adventures unaccompanied by personal commitment or love; she has no sense of marital fidelity and recognizes no maternal obligations to her offspring. If Sue's sexual energy is repressed, Arabella's is unfocused.

In the fiction of the American romantics Poe and Hawthorne the concept of the feminine and its place in the social order becomes especially pertinent because of the tendency of American romantic art to reflect the emerging nation's social, political, and cultural development. James Fenimore Cooper calls attention to the problem of the woman in American society in *The Prairie* (1827). America was at the beginning of the nineteenth century peculiarly masculine territory; the demands of settling the frontier—fighting the British and the Indians, exploring and clearing land, building and defending settlements—required rugged, masculine aggression, according to Cooper, and the few women who ventured West found life extremely difficult. But in *The Prairie* Cooper foresees another problem: once the land is claimed and cleared, masculine aggressiveness becomes sterile and self-destructive unless tempered by the more civilizing touches of the feminine. Hence his hero, Middleton, goes to New Orleans—the most European of American cities at the time—where he finds, rescues from kidnappers and a possessive Spanish father, and eventually marries the beautiful, Catholic, and sensuous Inez. As Joel Porte demonstrates in a brilliant study of the novel, Cooper places his hope for America's future on the union of Middleton and Inez—the Protestant and the Catholic, the aggressive and the submissive, the just and the merciful—in short, the procreative fusion of the male and sensuous female.[35] However, a

35 Joel Porte, *The Romance in America: Studies in Cooper, Poe, Hawthorne, Melville, and James* (Middleton, Conn., 1969), 47–50.

major obstacle to Cooper's idyllic vision emerges in the fiction of Poe and Hawthorne, as these two American "dark" romantics demonstrate the male's unwillingness to admit the fully developed woman into his society.[36] Both document the larger romantic tendency of the male to reduce the woman to a disembodied, narcissistic projection, a goddess who represents an intuitively glimpsed ideal and who reduces the male to an ineffectual supplicant. Hawthorne's fiction further exposes puritan America's fear of the woman—its belief that she, like Eve, is the supreme temptress in league with the devil—and its consequent attempt to de-feminize her before granting her access to his closed and sterile community.

Three Poe short stories—"Eleonora," "Morella," "Ligeia"—serve as companion pieces in their portrayal of the ideal woman who is a narcissistic projection of the masculine romantic protagonist.[37] The first is a poetic celebration of ideal love, ending somewhat optimistically as the narrator finds Ermengarde worthy of the love he had previously vowed eternally to the goddess Eleonora. But in "Morella" and especially in "Ligeia" the narrators are not so fortunate as their counterpart in "Eleonora": once separated from his ideal love, the narrator of "Ligeia," for example, can find satisfaction with the mortal Lady Rowena only after he has through an imaginative exercise of will transformed her into the departed Ligeia. In

36 In an overview of the concept or image of women in nineteenth-century American literature, Nina Baym gives very little attention to Poe's fiction; "Poe's women," Baym writes, "are purely theoretic figures and have no relation to female characterization" (232). Hawthorne receives slightly more discussion, but because of the scope of her essay, Ms. Baym can afford his work only generalized commentary, concluding that "Hawthorne was fascinated with the problem of strongly individualized women who try to live with integrity and self-respect in restrictive societies that define their sex as subservient and inferior" (225). See Nina Baym, "Portrayal of Women in American Literature, 1790–1870," in *What Manner of Woman: Essays on English and American Life and Literature*, ed. Marlene Springer (New York, 1977), 211–34.

37 Claudia Morrison calls "Morella" a "dream rehearsal" for the more fully developed "Ligeia." See Claudia Morrison, "Poe's 'Ligeia': An Analysis," *Studies in Short Fiction*, IV (1967), 236.

all three stories the love between the hero and his narcissistic ideal includes erotic elements, but in no instance does the eroticism involve fertility; the sexual union takes place in an imaginative construct resembling Keats's "elfin grot"—an ideal, timeless dimension that renders procreation unnecessary.

The narrator of "Eleonora" is the last descendant of a family line "noted for vigor of fancy and ardor of passion."[38] Highly imaginative, he is deemed "mad" by mortal men, but his madness grants him "glimpses of eternity" which "penetrate, however rudderless or compassless, into the vast ocean of the 'light ineffable'" (IV, 236). Traversing this "vast ocean," the narrator in his youth falls in love with Eleonora, "the sole daughter of the only sister of my mother long departed" (IV, 237). Eleonora is the romantic hero's narcissistic "earthly analogue," dwelling with him in the edenic metaphor of his imagination labeled "the Valley of the Many-Colored Grass": "No unguided footstep ever came upon that vale; for it lay far away up among a range of giant hills that hung beetling around about it, shutting out the sunlight from its sweetest recesses" (IV, 237). There they lived alone, "knowing nothing of the world without the Valley" (IV, 237).

The narrator's description of "the Valley of the Many-Colored Grass" links it to *Alastor*'s cove. Through the middle of the valley runs the "River of Silence" flowing "from the dim regions beyond the mountains at the upper end of our encircled domain": "No murmur arose from its bed, and so gently it wandered along, that the pearly pebbles upon which we loved to gaze, far down within its bosom, stirred not at all, but lay in a motionless content, each in its own old station, shining on gloriously forever" (IV, 237–38). In paradise even rivers are static. The whole valley speaks in "its exceeding beauty . . . of the love and the glory of God" (IV, 238);

---

38 James A. Harrison (ed.), *Complete Works of Edgar Allan Poe* (17 vols.; New York, 1902), IV, 236. All references to Poe's fiction are to this edition and appear parenthetically in the text.

indeed, a "voluminous cloud" encloses the entire cove "within a magic prison-house of grandeur and of glory" (IV, 239).

Within the edenic paradise Poe's hero finds his ideal love: "Love entered within our hearts . . . one evening at the close of the third lustrum of her life, and of the fourth of my own . . . we sat, locked in each other's embrace, beneath the serpent-like trees, and looked down within the waters of the River of Silence at our images therein" (IV, 238–39). The link to Narcissus is, of course, explicit. Blessed by "the god Eros" the couple "breathed a delirious bliss over the Valley of the Many-Colored Grass," absolutely transforming the valley into a Keatsian "elfin grot":

A change fell upon all things. Strange brilliant flowers, star-shaped, burst out upon the trees where no flowers had been before. The tints of the green carpet deepened; and when, one by one, the white daisies shrank away, there sprang up, in place of them, ten by ten of the ruby-red asphodel. And life arose in our paths. . . . The golden and silver fish haunted the river, out of the bosom of which issued, little by little, a murmer that swelled, at length, into a lulling melody more divine than that of the harp of Aeolus. (IV, 238–39)

Lest we are tempted to perceive Eleonora as the hero's first mortal love, Poe's narrator clearly elevates her into a transcendental dimension. Like Ligeia, Eleonora has no specific features; her beauty simply exceeds all comparison: the "River of Silence" is "brighter than all save the eyes of Eleonora"; and the "lulling melody more divine than that of the harp of Aeolus" is "sweeter than all save the voice of Eleonora." In short, Eleonora's loveliness "was that of the Seraphim" (IV, 239).

"A saint in Helusion," Eleonora is a goddess who like *Alastor's* veiled maiden commands from her devoted worshiper religious dedication:

I threw myself hurriedly at the feet of Eleonora, and offered up a vow, to herself and to Heaven, that I would never bind myself in marriage to any daughter of the Earth— that I would in no manner prove recreant to her dear memory. . . . And I called the Mighty Ruler of the Universe to witness the pious solemnity of my vow. (IV, 240)

Saintlike, Eleonora promises to guide her mortal lover, granting him protection and encouragement:

Because of what I had done for the comfort of her spirit, she would watch over me in that spirit when departed, and, if so it were permitted her, return to me visibly in the watches of the night; but, if this thing were, indeed, beyond the power of the souls in Paradise, that she would, at least, give me frequent indications of her presence; sighing upon me in the evening winds, or filling the air which I breathed with perfume from the censers of the angels. (IV, 241)

But like all of the romantic heroes, Poe's narrator tragically cannot sustain access to the "elfin grot"—Eleonora must pass on to a transcendent dimension, leaving the mortal hero on the "cold hillside"; "as I pass the barrier in Time's path formed by the death of my beloved, and proceed with the second era of my existence, I feel that a shadow gathers over my brain" (IV, 241). Immediately the cove is transformed: the "voluminous cloud uprose" taking away "all its manifold golden and gorgeous glories from the Valley of the Many-Colored Grass." And reluctantly the Adamic hero must depart from Eden with only the memory of his blessed Eve: "I left it forever for the vanities and the turbulent triumphs of the world" (IV, 242).

For a long while the hero remains "true to [his] vows," aloof from the "pomp and pageantries of a stately court, and the mad clangor of arms, and the radiant loveliness of woman" (IV, 243). Eventually, however, he seemingly breaks his vow to Eleonora, surrendering in love to Ermengarde—who comes to the "gay court of the king I served" from "some far, far distant and unknown land" (IV, 243). Yet Ermengarde is no mere mortal either; a "seraph," an "angel," she possesses a beauty which commands the hero's adoration: "I bowed down without a struggle, in the most ardent, in the most abject worship of love. What indeed was my passion for the young girl of the valley in comparison with the fervor, and the delirium, and the spirit-lifting ecstasy of adoration with which I poured out my whole soul in tears at the feet of the ethereal Ermengarde!" (IV, 243). Indeed, in last analysis Ermengarde seems the earthly repository of the disembodied Eleonora: "Oh divine was the angel Ermengarde! and as I looked down into the depths of her memorial eyes I thought only of them—and *of her*" (IV, 243). Still the devoted slave of the "Spirit of Love," the narrator receives from Eleonora absolution for breaking his earlier vow; he has simply replaced one goddess with another, forever in search of a disembodied, ideal love which for a time enters a mortal realm in the image of a woman.

Morella and Ligeia possess physical characteristics that link them to the spirit of ideal love embodied in Eleonora. According to her narrator-husband, Ligeia is an extraordinarily beautiful woman with black hair and eyes but with fair skin "rivalling the purest ivory"; her face is so beautiful that no woman "ever equalled her" (II, 250). Morella too is very beautiful, sharing with Ligeia a "high forehead," "ringlets of silken hair" and a sweetly musical voice (II, 32). But the heroines' "classic" beauty serves only to dehumanize them. Like the lady in Poe's poem "To Helen," Ligeia is "statue-like" in appearance: her hands like "marble," her skin "purest ivory," her body always in "repose." Ligeia's voice is "dear music" and her facial beauty "the radiance of an opium-dream—an airy and spirit-lifting vision more wildly divine than the phantasies which hovered about the slumbering souls of the daughters of Delos" (II, 249–50). Ligeia's mouth seems more sensuous, as it is "soft," "voluptuous" and has "color"; such hints of sensual warmth lead Joel Porte to see Ligeia as an imaginative erotic playmate, "the 'Lilith' of every Adam's most febrile dreams, who offers the fruit of infinite pleasure and gratification reserved for the gods."[39] But as sensual as her mouth might appear, its teeth are "heavenly" and give off a "holy light"; and her chin has "the spirituality, of the Greek—the contour which the god Apollo revealed but in a dream" (II, 251). From the outset the narrator focuses on Ligeia's spirituality, her "intensity" of soul; her body is "slender" and "somewhat emaciated," her steps "incomprehensibly light and elastic," her very presence fleeting and insubstantial: "She came and departed as a shadow" (II, 249).

"The haunting expression" of Ligeia's eyes, which are "far larger than the ordinary eyes of our own race" (II, 251), reveal the depth

39 Porte, *The Romance in America*, 72.

of her soul. But because Ligeia is the narrator's mirror image, her eyes grant the hero a glimpse of his own interior consciousness; he becomes obsessed in his desire to fathom the mysterious depths of Ligeia's reflecting eyes, beseeching, "What was it . . . which lay far within the pupils of my beloved?" (II, 251). Like other Poe characters—Usher, Egaeus, or the demented narrator of "The Tell-Tale Heart"—the hero in his projected introspection finds only horror and depravity. Morella's "meaning eyes" appropriately "sicken" the "soul" of her husband (II, 29), for they reflect the deep-seated malignity of his own soul.

Like most nineteenth-century American authors, Poe seems most reluctant to treat sexuality as a natural component of a healthy feminine nature. His poems "Al Aaraaf" and "The Colloquy of Monos and Una" portray sexual passion as a disease of impure nature;[40] Roderick Usher and the narrator-husband of "Morella" both locate the source of their spiritual maladies in the uncontrollable, unnatural sexual desire for the temptress woman; Ligeia's poem "The Conqueror Worm" presents the case from a feminine perspective, employing a powerful phallic metaphor to equate sexuality with man's exploitation of the woman and his own inevitable decay. Because sex is simultaneously an alluring, vital life force and a dangerous, evil and destructive phenomenon, Poe's ideal woman becomes an impossible blend of the ethereal and the sensuous; she reflects the hero's conflicting impulses and paradoxical desires. The woman must be pure of soul while sensuous and provocative. Ligeia's beauty is "of beings either above or apart from the earth," though she is "the most violently a prey to the tumultuous vultures of a stern passion." Eleonora is "a maiden artless and innocent"; Morella's face is "holy, and mild, and eloquent" (II, 32); Eulalie is "fair," "gentle," "modest," even "blushing"; and Helen is "clad all in white." But this same pure Helen is pictured "reclining . . . upon a

40 Daniel Hoffman, "I Have Been Faithful to You in My Fashion: The Remarriage of Ligeia's Husband," *Southern Review*, n.s., VIII (1972), 91.

violet bank," and the virginal eye of the "blushing" Eulalie is para-doxically "violet," a "matron eye."[41]

As wife and lover the woman occupies a similarly ambiguous role. Poe's heroes seem to need the idolatrous worship of their women to sustain their dangerously weak self-esteem, and for the most part they receive it: Ligeia "would . . . pour out before me the overflowing of a heart whose more than passionate devotion amounted to idolatry" (II, 255); Morella "shunned society, and, at-taching herself to me alone, rendered me happy" (II, 27); Berenice's cousin plans to marry her because "I called to mind that she had loved me long"; Annabel Lee "lived with no other thought/ Than to love and be loved by me"; "Ulalume" offers the supreme vision of Poesque narcissicism in the image of the poet kissing Psyche, the personification of his soul. Such narcissistic love proves destructive to the hero's ability to function in a real, dynamic world. The blonde, staid, and conventional Lady Rowena finds the narrator of "Ligeia" impossible to live with; she "shunned me and loved me but little," shattering the fragile masculine ego of the husband and caus-ing him to "loathe" her "with a hatred belonging more to demon than to man" (II, 261). The supreme egotism of the Poe narrator serves as a psychological defense against dark suspicions of his own depravity, and the idolatrous worship of the constructed ideal woman shields him from his own inferiority of soul. Thus the nar-rator of "Ligeia" retreats from the real Rowena into an imaginative fantasy world, becoming "a bounded slave in the trammels of opium." The power of his imaginative will enables him to recall Ligeia from the dead to enact his fantasies; ultimately the lure of the imaginative world completely consumes him, however, resulting in the destruction of the "real" woman and her subsequent transfor-

---

41 The "eye" suggests female sexuality, specifically the vagina. Interestingly, Mo-rella is the feminine of "morello," a species of wild cherry—a symbol of the virgin's genitals. References to the poems are to Floyd Stovall (ed.), *The Poems of Edgar Allan Poe* (Charlottesville, Va., 1965): "Eulalie—A Song," p. 100; "To Helen," p. 114.

mation into the hero's imaginative construct, Ligeia. Significantly the name Ligeia derives from "ligeance," "the jurisdiction or territory of a liege lord."

Psychoanalytic critics of Poe's fiction such as Daniel Hoffman, Marie Bonaparte, Claudia Morrison, and Joseph Wood Krutch approach the problem of Poe's concept of women from a biographical perspective, reducing everything to Poe's supposed fear of sex. Hoffman writes: "The very thought of consummated marriage struck Poe's imagination with terror . . . he was beset by redoubled fears of committing incest and of connubial non-performance." For Hoffman, "Ligeia" and "Morella" dramatize Poe's fears of "incest and impotence."[42] Bonaparte, Morrison, and Hoffman identify the transfer of the husband's love in both stories as "Poe's guilty transferral of love" from his real sweethearts to his dead mother."[43] Similarly, according to the psychoanalytic critics, Poe's heroes suffer terribly from a fear of impotence. Ligeia, according to Hoffman, is a vital woman desiring sexual relations with her husband: "What can an impotent lover do when his beloved is aroused 'to the tumultuous vultures of stern passion'? . . . He can solve everything by wishing her dead so hard that she dies."[44] Poe's heroes seem always to desire a woman who is dead, such as "the long lost Lenore," or one like Ligeia who is supernaturally positioned somewhere between life and death—a woman who is, in short, an imaginative construct. Only such women can satisfy the hero's contradictory desires.

Undercutting this biographical explanation of Poe's portrayal of women is the fact that in his characterization of women Poe operates well in the mainstream of romantic gothic fiction. In describing Emily St. Aubert—the heroine of Anne Radcliffe's *The Mysteries of Udolpho*—Eino Railo writes that the prototypical gothic heroine "breathes

---

42 Hoffman, "I Have Been Faithful," 89–90.
43 Morrison, "Poe's 'Ligeia,'" 237; Marie Bonaparte, *The Life and Works of Edgar Allan Poe: A Psychoanalytic Interpretation* (New York, 1971), 223; Hoffman, "I Have Been Faithful," 103.
44 Hoffman, "I Have Been Faithful," 94–95.

a fine femininity, a tender and sacrificial maternal spirit, fighting the battle of life with the weapons of resignation and tears, and bringing to love everything that is divine, passion excluded."[45] Ultimately, Poe's fiction might most profitably be approached as a dramatization of the romantic conflict between the real and the ideal. Rarely does the Poe narrator make any attempt to distinguish fantasy from reality. The narrator of "Ligeia" falls prey to "a crowd of unutterable fancies" (II, 267), as he concentrates upon "assumptions and aspirations which mortality had never before known." The narrator of "Morella," referring to his metaphysical studies under his wife's guidance, admits that "in all this . . . my reason had little to do" (II, 28). Like the narrator of "Berenice," both men suffer from "distempered vision," which renders them incapable of distinguishing reality from fantasy. When confronted by Rowena—who is grounded in reality—Poe's narrator is confused: "She spoke . . . of sounds which she *then* heard, but which I could not hear—of motions which she *then* saw, but which I could not perceive" (II, 262). His relationship with Rowena commences "in a moment of mental alienation," a temporary lapse into the realm of reality that is soon reversed by the hero's total absorption into the ideal Ligeia.

A close reading of "Ligeia" and "Morella" suggests that the two women have no concrete existence at all; they are simply imaginative constructs providing the hero with a retreat from the demands of reality. Far from being the lusty, physical woman Hoffman takes her for, Ligeia is "an airy and uplifting vision," "the radiance of an opium dream," "the shadow of a shade." In "Berenice," the "inner apartment" of the narrator's library becomes a metaphor for the center of his consciousness, into which he withdraws to indulge his monomania; similarly, Ligeia always appears before her husband in his "closed study." The empty grave in "Morella" testifies that the hero's beloved in that story simply had no body to bury. As the narrator of "Ligeia" questions, is not the ideal woman "a caprice of

---

45   Eino Railo, *The Haunted Castle* (London, 1927), 291.

my own—a wildly romantic offering on the shrine of the most passionate devotion?" (II, 249).

The psychological disintegration of Poe's heroes, their inability to sustain a meaningful love relationship within a community, and their unwillingness to allow the woman human qualities all point to the personal and social failure of romantic narcissistic love. The ideal woman in Poe's art is no woman at all, but a disembodied shadow of the hero's intuitive glimpses of a remote transcendental dimension. And the male's infatuation with this creature of his own making renders him sterile and hopeless in a communal setting; furthermore, it initiates a process that culminates in his psychological undoing.

The tragic tendency of the nineteenth-century male to prefer the visionary embodiment of his own creation to the complex, vibrant, and human female becomes a major theme in the fiction of Nathaniel Hawthorne. In "The Birthmark," for example, Aylmer destroys his beautiful wife in a monomaniac attempt to remove a facial blemish that, because all of her prior lovers had wanted to kiss it, stands as a symbol of both her sexuality and humanity. The self-righteous young hero of "Young Goodman Brown" likewise has great difficulty coping with his wife's human sexuality. Rejecting Faith's subtly veiled suggestive plea that he stay home in bed with her rather than rendezvous with Satan in the forest, Brown enters the devil's domain only to overhear erotic whisperings of religious leaders about a comely young woman who later turns out to be Faith, his wife. Having placed her on a pedestal, free of base urges, Brown is absolutely unnerved and effectively destroyed to learn that others regard Faith as a sexual being, and that she does, in fact, possess a sexual drive. In his 1851 novel, *The Blithedale Romance*, Hawthorne gives this theme sustained attention.

The Blithedale Romance chronicles the doomed attempt to realize the imagined ideal world within an actual spatial and temporal context. The narrator, Miles Coverdale, is a "frosty bachelor"—emotionally detached and heretofore unfruitful—who leaves the comfortable warmth of fireside at home to plunge "into the heart of the pitiless snow-storm, in quest of a better life."[46] But the Blithedale reformers fail to realize their aspirations, in large part because they are unable to yoke together a kindling desire for renovation with the implacable facts of human nature. Images of fire suggest the warm glow, the illumination, of Blithedale's inspiration; images of ice define Blithedale's still-born realization in the principals directly involved in the socialist scheme. The two pair of image patterns coalesce to characterize the experiment's stormy beginning. Although conceived in April, the utopia's birth is announced by an unseasonable snowstorm—a "symbol of the cold, desolate, distrustful phantoms that invariably haunt the mind . . . to warm us back within the boundaries of ordinary life" (18). The striking contrast between the cold, snow, and ice outside the Blithedale cabin and the seeming warmth around the fire inside suggests that the utopian attempt to take the cold ideal and thaw it in a mortal realm is doomed, because the warmth, like everything else at Blithedale, is illusory:

The stanch oaken-logs were long ago burnt out. Their genial glow must be represented, if at all, by the merest phosphoric glimmer, like that which exudes, rather than shines, from damp fragments of decayed trees, deluding the benighted wanderer through a forest. Around such chill mockery of a fire, some few of us might sit on the withered leaves, spreading out each palm towards the imaginary warmth, and talk over our exploded scheme for beginning the life of Paradise anew. (9)

This tension between the ideal and the real—the imaginary and the mortal—works through the two central female characters in the novel and the relationships they bear to the males of the Blithedale group. Zenobia and Priscilla offer to every major male character a choice, as Joel Porte expresses it, "between sexual truth and sentimental deception . . . dusky passion and marmoreal virtue."[47]

Zenobia, "an admirable figure of a woman" with a hand "which was very soft and warm," is clearly the epitome of mortal, though enlightened, femininity: "We seldom meet with women, now-a-

---

46 Nathaniel Hawthorne, *The Blithedale Romance*, vol. III of *The Centenary Edition of The Works of Nathaniel Hawthorne*, 10. Subsequent references are to this edition and appear parenthetically.

47 Porte, *The Romance in America*, 133–34.

days, and in this country, who impress us as being women at all; their sex fades away and goes for nothing, in ordinary intercourse. Not so with Zenobia. One felt an influence breathing out of her, such as we might suppose to come from Eve, when she was just made, and her creator brought her to Adam, saying—'Behold, here is a woman!" (17). As the symbol of passionate femininity and life— "womanliness incarnated," Coverdale labels her—Zenobia stands amidst the prevailing atmosphere of stasis and rigidity. Her most striking aspect is the new "hot-house flower" she wears daily, a "flower . . . such as appeared to have sprung passionately out of a soil, the very weeds of which would be fervid and spicy" (45). Although she too masquerades, Zenobia is the "first comer" (Eve) whose warmth "beamed upon us all" (16). Coverdale notes that one glance of her heated vitality might "melt [Hollingsworth] back into a man" (101); her transforming powers affect even Priscilla, whose "big [tear] drops began to ooze out from beneath her eyelids" (29) as she gains Zenobia's acceptance. Melting in Zenobia's heat, the static figures are subject to the fluidity of time: even Hollingsworth compares Priscilla to "the first fruits of the world" whose secrets "will be melted out of her" (30).

The aspiring creative artist, Coverdale, is at first drawn to Zenobia's sensuality, then repelled by it: "I most ungratefully began to wish that she would let me alone." A "high-spirited Woman, bruising herself against the narrow limitations of her sex," Zenobia makes others uncomfortably aware of the futility of their attempt to capture their imaginary vision. "The presence of Zenobia," the narrator confesses, "caused our heroic enterprise to show like an illusion, a masquerade, a pastoral, a counterfeit Arcadia" (21).

But Zenobia's vitality is doomed at Blithedale, for the masculine ego is unwilling to accommodate it. Roy Male points out that the two central men subconsciously try to destroy her, "Coverdale by his incessant probing, his cool dissection, and Hollingsworth by making her a tool in his conspiracy."[48] Though she is Queen of the

---

48 Male, *Hawthorne's Tragic Vision*, 147.

May, at Blithedale May-Day is a movable feast, and thus, as Daniel Hoffman contends, "loses its function," becoming "a masquerade" because it "does not observe the return to life of the world after the near-death of winter."[49] Voluptuous, sensual, and in love, Zenobia would seem an appropriate May queen indeed; but at Blithedale there is no king. Hollingsworth ignores her for the visionary, disembodied Priscilla, and the proud but unfulfilled Zenobia drowns herself. The whole community—which records no harvest in the fall—is sterile, for "nature does not condone such failures of the ritual marriage that celebrates her fecundity."[50] Zenobia tells Hollingsworth, "Let man be but manly and godlike, and woman is only too ready to become to him what you say" (124). But the male is intimidated by her and what she represents, and in refusing to grant Zenobia her humanity, becomes responsible for her death. Appropriately Zenobia's mutilated corpse is "the marble image of a death-agony"; denied her humanity, she is reduced to stone: cold, aloof, sterile, dead.

Zenobia's antithesis is Priscilla, "the weakly maiden, whose tremulous nerves endow her with sibylline attributes." Possessing "slender and shadowy grace, and those mysterious qualities which make her seem diaphanous with spiritual light," Priscilla is the product "man has spent centuries in making" (122). She is, in other words, the veiled maiden of Shelley's *Alastor* or the Amélie of *René*: "a slight mist of uncertainty still floated about Priscilla, and kept her, as yet, from taking a very decided place among creatures of flesh and blood" (49). "Enshrouded within the misty drapery of the veil," Priscilla enters Blithedale out of the snow, covered with ice: "a slim and unsubstantial girl . . . doomed to wander about in snow-storms" (26–27). The imagery suggests, Porte claims, "the essential frigidity of her perpetually chaste and unsexual nature."[51] Priscilla is, however, the woman the nineteenth-century romantic hero can love—the frozen, abstracted, purified embodiment of a chaste ideal.

49 Hoffman, *Form and Fable in American Fiction*, 211.
50 *Ibid.*, 208.
51 Porte, *The Romance in America*, 128.

Like Sue Bridehead or *Alastor*'s veiled maiden, Priscilla emasculates her lovers; she offers them a symbol of her sexuality in the beautiful silk purses she manufactures whose "peculiar excellence . . . lay in the almost impossibility that any uninitiated person should discover the aperture" (35). Admitting that he loves Priscilla not for who she is but for "the fancy-work with which I have idly decked her out" (100), Coverdale illuminates the veiled maiden's devastating charm: she possesses no identity of her own, becoming instead an embodiment of the spiritual ideal generated within the imagination of her suitors and consequently commanding from them a devotion that renders them sterile within a human community.

It is Hollingsworth who emerges as the heroic personality in the Blithedale escapade. An implacable idealist whose singular vision gives focus to the utopian experiment, Hollingsworth appears initially "quite as much like a polar bear as a modern philanthropist" (26). Hollingsworth's character seems capable of some fireside warmth when he tends to the ailing Coverdale; however, this warmth, like the original hearthfire, proves brief and illusory. He renders assistance not out of human love for an afflicted brother but because he sees Coverdale as an adjunct to his visionary plan. Eventually Coverdale discovers Hollingsworth to be "off his moral balance . . . by his great excrescence of a philanthropic scheme" (100)—caught in a heated monomania that results in his rejection of the fiery Zenobia and subsequent union with the illusory Priscilla, and leaves him with "frozen hopes" (224). Coverdale condemns Hollingsworth's "masculine egotism," which "centered everything in itself, and deprived woman of her very soul, her inexpressible and unfathomable all, to make it a mere incident in the great Sum of man" (123), and finally left him with "a heart of ice" (225).

Unfortunately Hollingsworth's monomaniacal vision freezes all human relationships: "By-and-by, you . . . grew drearily conscious that Hollingsworth had a closer friend than ever you could be . . . the cold, spectral monster . . . [of] his philanthropic theory" (55). To Coverdale, Hollingsworth is a "dragon"; Zenobia, outcast and even "murdered" by the "iron man," accuses Hollingsworth of subverting his humanity to lifeless aims: "Are you a man? No; but a monster! A cold, heartless, self-beginning and self-ending piece of mechanism!" (218). Ironically, Hollingsworth's fall results from his pursuit of the Veiled Lady, who like the devil Westervelt, is "stifled with the heat of a salamander-stove" (34). The principals crave heat, but theirs is a hellish desire resulting in "frozen hopes." So possessed is Hollingsworth by the "cunning devil" within him, he becomes "immolated" by his obsession (166).

The frustrated Blithedale experiment is consonant with all romantic attempts to achieve a Resurrection without Good Friday. Its participants prove unable to reconcile their dynamic, mortal nature with an abstract, permanent (frozen) vision of reform. As the pathetic artist in utopia, Coverdale stands witness to Blithedale's moral significance; but he too falls victim to the irresistible allure of the insubstantial veiled lady. He is not creative artist so much as he is voyeur, "washing his hands" of the Hollingsworth-Zenobia affair (171), and longing "for a catastrophe" (157). Although fanciful retreats from the mainstream of life do not veil the rigid truths of the human heart, Coverdale as artist remains content to communicate in "glittering icicles instead of lines of fire" (224).

The consequences facing a social order that requires its members to surrender sexual differences come into clear perspective in Hawthorne's 1850 novel, *The Scarlet Letter*. The "Custom House" section that prefaces the novel provides insight into contemporary Salem, confronting the reader with the central fact of Salem's decay. What was once "a bustling wharf" is "now burdened with decayed wooden warehouses, and exhibits few or no symptoms of commercial life."[52] Even the mirth of the town's inhabitants "resembles the phosphorescent glow of decaying wood." Across from the "delapidated wharf" stands the customhouse; its central room is "cobwebbed, and dingy with old paint; its floor is strewn with gray sand,

---

52 Nathaniel Hawthorne, *The Scarlet Letter*, vol. I of *The Centenary Edition of The Works of Nathaniel Hawthorne*, 4. Subsequent references appear parenthetically.

in a fashion that has elsewhere fallen into long disuse; and it is easy to conclude, from the general slovenliness of the place, that this is a sanctuary into which womankind, with her tools of magic, the broom and mop, has very infrequent access" (7). The implication here is that the decay and sterility of contemporary Salem directly result from its failure to grant access to the principle of femininity, or "womankind."

Because of the prominent role played by his ancestors in the persecution of women in early New England, Hawthorne accepts personal responsibility for Salem's decline. The Quakers, Hawthorne informs us, remember in their histories his first American ancestor, "and relate an incident of his hard severity towards a woman of their sect, which will last longer, it is to be feared, than any record of his better deeds" (9). This first progenitor's "son, too, inherited the persecuting spirit, and made himself so conspicuous in the martyrdom of the witches, that their blood may fairly be said to have left a stain upon him" (9). The mention at the close of chapter 1 of the "sainted Ann Hutchinson"—a seventeenth-century woman persecuted by men like Hawthorne's ancestors—serves to remind the reader of Hawthorne's personal involvement in the tale unfolded in the novel; Hawthorne, "as their representative," assumes the guilt of his ancestors, and hopes to expiate such guilt through the novel, *The Scarlet Letter*.

Significantly, Hawthorne is able to write his novel only after leaving the customhouse, for while ensnared by affairs there he is alienated from traditional sources of fertility and creativity—nature and art. John Crowe Ransom contends that puritanism "lopped off from religion the aesthetic properties which . . . loving artists had given it."[53] Hence in the customhouse section of the novel, Hawthorne confesses the guilt he feels in his choice of vocation as artist, a vocation that links him to Hester, who "artistically" embroiders her scarlet *A*. His creative forces are unleashed only by the discovery of the scarlet *A*, the embroidered emblem of Hester's art and

53 John Crowe Ransom, *The World's Body* (Baton Rouge, La., 1968), 64–65.

symbol of her fertility that had been hidden and repressed within the customhouse itself.

The novel opens drawing a clear contrast between the feminine protagonist, Hester, and her social order that denies or subverts the feminine impulse. The "virgin land" of the new country, instead of becoming an instrument of love and procreation, is allotted in part for a cemetery and prison. From the prison emerges Hester, who "never had . . . appeared more lady-like, in the antique interpretation of the term" (53). Juxtaposed to Hester stand her peers, a group of puritan women devoid of femininity: "The women, who were now standing about the prison-door, stood within less than half a century of the period when the man-like Elizabeth had been the not altogether unsuitable representative of the sex. They were her countrywomen; and the beef and ale of their native land, with a moral diet not a whit more refined, entered largely into their composition" (50). From such a jury Hester could hardly expect mercy (notably a feminine trait, associated in Catholic theology with the Mother of God); indeed, "meagre . . . and cold, was the sympathy that a transgressor might look for, from such bystanders at the scaffold" (50). One "hard-featured dame of fifty" protests that the male members of the community have been too merciful with Hester; another "autumnal matron" suggests branding Hester's forehead with a hot iron. Only one woman has sympathy for Hester—"a young wife, holding a child by the hand"; significantly, this woman perishes before the novel's close.

As Hester confronts the descendants of the "man-like Elizabeth," she sports the "A," "so artistically done, and with so much fertility and gorgeous luxuriance of fancy" (53) that it makes Hester "a figure of perfect elegance." The neatly embroidered A is the object that most disturbs the women of Salem, for in its artistic beauty the A becomes an embodiment of Hester's femininity while symbolizing her passion and shame.

Dimmesdale finds in Hester the quality of mercy absent in the hearts of the women of the community, referring to the "wondrous strength and generosity of a woman's heart" when Hester declines to reveal her lover's identity. Hawthorne reinforces the parallel between Hester and the quality of mercy by comparing the heroine to "the image of Divine Maternity" (56). Hester's "maternity" is immensely important, as it is her relationship to her illegitimate child that keeps her from a rendezvous with Mistress Hibbins, the witch who attempts to lure Hester into a satanic realm. Though sinful—and Hester is the first to acknowledge her wrongdoing—the heroine presents a regenerating alternative to the decay and sterility inevitable in a society that fails to foster the feminine impulse.

In *The Blithedale Romance* and *The Scarlet Letter* Hawthorne exposes a major deficiency in nineteenth-century American culture. Fostered both by the puritan repression of the feminine principle and the genteel tradition's etherealization of the woman, the denial of the "eternal feminine" celebrated at the close of Goethe's *Faust* had become a characteristic of American life. Henry Adams writes of nineteenth-century America:

The Woman had once been supreme; in France she still seemed potent, not merely as a sentiment, but as a force. Why was she unknown in America? For evidently America was ashamed of her, and she was ashamed of herself. . . . the monthly-magazine-made American female had not a feature that would have been recognized by Adam. . . . An American Virgin would never dare command; an American Venus would never dare exist.[54]

But America's denial of the feminine impulse is only an intensification of a tendency in romanticism at large. Committed to a self-generated vision, the romantic hero is tragically impatient with a vital, organic reality; rather, he yearns toward union with a static ideal that lies beyond mortal reach. Thus he is rendered impotent in a real world, sterile and doomed to extinction.

54 Henry Adams, *The Education of Henry Adams*, intro. D. W. Brogan (Boston, 1961), 384–85.

VI

Incest and American Romantic Fiction

I suppose it is a commentary on our age that the man at the gate in "Ode to the Confederate Dead" never quite achieves the illusion that the leaves are heroic men, so that he may identify himself with them, as Keats and Shelley too easily and too beautifully did with nightingales and west winds. More than this, he cautions himself, reminds himself repeatedly of his subjective prison, his solipsism, by breaking off the half-illusion and coming back to the refrain of wind and leaves.

Allen Tate, "Narcissus as Narcissus"[1]

In his essay "Narcissus as Narcissus" (1939) Allen Tate states that the subject of his poem "Ode to the Confederate Dead" is "solipsism, a philosophical doctrine which says that we create the world in the act of perceiving it; or about narcissism, or any other *ism* that denotes the failure of the human personality to function objectively in nature and society."[2] Tate focuses in his essay—and even more poignantly in his poem—on a problem besetting the American artist since the nation's beginning: how does the American reconcile the desire for excessive individualism with the demands made upon him by the emergent social order? The founding of the American Republic appropriately coincided with the rise of romanticism in Europe, both drawing their inspiration from the Enlightenment; and

---

1 Allen Tate, "Narcissus as Narcissus," *Essays of Four Decades* (Chicago, 1968), 599.

2 *Ibid.*, 595–96. Strictly speaking, solipsism is a philosophical term referring to the epistemological theory that holds that the self is the sole source of knowledge. But as Tate suggests, in literature solipsism has other related connotations. Hence when I use the term I have in mind the excessive introspection and self-absorption that renders the individual incapable of functioning "objectively in nature and society."

one could assert, without stretching the point too greatly, that in the American experiment in democracy the romantic tendency toward solipsism received its logical political manifestation. Rousseau, René, or Werther could repudiate traditional institutions and posit the principle of order within individual consciousness without posing a great threat to the entrenched institutional framework of Europe; they were exceptional individuals whose behavior by definition was atypical. But in America, lacking established social and political institutions, self-absorption or solipsism was to be the characteristic response of both the intelligentsia and the common man. Even Thomas Jefferson—author of the Declaration of Independence and the third president of the United States—worked to ensure that neither church nor state gained control over individual lives; his phrase "that government is best which governs least" stood as an expression of American governmental philosophy for over a century.

But Jefferson did not envision anarchy as the logical outcome of his maxim. Working from the assumption that "enlightened self-interest" was inseparable from the communal welfare, Jefferson trusted that through education and cultivation the individual citizen would be prepared to serve the community, willing to practice "eternal vigilance."[3] Jefferson's assumption was that within a republican nation predicated upon the proposition that "all men are created equal" before the law, a "natural aristocracy" based on genius, talent, and virtue would surface to guide the fledgling country's destiny. Yet by the second decade of the nineteenth century, the nation's intellectuals had developed grave reservations concerning the actual working-out of Jefferson's vision. The "natural aristocracy" seemed powerless before the flood of democracy in practice, a phenomenon that in 1822 the eighteen-year-old Ralph W. Emerson equated with "vulgarity, with General Jackson and tobacco-chewing." Suppose,

3   See Robert E. Spiller *et al.* (eds.), *Literary History of the United States* (3rd rev. ed.; New York, 1963), 158–59.

Emerson conjectured on the eve of Independence Day, 1822, the American experiment proved only "that too much knowledge, & too much liberty makes them mad?" Even genius, that darling of the age, proved suspect. With the examples of Byron—whose genius "is blind, it sees not its true end"—and Napoleon—who "had an Aim & a Bad one"—in mind, Emerson became preoccupied with the fear of an heroic personality that finds "permissible or actually congenial sexual aberration or political domination."[4]

Hence, early in American literature the tension between solipsism and the pressing need for community in an emergent democracy becomes a fundamental concern of the artist, often coloring his portrayal of the heroic personality. The American "dark" romantics—William Hill Brown, Charles Brockden Brown, Poe, Hawthorne, Melville—adapt the metaphor of sibling incest to portray the dangers inherent in the narcissistic element of their heroes' quest for passionate self-fulfillment: absorption into self proves a sure avenue to dementia and eventual destruction. Furthermore, the work of each of these novelists reflects "the remarkable congruence of history and fiction" that Lewis P. Simpson sees as a hallmark of American fiction.[5] As Emerson so succinctly expressed it, the American political experience was predicated upon the assumption "that the nation existed for the individual" and its corollary, "the individual is the world"—ideas that, as we have noted in Chapter IV, emerged from the European Enlightenment and proved crucial in the formation of the romantic movement. Hence, in their exploration of the hero's psychological disintegration—occasioned by acute self-consciousness—the "dark" romantic writers not only call into question crucial theoretical premises of European romanticism but also cast doubt upon the possibilities for success of the American political experiment based upon these premises. The demise of the hero, in

4 The discussion of Emerson in this paragraph is indebted to Perry Miller, "Emersonian Genius and the American Democracy," *New England Quarterly*, XXVI (March, 1953), 28–30.
5 Simpson, "John Adams and Hawthorne," 1.

other words, reflects the demise of a social and political order that places insufficient emphasis on the Vergilian notion of *civitas*.

In their portrayal of incest as self-destructive, the American romantics differed from their counterparts in France and England who, by and large, pictured sibling incest as a regenerating alternative to conventional, sterile morality. Incest is "only crime of convention," Shelley writes in his preface to *Laon and Cythna*; he introduces it into his poem "to break through the crust of outworn opinions on which established institutions depend."[6] A far more sinister brand of incest underlies Shelley's *The Cenci*, for the count's sadistic rape of his virtuous daughter epitomizes his brutally repressive exercise of psychological and physical control. But sibling incest rarely assumes this sort of satanic coloring in English and French romanticism: the sister-soul in Shelley's "Epipsychidion," Astarte in Byron's *Manfred*, and Amélie in Chateaubriand's *René* serve as sources of inspiration and consolation to weary romantic heroes.[7] The relationship between Agnes and her brother Lorenzo, in Matthew Gregory Lewis' *The Monk*, illustrates the pattern incest generally follows in English romantic literature and hence provides a convenient point of contrast to sibling incest as it is portrayed in American romantic fiction.

The theme of repression and its consequences is the central concern of Lewis' archetypically gothic novel, which charts Agnes' development from a state of artificial innocence in the convent of St. Clair to an understanding of her mortality and a mature acceptance of her flawed humanity. A beautiful, innocent girl whose "simplicity" offers "an advantageous contrast to the art and studied coquetry"[8] of most women, Agnes is at the novel's outset a young nun who—like Blake's Thel—is aware of the limitations imposed by her

---

6 Clark (ed.), *Shelley's Prose*, 320.

7 The best study of the theme of incest in English and European romanticism is Peter L. Thorslev, Jr., "Incest as Romantic Symbol." Thorslev does not discuss the theme as it appears in American literature.

8 Matthew Gregory Lewis, *The Monk* (New York, 1952), 144. Subsequent references are to this Grove Press edition.

innocence. She seeks experience by falling in love with the worldly Don Raymond, but her attempt to flee the nunnery with him fails and Agnes falls under the stern eye of Mother St. Agatha, the prioress. Addressed as "domina," the Prioress represents the repressive Church that seeks to enforce Agnes' debilitating innocence; she is motivated by a desire to make St. Clair "the most regular order in Madrid" (71), and steadfastly refuses to allow Lorenzo's "profane eyes" (213) to view the inside of the convent, even though she tells him that his sister lies dying within its walls. But the Church is unable to keep the world outside its domain. Posing as the gardener's helper, Raymond gains access to the convent and seduces Agnes in the garden.

Agnes is ill-prepared to cope with the conflicting psychological tensions which worldly experience brings. She desires the passion occasioned by her love for Raymond, yet she is inhibited because she takes seriously her vows to the Church. To her worldly lover Agnes is "beloved," but to the prioress she is a "prostitute" and "criminal." Split by allegiance to both realms, Agnes is unable to reconcile the discordant quality of her life; she pleads for "mercy," but is told that "mercy would be criminal" (70). Tragically, Agnes learns that all human actions have consequences: she is pregnant with Raymond's child.

Locked in a crypt as punishment for her crime of "incontinance," Agnes enters a nightmarish, purgatorial world which forces her to confront her repressions and to construct her identity. Built by the Church, the crypt suggests Agnes' repressive inhibitions which insulate her from human intercourse. Because she proved too weak to fulfill her vow to control human passion, Agnes shares affinity with the "mouldering bodies" in the crypt—the physical emblem of all who labor under the burdens of the flesh. But Agnes is reluctant to accept her humanity, to admit that she is not divine like the marble saint that rests directly above her. Only with the birth of her child does Agnes learn her identity and the value of her suffering.

A symbol of her sin and of her love, the child is like the albatross in Coleridge's *The Rime of the Ancient Mariner*: a physical manifestation of transgression and guilt that assumes redemptive qualities. The child offers Agnes a choice, for she could reject the infant and deny both her sin and her humanity. But when Agnes delivers her "wretched burden" she offers "prayers for its safety . . . bathes it with tears" (393), and struggles to preserve its fragile life. The baby's death illustrates to Agnes that all human life is conceived in sin and is mortal, including her own. Embracing the corpse, "holding it to her bosom . . . lamenting it, loving it, and adoring it," Agnes accepts the child though it is a "mass of putridity." Psychologically and spiritually, Agnes is ready for release from her purgatory.

The physical release is occasioned by her brother, Lorenzo. Frantically searching for his sister throughout her captivity, Lorenzo is his sister's alter ego; his union with her delivers Agnes from the repressive forces inhibiting her. Lorenzo discovers Agnes by manipulating a sacred, forbidden statue that serves as a door to Agnes' cell; in other words, he opens the door only by repudiating the strictures of the Church, the symbol of repression throughout the novel. Freed through union with her brother, Agnes leaves the convent to embark upon a satisfying life: her remaining years "were happy as can be those allotted to mortals, born to be the prey of grief, and sport of disappointment" (400).

The relationship of Agnes to Lorenzo mirrors the pattern of most incestuous loves in English and French romanticism: of René and Amélie, Laon to Cythna, Manfred to Astarte, the poet to his "sister soul" in "Epipsychidion." Though at times the hero (or heroine) meets his demise, the destruction is more the result of a world toxic to acute sensibility of soul than of the relationship itself; indeed, the incestuous relationship, in most instances, provides solace and spiritual inspiration to the world-weary romantic hero. But early nineteenth-century America was not France or England—it lacked the cohesiveness and order provided those countries by established institutions. Rather, America more closely resembled Germany, which was also at the time a loose collection of city-states lacking the literary, political, or religious cohesiveness characteristic

of its more prosperous neighbors.[9] Like their American counterparts, German artists too gave incest harsh treatment: Tieck's *Der
blonde Eckbert*, Schiller's *Die Braut von Messina*, and Grillparzer's *Die
Ahnfrau* all portrayed incest as an unconscious act—as in *Oedipus*—
the recognition of which invariably led to dementia and death. The
point I hope to demonstrate in the remainder of this chapter is that
incest in American gothic fiction is more than ornamental trapping
designed to intensify terror and titillate the reader;[10] rather, it is
central in the American artists' attempt to convey the self-destructive element implicit in the nation's experiment in deocracy. Democracy is fine if the soul is as the man of the Enlightenment or the
optimistic romantic conceived it: a "belle âme" governed by reason
and divinely inspired. But if the self is a morass of psychological
disorder too weak to bear scrutiny, then democracy becomes an experiment in terror.

The first American novel, William Hill Brown's *The Power of
Sympathy; or, The Triumph of Nature* (1789), appeared in Boston as an
anonymous work seemingly cast in a Richardsonian mold. Dedicated to "the Young Ladies of United Columbia," the novel ostensi-
bly was "intended to represent the specious CAUSES, and to Expose
the fatal CONSEQUENCES, of SEDUCTION."[11] The novel's sentimental
overtones and obvious indebtedness to the popular Samuel Richardson have led most scholars to treat *The Power of Sympathy* as a his-
torically important but intrinsically wretched example of the sentimental novel in America.[12] Overly conscious, belabored didacticism
and flat, dull characterization do indeed render the novel tedious;

9 Furst, *Romanticism in Perspective*, 31–38.
10 The Englishman Horace Walpole wrote that he introduced incest into *The Mysterious Mother* because "I was desirous of striking a little out of the common road,
and of introducing some novelty on our stage." See Thorslev, "Incest as Romantic Symbol," 43.
11 William Hill Brown, *The Power of Sympathy*, ed. William S. Kable (Columbus,
Ohio, 1969), 3. The quotation is from the original title page from Brown's novel.
All parenthetical references are to the Kable edition.
12 Herbert R. Brown, *The Sentimental Novel in America, 1789–1860* (Durham, N.C.,
1940), 44–45; Alexander Cowie, *The Rise of the American Novel* (New York, 1948),

but the introduction of the theme of incest contributes an element of irony to the novel that undercuts its sentimentality and foreshadows basic themes in the American gothic novel for the next hundred years.

The novel's notorious subplot—which Brown tells us is "Founded in Truth"—gives a thinly disguised rendition of a local scandal: the illicit affair of Ophelia and her brother-in-law parallels the affair of Frances Apthorp and her brother-in-law, Perez Morton—both from socially prominent Boston families. Like Ophelia, Miss Apthorp committed suicide via poison; and she did so less than five months prior to the publication of the novel. The frontispiece of the novel's first volume, a graphic woodcut depicting the death agony of a young woman and bearing the caption, "O Fatal! Fatal Poison!" alarmed the Apthorp and Morton families and led to an attempt to suppress the novel.[13] The subplot serves in the novel as an exemplum designed to point out the fatal consequences of seduction, and as such it fits well into a Richardsonian pattern of titillating readers and placating moralists. Although Brown, like Richardson, renders a vivid portrayal of the evil of seduction, the world he pictures is not one to reward an unwavering reliance on natural, heart-felt virtue. Indeed, the central plot of *The Power of Sympathy* reveals that the resemblances between this novel and the novels of Richardson are in the last analysis superficial.

The central love affair between Harrington and Harriot, in fact, contrasts with the love liaison portrayed in the subplot in that it is genuine and to a certain extent ethereal. At first Harrington has only improper designs on Harriot; his "scheme of pleasure" includes only seduction. Harrington writes to Worthy that he is "not so much of a republican as formally to wed any person of this class"; instead he merely plans "to take this beautiful sprig, and transplant it to a more favourable soil, where it shall flourish and blossom under my own

10–12; and William S. Osborne, "Introduction," to William Hill Brown, *The Power of Sympathy and The Coquette* (New Haven, Conn., 1970), 12–14.

13   Herbert Brown, "Introduction," to William Hill Brown, *The Power of Sympathy; or, The Triumph of Nature*, ed. Herbert Brown (Boston, 1961), xi–xii.

auspices. In a word, I mean to remove this fine girl into an elegant apartment, of which she herself is to be the sole mistress" (13). But Harrington's first glimpse of Harriot leads him to the first rung in a Platonic ladder of love. At first driven by a lustful desire for her physical beauty, he gradually ascends to an awareness of her finer qualities and a love for her that is eternal. So powerful is his love, in fact, that Harrington abandons plans to seduce Harriot and intends to marry her; so profound is his remorse over the barriers to their union that he commits suicide at the novel's close, a copy of Goethe's *The Sorrows of Young Werther* lying on his bedside table.

And this is where Brown and Richardson part company. Central to Richardson's concept of virtue is the unwavering faith that virtuous abstinence and deepened love will merit a pleasing and prosperous result. Pamela resists Squire B. in part because her culture has trained her to believe that in the end her virtue will meet with tangible reward. Harrington and Harriot, however, do not fare so well. Just as they are set to consummate their patient and virtuous love, they are visited by the sins of their parents; they learn that because of an adulterous affair between the senior Harrington and Harriot's mother, Maria, they are brother and sister. Drawn together by "the power of sympathy," the pair tragically learns that theirs is not the best of all possible worlds, that the heart is not a valid gauge of moral behavior. The idealistic dream of "rational love" proves to be an illusion; as the *raisonneur* Worthy expresses it: "Reason is taken from the helm of life—and Nature—helpless, debilitated Nature . . . splits upon the rocks" (170).

In last analysis *The Power of Sympathy* is as antisentimental as New England puritanism. Set in the idyllic natural environs of Belleview, the novel suggests both the biblical myth of the Garden and the popular eighteenth-century conception of America as the New Eden offering an opportunity for the realization of dreams emerging from the European enlightenment. Belleview resembles Mettingen (*Wieland*) or Saddle Meadows (*Pierre*)—a natural paradise seemingly free of the corruption of the outside world; as Mrs. Holmes writes: "Nature is every where liberal in dispensing her beauties and her variety—and I pity those who look round and declare they see neither" (19). From the midst of the Garden, however, comes the news that precipitates the novel's tragedy. Mrs. Holmes reveals the sibling relationship of the lovers, and the two are caught up in and destroyed by the sins of their father. The elder Harrington's adulterous affair with Maria becomes the equivalent of the puritan concept of original sin; and it is neatly counterpoised by the son's illicit affair with Maria's daughter. As Leslie Fiedler points out: "Seduction for Brown finally becomes the symbol of the uncontrollable demonic element in life, which lays waste the civilized but natural haven of Belleview."[14] The "enlightened" Christian theory of forgiveness crumbles before the inscrutable and endless effects of sin.

Incest in *The Power of Sympathy* thus is employed to reinforce a theme that recurs in Brockden Brown's *Wieland*, Melville's *Pierre*, Hawthorne's "Alice Doane's Appeal," and Faulkner's *Absalom, Absalom!*: the sins of the father return to haunt and eventually to destroy the son. Contrary to the popular myth about America, the "New Adam" can never have a "fresh start"; as Quentin Compson in Faulkner's *Absalom, Absalom!* discovers, the past of our fathers is one with our present. The essential premise of sentimental Christianity that love rights the wrongs of this world and makes us better men disintegrates before the puzzle of incest. Harrington, like Goethe's Werther, looks to the afterlife as a means of legitimizing his illicit passion: "Let the tears of sorrow blot out my guilt from the book of thy wrath" (179), he prays. "In Heaven—there alone is happiness—there shall I meet her—there our love will not be a crime" (157); but in this life love has little effect when faced with the overwhelming fact of man's innate depravity.

Brown further undermines Richardson's sentimental vision in his implication that nature runs counter to order and morality. A frightening and often overlooked aspect of *The Power of Sympathy* is that the brother and sister are inevitably drawn together by nature.

14 Fiedler, *Love and Death in the American Novel*, 119.

Harrington tells Worthy that he will plead the "dictates of Nature" in his attempt to seduce Harriot. After she discovers that her love for Harrington is incestuous, Harriot writes: "Allied by birth, and in mind . . . the sympathy which bound our souls together, at first sight, is less extraordinary. . . . Shall we strive to oppose the *link of nature* that draws us to each other?" (153). The natural incestuous union of the two devastates the facile Rousseauistic assumption that nature should provide an intuitive moral conscience; indeed, following the natural impulses of the heart leads one into a morass of sin and moral disorder.

In his seminal discussion of the nature and implications of American puritanism, Perry Miller notes that "what is persistent, from the covenant theology (and from the heretics against the covenant) to Edwards and to Emerson is the Puritan's effort to confront, face to face, the image of a blinding divinity in the physical universe, and to look upon that universe without the intermediacy of ritual, of ceremony, of the Mass and the confessional."[15] The psychological danger generated from puritan solipsistic practices becomes a favorite theme of early American novelists—especially Hawthorne and Melville—but nowhere does it receive fuller consideration than in Charles Brockden Brown's *Wieland; or, The Transformation* (1798). The novel's subtitle, "An American Tale," suggests that Brown constructs a fable attempting to explain a condition at the heart of American society. A gruesome horror tale of mystery and violence, *Wieland* specifically illuminates the inevitable results of solipsism occasioned by religious mania; more generally, the novel explores the consequences of an individual's attempt to fashion his life according to self-generated ideals that lack an institutional base.

As in *The Power of Sympathy*, the Wieland children (Theodore and Clara) unwittingly labor under a curse bequeathed by their father. The elder Wieland, doomed as an orphan to the difficult life of an apprentice, leaves his native Germany to settle near Philadel-

---

15   Perry Miller, *Errand into the Wilderness* (New York, 1964), 185.

phia, where he acts as a Christian missionary to the Indians. Introspective by nature, the elder Wieland becomes increasingly fanatic in his religious devotion and practice. Clara says that her father's "mind was in a state peculiarly fitted for the reception of devotional sentiments."[16] But for Wieland devotion was "a silent office" that "must be performed alone" (11); the extreme manner of his religious devotion Wieland adopts "not, accurately speaking, because it was the best, but because it had been expressly prescribed to him" (12), presumably by God. In an attempt to expiate an unmentioned curse or crime, Wieland engages in a personal crusade to convert the Indians of North America to Christianity. "The license of savage passion, and the artifices of his depraved countrymen" (11) render Wieland unsuccessful in his missionary work, and despite his material prosperity—a sign to the orthodox puritan community that Wieland enjoys God's favor—the elder Wieland considers himself a failure, unable to implement his self-appointed task.

The elder Wieland engages in solitary religious fanaticism and self-deprecation until, in a state of agitated depression, he becomes convinced of his impending doom—which he attributes to religious retribution. Clara, as narrator, assumes that her father's dejection results from his failure with the Indians; however, there is solid evidence to suggest that the ordeal with the Indians was a delay tactic devised by Wieland in hopes of appeasing a God who had commanded him to perform a specific, unmentioned task which Wieland proves unable to fulfill:

Suddenly the sadness that constantly attended him was deepened. Sighs, and even tears, sometimes escaped him. To the expostulations of his wife he seldom answered any thing. When he deigned to be communicative, he hinted that his peace of mind was flown, in consequence of deviation from his duty. A command had been laid upon him, which he had delayed to perform. He felt as if a certain period of hesitation and reluctance had been allowed him, but that this period was passed. He

16 Charles Brockden Brown, *Wieland; or The Transformation: An American Tale*, vol. I of *The Novels and Related Works of Charles Brockden Brown*, ed. Sydney J. Krause *et al.* (6 vols., projected; Kent, Ohio, 1977—), 8. Subsequent references appear parenthetically to this edition.

was no longer permitted to obey. The duty assigned to him was transferred, in consequence of his disobedience, to another, and all that remained was to endure the penalty. (12–13)

Having failed in his attempt to convert the Indians, which had been his self-appointed mission to appease a God who had commanded something else, Wieland comes to believe that his mysterious offense is "incapable of expiation." One day the elder Wieland mysteriously bursts into flames and perishes. Brown tries to explain the death as spontaneous combustion; Clara calls it a mystery and pushes it out of her mind. Perhaps the death might plausibly be explained as a schizophrenic suicide, violent and grotesque yet capable of being projected onto an external force. Theodore Wieland, however, regards the death of his father as the inevitable outcome of "a direct and supernatural decree" (35). As the novel develops, we learn that Theodore is the "another" to whom the duty assigned to the elder Wieland was transferred; the specific "command" which the father proved incapable of fulfilling is, we later discover, the destruction of the family life.[17]

Though the children labor under the shadow of their father's death, they lead an essentially idyllic childhood. Spared "the corruption and tyranny of colleges and boarding schools," the Wieland children receive an education "modelled by no religious standard" (20; 22). Larzer Ziff points out that Clara and Theodore begin their adult lives "free from either the aristocratic restrictions placed upon the grandparent (they prefer rusticity), or the religious prejudices of the parent (they have received an enlightened education).[18] Subjected to little restraint or control, Theodore and Clara have no opportunity to test their views and attitudes in the real world. They seem, in Clara's eyes, model children who became model adults. But theirs is a solipsistic life, and brother and sister gradually be-

17　Fred Lewis Patee asserts that the elder Wieland's divine mission—never delineated in the novel—is "by inference the sacrifice of his family." Fred Lewis Patee, "Introduction," *Wieland or The Transformation Together with Memoirs of Carwin the Biloquist: A Fragment* by Charles Brockden Brown (New York, 1926), xi.

18　Larzer Ziff, "A Reading of *Wieland*," *PMLA*, LXXVII (March, 1962), 57.

come only vaguely differentiated halves of a single person. Significantly, they are inseparable; when Wieland—"who was wont to love Clara with a passion more than fraternal"—becomes attached to Catherine, so does Clara.[19] The three "withdrew . . . from the society of others, and found every moment irksome that was not devoted to each other" (21). When Wieland and Catherine are wed and located at Mettingen, Clara accompanies them, living somewhat apart only as a means of self-denial. Their life at Mettingen is but a prolongation of their childhood. Interestingly, the three enact plays, sing, make historical speeches and have their best banquets together on the very spot of the father's hideous death; hence their lack of seriousness about life achieves its greatest expression upon a spot that denies simultaneously the realities of death and suffering which have influenced them so profoundly. Into their idyllic existence comes Pleyel—Catherine's brother—who is welcomed joyfully. Their relationships are based upon idealized, childlike visions of perfect companions: to Clara, Catherine is beautiful and nearly perfect; Theodore is serious, pure, and given to reflection; Pleyel is boisterous and inclined to mirth; Clara is virtuous and above reproach.

But gradually the reality of the evil embodied in the father's death begins to assert itself. Theodore, whom Clara says thought proper to repose on the props of "moral necessity, and calvinistic inspiration" (25), grows increasingly introverted and brooding. Clara too has momentary intimations of danger, notably in a dream in which her brother beckons her into an abyss. The dream becomes a vehicle for expressing Clara's subconscious, for crystallizing on one level her latent incestuous love for Theodore and on another the more general curse under which the entire family labors. "What

19 There is some scholarly dispute regarding the relationship between Theodore and Clara. Leslie Fiedler insists that it is incestuous (*Love and Death in the American Novel*, 36), as does Larzer Ziff ("A Reading of *Wieland*," 54). But William Manley asserts that there is no evidence of incest in the novel—see his "The Importance of Point of View in Brockden Brown's *Wieland*," *American Literature*, XXXV (1963), 311–21.

monstrous conception is this," Clara reflects upon her vision: "My brother!" Unable to cope with glimpses of disturbing psychological and metaphysical truths, Clara concludes: "Ideas exist in our minds that can be accounted for by no established laws" (87). Clara quickly suppresses her irrational dream, and placidly continues to assume that her idyllic Mettingen is the best of all possible worlds.

For a time Clara's life is one with that of her brother and sister-in-law: she appears to have married them both. Only after Pleyel has been assimilated into the group does she consider him a potential husband, and even then their relationship is neither mature nor sexual; rather, it is an outgrowth of the symbiosis that already exists, still sentimental and removed from reality. With the entrance of the satanic Carwin, the tragic stage is set. In their blissful ignorance the four react to every pitfall the irresponsible harlequin creates: when Pleyel hears a voice in the night reveal that his baroness is dead, he believes it. There is no anchor in reality, no means of filtering sensory experience. They are still children, and when events build toward the destruction of their lives they can find no means of unraveling the mysteries or of communicating meaningfully about them—despite their professed devotion to the life of reason.

When Clara goes to Wieland to eliminate any doubts about her virtue that Pleyel may have planted, he seems to believe her—he must! She is but a part of him in his undifferentiated childlike view of reality; if she is polluted, so then is he. Yet a seed of doubt has been planted in an already unstable thought process. In his belief that one must have his life in order, the solipsistic Wieland decides that if he is polluted he must act to undo the evil; he is unable to tolerate the ambiguity of guilt. Wieland allows Clara to go off to prove her virtue, but when Clara does not return at the appointed hour, Wieland becomes distraught. Suspicious that his sister might be guilty, Wieland goes to look for her; when he does not find Clara in her room, he become sure of her guilt. In his anguish Theodore perceives an answer: he is commanded by God to sacrifice his wife. Out of his confusion and sense of depravity—heightened by years of isolation—emerges a divine mission, such as occurred to his father years before. Theodore drags Catherine to Clara's house, kills her in Clara's bedroom, and leaves the body on Clara's bed: at this moment Wieland cannot separate Catherine and Clara, just as he has been unable to do in the past. As he carries out yet further commands, Wieland's acts are brutal and fierce: the lines of his daughter Louisa's face are completely obliterated by his violence. These are acts of schizophrenic rage; Wieland has turned outward what his father had turned in upon himself. After years of playing at life, Wieland gives vent to pent-up rage and passion in one insane outburst.

Clara can no more find fault in her brother than he can tolerate it in her. She too resorts to a number of defenses to deal with the destruction of her storybook world: she faints, she attributes to Wieland virtuous motives that have simply been misguided, she focuses all of her horror on Carwin. Even when threatened by her brother, Clara believes it a passing whim, easily dispelled by blaming Carwin's "heavenly" voices. She obliviously drops the penknife to the floor, providing Wieland with a new stimulus for his fancies; he is convinced that he must kill Clara to fulfill a heavenly behest: "Father! I thank thee. This is thy guidance," Wieland exclaims. "Hither thou hast led me, that I might perform thy will. . . . Poor girl! a dismal fate has set its mark upon thee' (218). When Wieland is dead at her feet, Clara imagines that she will follow him naturally—in the style of her mother and grandmother before her—for Wieland is, indeed, her first love. Though at the end of the novel Clara seems to have transcended her ordeal, she instead retreats back into her fantasy creation. She continues her symbiotic existence with Pleyel—the only remaining member of the group—and all else she erases from her mind. Clara believes that her virtue, courage, and keen thinking have saved her; rather, her schizoid approach to life renders her immune to the full horror of her ordeal.

Scholars have long noted the major influence of German literature on Brown and specifically on *Wieland*. Brown played a crucial role in the dissemination of German books in America, reading widely in available English translations of German fiction, poetry, drama and arranging for the publication of "more items of German literary intelligence than any other contemporary American."[20] Harry Warfel has shown unmistakable ties between *Wieland* and Cajetan Tschink's *Geisterseher*, translated in 1795 by Peter Will as *The Victim of Magical Delusion* and appearing serially in volume II of the *New York Weekly Magazine* (1796–97)—where Brown read of the factual incident which was to form the core of *Wieland*, a religious fanatic's murder of his entire family in upstate New York.[21] From Tschink, Brown adopted what Warfel labels "the theme of *Wieland*": the manipulation of the religious enthusiast by the intelligent, calculating ventriloquist, Carwin.

But Warfel's 1940 article stresses too greatly the importance of the single source, *The Victim of Magical Delusion*. The theme of *Wieland* does not revolve around Carwin, as Warfel contends. An interesting though sketchily developed character, Carwin finally is a mere catalyst whose primary importance lies in the fact that Clara uses him as a scapegoat for evil she finds inexplicable. Rather like Goethe's Mephistopheles, Carwin is an impish pawn of a force he does not comprehend; however, whereas Goethe's devil serves a benevolent deity to occasion the hero's salvation, Carwin is the agent through whom an incomprehensible, metaphysical evil wreaks the destruction of the psychologically unbalanced Theodore. The juxtaposition of *Wieland* to Tschink's work leads Warfel to conclude that "Brown wrote *Wieland*, among other reasons, to approve the wisdom of a rationalistic approach to seemingly inexplicable or supernatural phenomena."[22] If this were indeed Brown's purpose, then we must conclude that he is not entirely successful. Pleyel and Clara make a rationalistic retreat from the implications of their ordeal which seems more escapist and delusory than enlightened, though perhaps their approach is the only one that allows survival. Indeed, the theme of incest in the novel coupled with the implications of the

20   Harry Warfel, "Charles Brockden Brown's German Sources," *Modern Language Quarterly*, I (September, 1940), 357.
21   *Ibid.*, 361.
22   *Ibid.*, 357; 362–63.

novel's title call into question the viability of an enlightened, rational approach to a universe that is mysterious, inexplicable, and permeated with evil.

The title of Brown's novel—*Wieland; Or, The Transformation*—implies that the novel is not about Carwin but about one of the Wieland family. But which one? Each undergoes a "transformation," but, significantly, the novel is not entitled *Theodore Wieland*, *Clara Wieland*, *Wieland the Elder*, or even *The Wielands*—as might seem appropriate if the novel were but the history of a single family. Instead, the emphasis at the novel's outset on the ancestral history of the Wieland family suggests that the word *Wieland* is used as a specific instance of *ancestor* and includes an entire family line perpetuated in successive transformations (or generations), though branching in two distinct directions: the religious-mystic, with its motifs of mission, guilt, divine command, and retribution; and the artistic, refined by reason, sensibility, and a certain degree of mirth. To the former belong the elder Wieland and Theodore; to the latter, the "modern poet" referred to in the novel's first chapter, Christoph Martin Wieland—the contemporary author of *Oberon* who espouses the values and aspirations of the European Enlightenment despite the pietism of his upbringing—and, to a certain extent, Clara.

The "temple" erected on the family estate at Mettingen reflects both branches of the family line. The converted temple of the elder Wieland, with its starkness mellowed by furnishings (including a bust of Cicero), music, dramatic performances, and conversations, becomes the *salon* of a modern generation; a symbol of the enlightened sensibility of the children, the temple reflects their refusal to confront the reality of the mysterious curse that claimed their father's life and that eventually is to threaten the entire family line with extinction. The original temple, built by the religious mystic Wieland, leads the reader back via the piety of the Middle Ages (the twelfth-century Albigenses) to an even earlier mythological origin: to the original ancestor Wieland, the German name of Wayland the Smith.

The story of the original Wieland appears in many versions in

German, Icelandic, and Anglo-Saxon mythology (e.g., in the *Völundarkvida* and in *Beowulf*). It is likely that Brown, an avid proponent of German literature and thought, would have encountered the German name Wieland somewhere in his reading, particularly at a time when romantic zeal was reappropriating Nordic mythology and when translations from the *Edda* were appearing in American magazines. The "Wieland the Smith" motif introduces the idea of the slaughter of children as just retribution for the sins of the father. Wieland, after having killed the king's sons and seduced his daughter, leaves behind him the silver cups he artfully wrought out of the boys' skulls and the progeny sprung from his union with the king's daughter. Wieland then disappears, according to the version in the *Edda*, lifting himself off his prison island on wings.[23]

The saga leaves open-ended a possible sequel. An artist like Brown, if familiar with the legend, might well conceive of the sons of Wieland and their descendants laboring under a curse until the murder of the princes was avenged—either by a voluntary sacrifice of children of the Wieland line, or by the extinction of that line. This is, I think, the command received by the elder Wieland, "which he had delayed to perform" and "was transferred, in consequence of his disobedience, to another," the son Theodore. Several curious facts surrounding the mysterious death of the elder Wieland call to mind the Wieland saga from the *Edda*. Though he is engulfed by flames, Wieland's hair and feet, we are told, somehow remain unseared; in the saga, hair and feet are explicitly mentioned as being severed from the boys' bodies by Wieland. Too, the body of the elder Wieland putrifies rapidly, as if Brown wanted to imply its antiquity; the ravages of time occur all at once at the onset of death, suggesting that the successive generations were reincarnations of a single "ancestor." The same fire that engulfs the elder Wieland similarly consumes the son; Clara notes of Theodore, just before he stabs himself to death: "His eyes were without moisture, and gleamed with the fire that consumed his vitals" (231).

23 *The Poetic Edda*, trans. Henry Adams Bellows (Princeton, N.J., 1936).

As in *The Power of Sympathy*, the children of the Wieland family line suffer the dire consequences of their ancestor's original crime. But they do so, Brown implies, only because they fall prey to the puritan habit of introspection, which occasions discovery of the inherent evil that lay dormant and untapped while insulated by an enlightened or rationalistic frame of mind. The fates of Theodore and Clara testify to Brown's distrust of the absorption into self characteristic of the romantic hero. The incest motif and appropriation of the Wieland the Smith legend enforce the pervasive nature of evil in Brown's universe; but if one cannot escape evil, he need not dwell upon it. The two branches of the family line offer contrasting approaches to the legacy of evil that engulfs all. Submission to one, the religious-mystic, leads to the tragedy of psychological disintegration and extinction, for the individual activates the always potential evil force through solipsistic cultivation of it. But affirmation of the other, the enlightened world view that allies art and reason, offers the possibility of escape. The enlightened approach to life does not eradicate evil; it simply directs the individual's consciousness from it to the external world which affords channels for the meaningful exercise of psychic energy. The Wieland line is not extinguished in Brown's novel; it survives in Clara, but only because, part of her dead, she abandons the old locale and takes on a new name. Cleansed by the fire that destroys her home, Clara reverses the pattern initiated by her father: like her original ancestor in the Wieland saga, Clara escapes retribution by growing wings, so to speak, and lifting herself off across the ocean—far removed from the psychologically closed "island" of Mettingen.

Nathaniel Hawthorne's early short story, "Alice Doane's Appeal" (1835), makes explicit a dimension of solipsism implicit in *Wieland*: the self-destructive tendency towards self-absorption is a historical legacy bequeathed to all Americans by New England puritanism. As critics generally have pointed out, "Alice Doane's Appeal" conveys to its readers a sense of inherited historical guilt, encouraging us to "assume the moral responsibilities, the guilt and

righteousness" arising from out national past.[24] The story operates
on three levels. There is first the tale of Leonard Doane, his incestuous love for his sister and his fratricide occasioned by sexual jealousy; secondly, there is the recounting of the puritan witchhunts, as
Hawthorne urges us to recall the spot "where guilt and phrenzy
consummated the most execrable scene, that our history blushes to
record;"[25] and finally, there is the narrative framework in which the
author tries to interest two dull-witted ladies in his personal attempt
to make sense of his past. Here Hawthorne resembles Quentin
Compson in Faulkner's *Absalom, Absalom!*, another sensitive young
man who finds that in piecing together the past of Henry Sutpen (a
past which like that of Leonard Doane's includes incest and fratricide) he has constructed his personal psychic history. As Frederick
Crews has demonstrated, the three levels of "Alice Doane's Appeal"
are intimately related.[26]

In its broad outlines the central plot of Hawthorne's story shares
direct affinities with *Wieland*. The introspective protagonist, Leonard Doane, like Wieland is "characterized by a diseased imagination
and morbid feelings" (270). Orphaned at an early age, Leonard's
only real human contact is with his sister Alice, "beautiful and virtuous, and instilling something of her own excellences into the wild
heart of her brother" (270). But Alice's "excellence" is not sufficient
"to cure the deep taint of his nature." Obviously their relationship
is a mirror of Leonard's solipsism: "The young man spoke of the
closeness of the tie which united him and Alice, the concentrated

---

24 Roy Harvey Pearce, "Hawthorne and the Sense of the Past, or, The Immortality
of Major Molineux," *ELH*, XXI (December, 1954), 337–340. Leslie Fiedler suggests that the story is a "parable of the American Revolution" (*Love and Death in
the American Novel*, 43).

25 Nathaniel Hawthorne, "Alice Doane's Appeal," in Vol. XI of *The Centenary Edition of The Works of Nathaniel Hawthorne*, 267. Parenthetical citations are to this
edition.

26 Frederick Crews, *The Sins of the Fathers: Hawthorne's Psychological Themes* (New
York, 1966), 44–56.

fervor of their affection from childhood upwards, their sense of lonely sufficiency to each other" (271).

The smug complacency of Leonard's solipsistic world shatters with the appearance of Walter Brome, who like William Wilson's counterpart in Poe's short story appears from nowhere to thwart the protagonist's secret desires by making him conscious of them. Brome courts Alice and receives her love in return; Leonard's "discovery, or suspicion of a secret sympathy between his sister and Walter Brome" maddens him with jealousy. When Leonard discovers that Brome is his brother, his course of action becomes clear: he must murder the antagonist to preserve his sister's tainted virtue.

But in Walter Brome, Leonard finds crystallized his own guilt and depravity:

Searching . . . into the breast of Walter Brome, I at length found a cause why Alice must inevitably love him. For he was my very counterpart! I compared his mind by each individual portion, and as a whole, with mine. There was a resemblance from which I shrunk with sickness, and loathing, and horror, as if my own features had come and stared upon me in a solitary place, or had met me in struggling through a crowd. Nay! the very same thoughts would often express themselves in the same words from our lips, proving a hateful sympathy in our secret souls. . . . But my soul had been conscious of the germ of all the fierce and deep passions, and of all the many varieties of wickedness, which accident had brought to their full maturity in him. (271)

Again as in "William Wilson" the hero discovers himself inextricably bound to his newly discovered alter ego. In plummeting into the recesses of his consciousness Leonard discovers a truth that terrifies him and from which he can never escape: "The similarity of their dispositions made them like joint possessors of an individual nature, which could not become wholly the property of one, unless by the extinction of the other" (272). Aware of his dark psychic secrets, Leonard—like Wieland—must destroy his sister, the visible representative of his will: he was "moved also by dark impulses, as if a fiend were whispering him to meditate violence against the life of Alice" (274).

But Leonard does not have to kill Alice; the community does

that for him, burning her as a witch. As in *The Scarlet Letter*, the persecuted heroine becomes a symbol of the community's sin, a scapegoat for their personal evil. Frederick Crews writes: "As in Hawthorne's scenes of accusation generally, victims and persecutors are caught up in a collective shame, a cringing before the human spirit's war upon itself."[27] In other words, the sin the brother commits in murdering Walter has its counterpart in the sin of the community in their persecution of witches. The habit of introspection fostered by puritanism leads its adherents to a discovery of profound depravity within themselves; psychologically unable to bear the implications of their discovery, the community—like Wieland and Leonard—projects its guilt onto an outside force. The entire community is solipsistic; their perception of the exterior world is determined solely by their own natures. Hence Alice and those like her become mere abstract embodiments of personal depravity that must be expunged. The purity that seemingly results is thus a sham, as the powerfully suggestive image at the beginning of the story implies. Gallows Hill is emblematic of the Puritan community; covered with woodwax—"a deceitful verdure" that simulates grass and puts forth glorious yellow blossoms—the hill like the community seems beautifully radiant and pure from a distance. But, Hawthorne tells us,

the curious wanderer on the hill will perceive that all the grass, and every thing that should nourish man or beast, has been destroyed by this vile and ineradicable weed: its tufted roots make the soil their own, and permit nothing else to vegetate among them; so that a physical curse may be said to have blasted the spot, where guilt and phrenzy consummated the most execrable scene that our history blushes to record. (267)

Edgar Allan Poe's 1839 story "The Fall of the House of Usher" is a remarkably succinct symbolic representation of the decaying romantic artistic imagination. As in Coleridge's "Kubla Khan" we are given a privileged insight into the interior of the mind of the artist; Poe's story emerges, Richard Wilbur contends, "as a dream of

27 *Ibid.*, 46.

the narrator's, in which he leaves behind him the waking, physical world and journeys inward toward his *moi intérieur*, toward his inner and spiritual self."[28] The House of Usher becomes, Daniel Hoffman asserts, "a profound and intricate metaphor of the self";[29] the narrator travels "through many dark and intricate passages" before finally discovering the "studio of the master."[30] The "studio" is of course the artist's soul; the "master" is Roderick Usher.

Usher then emerges as the vision at the end of the narrator's solipsistic excursion into the recesses of consciousness. As in other Poe stories—notably "William Wilson" and "Ligeia"—the vision is presented as clearly distinct from the protagonist. Roderick has his personal psychic history and bizarre characteristics that differentiate him from the overtly rational narrator; yet he is important to the narrator for he provides a glimpse of the effects of solipsism on the artistic imagination. The narrator is able to escape the house and to retreat back into rationality. Rather like Clara Wieland, Poe's narrator survives and functions because unlike Usher he does not succumb to the prison of the self; he blithely ignores the evil pervading the soul, the evil with which the acutely sensitive Usher could not cope.

The narrator of Poe's tale informs us that the appellation "House of Usher" includes, "in the minds of the peasantry who used it, both the family and the family mansion" (275). The house, with its "bleak walls . . . vacant eye-like windows . . . a few rank sedges" surrounded by "a few white trunks of decayed trees" (273), becomes as Richard Wilbur demonstrates, "in allegorical fact, the physical body of Roderick Usher, and its dim interior *is*, in fact, Roderick Usher's visionary mind."[31] Most significantly, the house embodies Roderick's solipsism; just as its tenant's "reserve had been always excessive

28   Richard Wilbur, "The House of Poe," in Robert Regan (ed.), *Poe: A Collection of Critical Essays* (Englewood Cliffs, N.J., 1967), 108.
29   Daniel Hoffman, *Poe Poe Poe Poe Poe Poe Poe* (Garden City, N.Y., 1972), 302.
30   Edgar Allan Poe, "The Fall of the House of Usher," in James A. Harrison (ed.), *The Complete Works of Edgar Allan Poe*, II, 277. Parenthetical references are to this edition.
31   Wilbur, "The House of Poe," 107.

and habitual," so the house seems cut off from the outside world: "About the whole mansion and domain there hung an atmosphere peculiar to themselves and their immediate vicinity—an atmosphere which had no affinity with the air of heaven, but which had reeked up from the decayed trees, and the grey wall, and the silent tarn" (276). Isolated and self-sufficient, the house seems stable—"the fabric gave little token of instability"; but to the eye of a "scrutinizing observer" there appears a "barely perceptible fissure, which, extending from the roof of the building in front, made its way down the wall in a zigzag direction, until it became lost in the sullen waters of the tarn" (277). This fissure, which later is to rip the house open, foreshadows the split in Roderick's soul occasioned by his incomprehensible love for his sister, Madeline.

Roderick's incestuous passion for Madeline is apparent to all except the narrator. Usher's malady, he tells the narrator, is "a constitutional and a family evil, and one for which he despaired to find a remedy" (281); it can be traced "to the severe and long-continued illness—indeed to the evidently approaching dissolution—of a tenderly beloved sister—his sole companion for long years—his last and only relative on earth" (281). As is the tradition in romantic literature, Roderick is drawn to his sister because she is his mirror image, or at least she represents a portion of himself: "A striking similitude between the brother and sister now first arrested my attention; and Usher . . . murmured out some few words from which I learned that the deceased and himself had been twins, and that sympathies of a scarcely intelligible nature had always existed between them" (288–89).

Unlike incestuous love for René or Manfred, the aspect of Roderick represented by Madeline is hardly regenerating. Like Pierre's love for Isabel, Usher's love for Madeline becomes, as Joel Porte states, symbolic of Usher's narcissistic "infatuation with his own psyche—a destructive involvement with his own unconscious which is at once the romancer's inspiration and his undoing."[32] Usher's poem, "The Haunted Palace," emerges as an allegorical portrayal of

32 Porte, *The Romance in America*, 67.

the hero's psychic history, and as such illuminates the relationship of Roderick and Madeline. As the narrator suggests, the poem insinuated "the tottering of his lofty reason upon her throne" (284). The poem relates the tale of a "Radiant palace . . . / In the monarch Thought's dominion" that has been destroyed by "evil things, in robes of sorrow" (we might recall here that at the end of the story "the lofty and enshrouded figure of the lady Madeline" appears with "blood upon her white robes"). The loss of reason is revealed in the poem by a shift from "Spirits moving musically/ To a lute's well-tuned law" to "Vast forms that move fantastically/ To a discordant melody"—the shift, Porte contends, from "lawful music" to the "wild fantasias" of Usher's improvisations.[33] The "Haunted Palace" hence becomes a projection of Usher's fate as romantic artist: he optimistically begins his journey into the soul in search of artistic materials but inevitably ends in madness and despair as he discovers the evil lurking in himself.

Usher's plight as the romantic artist trapped in the recesses of his own consciousness foreshadows developments in Poe's aesthetic theory. Increasingly Poe held the romantic aesthetic suspect, and by 1845 he had grown outright critical of what Robert D. Jacobs calls "the expressivist tendencies of romanticism."[34] The artist's first responsibility, Poe argued by 1845, is universality of appeal and intelligibility. Usher's improvisations are emblematic of the art produced by those poets in England who claimed affinity with Shelley: "From the ruins of Shelley there sprang into existence, affronting the Heavens, a tottering and fantastic pagoda, in which the salient angles, tipped with mad jangling bells, were the idiosyncratic *faults* of the great original."[35] The phrase "a tottering and fantastic pagoda . . . tipped with mad jangling bells," recalls the language of "The Haunted Palace": "the tottering of his lofty reason upon her throne" leads to an art producing "vast forms that move fantastically/ To a discordant melody." And in an 1845 review of the poems of Thomas Hood, Poe devastates the English poet in language recalling the nar-

33 *Ibid.*, 66.
34 Robert D. Jacobs, *Poe: Journalist and Critic* (Baton Rouge, La., 1969), 361.
35 Harrison (ed.), *The Complete Works of Edgar Allan Poe*, XII, 33.

rator's description of Roderick Usher in the 1839 tale. Hood's work, Poe argues, was "the result of vivid Fancy impelled, or controlled—certainly tinctured, at all points, by hypochondriasis." As artist, Hood's true province "is a kind of border land between the Fancy and the Fantasy"; his puns "are the hypochondriac's struggles at mirth—they are the grinnings of the death's-head."[36] Usher's music, the narrator informs us, consisted of "wild fantasias" which testify to "the tottering of his lofty reason upon her throne." And his painting, the product of "an elaborate fancy," elicits from the narrator indefinable feelings of dread: "There arose out of the pure abstractions which the hypochondriac contrived to throw upon his canvas, an intensity of intolerable awe, no shadow of which felt I ever yet in the contemplation of the certainly glowing yet too concrete reveries of Fuseli" (283).

Both Hood and Usher were "hyopchondriacs" and as a result their art was flawed. For Poe, genius reflected perfect mental health operating in accordance with natural law; as Jacobs points out, Poe thought "a work of art produced by a genius would have harmony and proportion as its leading features, because the mental equipment of the genius, his faculties, were balanced in their development and operation."[37] Poe gradually realized that art must bridge "the disgustful gulf of utter incongruity and absurdity, lit only by miasmatic flashes, into the broad open meadows of Natural Art and Divine Genius."[38] The introspective solipsism characteristic of Usher's aesthetic is, Poe argued, antithetical to artistic creation. It is this solipsism which Poe thought threatened the work of Nathaniel Hawthorne; thus Poe advised his respected contemporary: "Let him mend his pen, get a bottle of visible ink, come out from the old Manse, cut Mr. Alcott, hang (if possible) the editor of 'The Dial,' and throw out the window to the pigs all his odd numbers of 'The North American Review.'"[39]

Poe's story calls into question the primary assumption of the

36 *Ibid.*, XII, 215–16.
37 Jacobs, *Poe: Journalist and Critic*, 373.
38 Harrison (ed.), *The Complete Works of Edgar Allan Poe*, XII, 35.
39 *Ibid.*, XIII, 151–55.

first-generation romantics. Goethe, Chateaubriand, and Words-worth—taking their lead from Rousseau—saw the natural man as an essentially pure, divine creature whose only depravity was forced upon him by a debased social order. The solution to man's ills thus becomes a turning inward, where he can find an infinite reservoir of positive natural goodness. Poe, like Brown before him, sees the interior of man as a storehouse of evil far more destructive than the social order from which the romanticist escapes. His narrator—and the reader—is given a privileged glimpse of the fate in store for the solipsistic artist, and presumably in his departure from the house and what it represents he is able to transcend the lure of uncontrolled solipsism.

The fundamental romantic assumption of man's innate purity receives satiric parody and devastating rebuke in Herman Melville's 1852 novel *Pierre or, The Ambiguities*, for Melville employs the theme of incest to demonstrate the destruction of the romantic ideal. As Perry Miller argues, *Pierre* "sums up and turns inside out . . . the Byronic hero."[40] Full of the same moral self-righteousness characteristic of the New England abolitionists of the period, Pierre cuts himself off from family and friends in an ill-fated attempt to restore moral order. "The fool of Truth, the fool of Virtue," Pierre pursues "the endless, winding way,—the flowing river in the cave of man; careless whither I be led, reckless where I land."[41] He is foiled in his solipsistic quest because he cannot tolerate the ambiguity of his illicit love for Isabel; the resources of his soul that he marshals to Isabel's aid contain depths of depravity Pierre hardly expects. Thus Pierre calls attention to what Edward H. Rosenberry labels Melville's central dilemma: "Moral perfection and imperfection stood before Melville's straining vision as twin realities forever resisting all rational efforts to focus them in a single image."[42]

40 Perry Miller, *The Raven and the Whale: The War of Words and Wits in the Era of Poe and Melville* (New York, 1956), 305.

41 Herman Melville, *Pierre or, The Ambiguities*, ed. Henry A. Murray (New York, 1962), 126. Parenthetical references to *Pierre* are to this Hendricks House edition.

42 Edward H. Rosenberry, *Melville* (London, 1979), 96.

Just prior to beginning work on *Pierre*, Melville had completed an extended trip to England in 1850. The recent death of William Wordsworth was, we might imagine, a topic of conversation among literary people, and Melville, given his metaphysical bent, no doubt gave some thought to the significance and impact of the century's greatest English poet. In *Pierre*, Melville offers a history of the romantic movement that serves to parody the strain of romantic optimism running from Wordsworth through Shelley to Melville's contemporaries Emerson and Thoreau.[43]

The resemblances between Pierre's father and William Wordsworth are profound and intriguing. History tells us that the fact of Wordsworth's illegitimate daughter was unknown to the world until the publication of G. M. Harper's *Wordsworth's French Daughter* in 1921. It is of course possible that Melville learned of this well-kept secret from someone—perhaps Evert Duyckinck—during his 1850 stay in England, though it is unlikely that anyone who might have known would tell Melville yet keep the secret from the rest of the world. Mary Moorman, however, reports that there is some evidence to suggest that rumors and gossip pertaining to Wordsworth's French affair were widespread in London at the time; Christopher Wordsworth apparently thought preserving the secret to be a hopeless task, since he had heard the rumor "mentioned to him in a public street in London."[44] In any event, the elder Glendinning's illicit and hidden sexual relationship with the French girl during the French Revolution and his bastard offspring certainly call to mind the Wordsworth–Annette Vallon affair. But because I am unable to

43 Numerous scholars have noted the elements of parody in Melville's *Pierre*. Michael Davitt Bell contends that "portions of Pierre's career parody, and thereby subvert, the various literary works Pierre himself endeavors to cherish"—"The Glendinning Heritage: Melville's Literary Borrowings in *Pierre*," *Studies in Romanticism*, XII (Fall, 1973), 742. Edward H. Rosenberry argues that the "Church of the Apostles" presided over by Plinlimmon affords Melville an opportunity to satirize "the eternal illusion of utopian schemes for the perfection of man and society" (*Melville*, 97).

44 Mary Moorman, *William Wordsworth: A Biography, The Early Years, 1770–1803* (London, 1957), 182n.

find any direct proof that Melville knew of Wordsworth's secret life, I must admit the possibility that this parallel between Glendinning and Wordsworth is mere coincidence; if so, it is a remarkably shrewd fiction.

The two portraits of the elder Glendinning suggest the dual personality of Wordsworth. On public display is a "fine joyous painting, in the good-fellow, Flemish style"; this portrait depicts a man who possesses "all the nameless and slightly portly tranquilities," coated with "a thousand proprieties and polished finenesses" (84–85). Such is the endorsed record of a man who died "leaving behind him, in the general voice of the world, a marked reputation as a gentleman." The other, hidden, portrait is detested by Pierre's mother, though treasured by Dorothea. Painted by "a retired and solitary sort of youth," it captures the elder Glendinning shortly after his affair with a "too lovely young Frenchwoman," and haunts the son with "all those ineffable hints and ambiguities, and undefined half-suggestions, which now and then people the soul's atmosphere" (99). The fated attempt to explore these "ineffable hints and ambiguities" becomes the son's self-destructive quest for authentic identity.

There are other, less speculative, ties between Pierre's father and the great English romantic poet. Pierre's Aunt Dorothea—his father's sister—"offered up her morning and her evening rites, to the memory of the noblest and handsomest of brothers" (85–86); she, of course, recalls Wordsworth's devoted sister, Dorothy. Both the elder Glendinning and Wordsworth have wives named Mary. Pierre's childhood sweetheart, Lucy, is but the grownup girl of Wordsworth's early poems: she belongs "to the regions of an infinite day" (2).[45]

As the novel opens, Pierre is very much the "positive" romantic idealist.[46] His ancestral home, Saddle Meadows, is reminiscent of the Lake District or Nether Stowey—a divinely beautiful paradise

45 Michael Bell too notes the link between Lucy and the "innocent and pastoral Lucy of Wordsworth's poems"—see "The Glendinning Heritage," 749.

46 For a description of the qualities of the "positive Romanticist" see Morse Peckham, "Towards a Theory of Romanticism," 5–23.

intimating natural splendor and idyllic bliss: "the perfect mold of the delicate and poetic mind" (4). The "uncommon loveliness" of the region gives it the illusion of Eden, almost as if Coleridge's aborted utopian hopes of establishing a "pantisocracy" on the banks of the Susquehanna River had come to fruition in upper New York State. Even Pierre's description of a pine tree on the Saddle Meadows estate echoes Coleridge's early poem, "The Eolian Harp": "Hark, now I hear the pyramidical and numberless, flame-like complainings of this Eolean pine;—the wind breathes now upon it;—the wind,—that is God's breath" (46–47). At this point in his career, Pierre lacks the Keatsian awareness of melancholy—that more mature romantic understanding that pleasure and pain spring from the same source: "Not unto young Pierre, did there then steal that thought of utmost sadness; pondering on the inevitable evanescence of all earthly loveliness; which makes the sweetest things of life only food for ever-devouring and omnivorous melancholy." For this young Adam, there need be only an Eve—a sister—to make his Eden complete. Ironically, of course, the eventual appearance of the sister renders Eden lost forever. As Michael Bell writes, "the influences on Pierre's early life are Wordsworthian and . . . Pierre's renunciation of Wordsworthian Nature goes hand in hand with his renunciation of his family heritage."[47]

In Book X of *The Prelude*, Wordsworth calls attention to an intuitive moral vision that propels the hero in a valiant struggle for virtue "'mid the loud distractions of the world":

> A sovereign voice subsists within the soul,
> Arbiter undisturbed of right and wrong,
> Of life and death, in majesty severe
> Enjoining, as may best promote the aims
> Of truth and justice, utter sacrifice,
> From whatsoever region of our cares
> Or our infirm affection Nature pleads,
> Earnest and blind, against the stern decree.[48]

47 Bell, "The Glendinning Heritage," 751.
48 Hutchinson (ed.), *Wordsworth: Poetical Works*, rev. Ernest de Selincourt, 564, ll. 181–90.

For Wordsworth, the surrender to this "sovereign virtue" proves beneficent, as it is an infallible guide through the moral maze of mortal life. But for Pierre, such surrender results in his undoing.

Assured of the validity of his personal moral vision, Pierre dedicates himself to the monomaniac pursuit of a single, self-generated, ideal—the establishment of justice in a defective Eden, a world seriously out of tune with his personal vision of the good and the beautiful. Melville informs us that "there is dark, mad mystery in some human hearts, which, sometimes, during the tyranny of a usurper mood, leads them to be all eagerness to cast off the most intense beloved bond, as a hindrance to the attainment of whatever transcendental object that usurper mood so tyrannically suggests. . . . We think we are not human; we become as immortal bachelors and gods" (212). In his pursuit of justice, "Pierre was now this vulnerable god; this self-upbraiding sailor; this dreamer of the avenging dream" (212). Now cut off from what has proven to be an illusory paradise, Pierre identifies with Enceladus; in Pierre's dream, the armless Titan assumes "his own duplicate face and features." Pierre has moved from Wordsworthian child to Shelleyan hero—a Prometheus dedicated to the restoration of an ideal order through love. Agonizingly aware of chronometric excellence but chained to a world operating to different principles, Pierre is the prototype of the man described in the Phlinlimmon pamphlet: "he who finding in himself a chronometrical soul, seeks practically to force that heavenly time upon the earth; in such an attempt he can never succeed, with an absolute and essential success. And as for himself, if he seeks to regulate his own daily conduct by it, he will but array all men's earthly time-keepers against him, and thereby work himself woe and death" (249). Pierre is a man, like Emerson, who seeks truth "direct from God Himself" (193). And through Pierre, Melville conclusively demonstrates the failure inherent in the Romantic's quest to conform the world to his singular vision.

Scholars have long noted the resemblances between the later Pierre and the satanic tradition of romantic heroism. Henry A. Murray sees Pierre as parallel to Hawthorne's Hollingsworth; J. J.

Mogan links him to Byron's Manfred.[49] Though the theme of incest and Pierre's defiance provide a basis for Mogan's comparison, the quest of Melville's hero has a humanitarian dimension absent from Manfred's search for oblivion. Pierre fails in large part because his assumption of his own moral purity is false. Subconsciously assured that "womanly beauty, and not womanly ugliness, invited him to champion the right" (127), Pierre gradually becomes aware of his incestuous attachment to Isabel. And, as in Poe's story, the relationship comes to reflect the psychological instability and moral depravity that lurk beneath the veneer of Pierre's altruistic sacrifice.

Pierre's latent instability and moral depravity are foreshadowed in his relationship to his mother, which clearly has an underlying if unconscious erotic basis: the "romantic filial love of Pierre seemed fully returned by the triumphant maternal pride of the widow" (3). Desperately wanting a sister because "much that goes to make up the deliciousness of a wife, already lies in the sister" (6), Pierre adopts his mother as a substitute; he extends "lover-like adoration" (17) and calls her "Sister Mary" at every opportunity. The relationship that Pierre shares with his mother seems sacred, for even Lucy is an outcast when the three are together. After Isabel appears, Pierre readily transfers his affection from mother to sister; again, Lucy is an outsider. Melville reinforces this motif through parallel scenes at the opening and close of the novel. Early in the book Pierre and his mother are sitting at the breakfast table when interrupted by Lucy, who obviously is alienated from the sympathies flowing between mother and son. A similar scene appears at the novel's close, though Pierre's mother is replaced by Isabel. The sister has usurped the place of the mother, but Lucy is the constant outsider. Consumed by his solipsistic quest, Pierre ultimately is destroyed by his narcissistic infatuation with women who are mirror images of his own "belle âme"; unfortunately the extensions of his soul who so

49 Murray, (ed.), "Introduction," to Herman Melville, *Pierre*, lxxxvi; J. J. Mogan, "*Pierre* and *Manfred*: Melville's Study of the Byronic Hero," *Papers in Language and Literature*, I (1965), 230–40.

fascinate Pierre are not as pure as he naïvely assumes, and instead of delivering him from the shackles of a harsh and corrupt world, they trap him in intolerable moral ambiguity.

An interesting parallel might be developed between the American romantics Brown, Poe, Hawthorne, and Melville and their German counterparts in their portrayal of that exploitation of self I have called romantic solipsism, but such a comparison is beyond the scope of this chapter. What is discernible in the American situation, however, is the lack of a revered literary tradition, and the lack of a definable social order. The need for literary polity, as Lewis P. Simpson has pointed out, led to the establishment of the Boston Anthology Society and the Athenaeum, related groups dedicated to the transference of letters across the Atlantic,[50] but the major impetus in American romanticism came from individuals or groups who resisted transference and wanted to create a characteristic literature drawing its materials from the soul of the introspective artist. Emerson and Whitman exploited the self with full confidence that the voice of the soul was the voice of God; solipsism as a mode of perception offered no threat to those who were convinced that they were mere channels through which the tide of inspiration poured. But how different it was for those romantics whose explorations of the self revealed what Melville called the "blackness of darkness." If there were a community of the human psyche in America analogous to the community of the human condition specified in the Declaration of Independence, then what was found in one self was at least potential in all others; as Emerson asserted in "The American Scholar," "he then learns that in going down into the secrets of his own mind, he has descended into the secrets of all minds."[51] In his descent Emerson discovered "self-trust"; but what

---

50 For a discussion of the Boston Anthology Society and Athenaeum see Lewis P. Simpson (ed.), "Introduction," *The Federalist Literary Mind: Selections from the Monthly Anthology and Boston Review, 1802–1811, Including Documents Relating to the Boston Athenaeum* (Baton Rouge, La., 1962), 3–41.

51 Emerson, "The American Scholar," *Collected Works,* eds. Ferguson and Spiller, I, 63.

did the "dark romantics" find in their excursions into the recesses of the self? Brown found mania and self-delusion; Hawthorne found guilt and perverted conscience; Poe found the perverse will to self-destruction; and Melville found self-love masked behind the fairest appearances of filial and fraternal devotion.

In America then, it was possible to see solipsism as antithetical to that kind of voluntary cooperation among citizens demanded by emergent democracies. Usher and Pierre—both artists—illustrate the destruction of the artistic sensibility alienated from a viable social context. Wieland, Roderick, and Pierre, as defiant isolatoes, portray the self-destructiveness inherent in the attempt to regulate one's life according to a personal morality divorced from the demands and compromises required in an emergent social order.

VII

The Emersonian Anti-hero and the
Romantic Concept of Tragedy

Romantic literature offers protagonists of varying degrees of heroic
stature who envision an ideal order that by contrast renders the mortal realm they inhabit corrupt, boring, and disgusting. Various
modes of traditional heroic literature afford the romantic artist a
means of protesting established government, religion, education, or
social norms, but the base of such protest is typically a glimpse of
an ideal that commands the hero's allegiance. The romantic hero
embodies the *hamartia* that according to Hegel defines the tragic
hero, a commitment to a single moral claim that, no matter how
just, is merely partial and hence destructive of what Murray Krieger
calls "the unity of the moral world."[1] For Hegel, the tension between the demands imposed by formal, universal moral order and
the hero's monomaniacal commitment to a single segment of that
order forms the basis of classical tragedy; the defeat of the hero—no
matter how noble he may be—brings aesthetic pleasure because it
affirms the triumph of universal justice.[2] Krieger contends that, be-

---

1   Murray Krieger, *Visions of Extremity in Modern Literature*, vol. I of *The Tragic Vi-
    sion: The Confrontation of Extremity* (Baltimore, 1960), 5.
2   A. C. Bradley, *Oxford Lectures on Poetry* (London, 1909), 65–95.

ginning with the romantics, the "embracing frame" of universal moral law is lost; justice passes "from the universal to the rebellious individual," who is rendered unfit for society and its laws because he has glimpsed beyond them:

The tragic vision remains what it was, but it can no longer be made through tragedy to yield to an order and a shared religious vision. The ultimately absorbent power of tragedy, symbolic of the earned affirmation of universals, is gone, with the result that the solitary visionary is left unchallenged, except by the threats of uncomprehending and unsympathizing destruction at the hands of aroused ethical righteousness, the arm of social practicality.

What Krieger labels the "essence of the tragic vision" results when "our excommunciated ethical man, realizing the complete futility of human existence, cannot find a relationship with anything beyond it."[3]

Krieger's discussion of the modern tragic vision contributes to an understanding of romantic heroism and romantic tragedy, but it doesn't quite explain them. The problem is that the romantics serve as a bridge between traditional and modern world views; though they turn the emphasis away from the authority of a universal, socially sanctioned moral order to the individual's commitment to a self-generated ideal, romantic artists remain committed to universal—albeit transcendental—values by which they gauge their heroes' actions. When Krieger writes that "however well meaning, the individual may very well be doomed to pervert the absolute he claims to represent, since he has come to it as individual and particular, and thus as unsanctioned,"[4] he describes what might be seen as the norm for romantic heroes. Alex Zwerdling writes that the modern hero depends "on the individual, private code of the writer" who insists on his own "authority over common humanity."[5] What is remarkable about romantic heroes is their failure to live up to their creators' expectations. Those romantic heroes who devote their energies to the pursuit of an ideal almost invariably are frustrated,

3 Krieger, *The Tragic Vision*, I, 17–18, 20.
4 *Ibid.*, I, 12–13.
5 Zwerdling, *Yeats and the Heroic Ideal*, 7–8.

corrupted, and doomed in the process: caught in a debilitating solipsistic prison, the hero either falls short in his attempt to realize the ideal, ending up corrupting it and wreaking personal and social havoc; or, as is the case with Keats's heroes, momentarily achieves the ideal only to descend back into a mortal realm made all the more unbearable by that momentary achievement. Romantic heroes are, more often than not, employed to illustrate perversions of a heroic ideal. In romantic literature the line between the hero and the anti-hero is thin indeed. Implicit in the heroic ideal is the inevitability that moral man will fall short. Therein lies the crux of the romantic tragic dilemma.

The link between romantic heroism and the romantic concept of tragedy is evident in the writings of Emerson. Well-versed in German idealistic philosophy, English romantic poetry, and European mysticism, Emerson reflects the aesthetic center of American romanticism; not only do his essays, journal entries, public addresses, and poems consider at length and give expression to the full range of romantic concerns but his writing and posture as poet of the age either directly influence the other romantic writers of his generation or form a core of thought against which they react. Throughout his career Emerson is preoccupied with the nature and possibility of heroic action. "It is natural to believe in great men," Emerson writes in *Representative Men* (1850); "Our religion is the love and cherishing of these patrons. The gods of fable are the shining moments of great men."[6] But as he moved toward a definition of his heroic ideal, and measured himself and those he admired against it, Emerson came uncomfortably to realize that perhaps true heroism lies beyond the grasp of mortal men.

Behind Emerson's theory of heroism lies his concept of the "central" or "representative" man. In this book on heroism, *Representative Men*, Emerson quotes Swedenborg: "In our doctrine of Representa-

---

6 Emerson, *Representative Men*, vol. IV of *The Complete Works of Ralph Waldo Emerson*, ed. E. W. Emerson, 3–4. Subsequent references, indicated *RM*, appear parenthetically to this edition.

tives and Correspondences we shall treat of both these symbolical and typical resemblances . . . which correspond so entirely to supreme and spiritual things that one would swear that the physical world was purely symbolical of the spiritual world." The heroic spirit for Emerson is a constant transcendental force; men in the mortal world are heroes only insofar as they "represent" or mirror this transcendental ideal. Hence world history offers not separate individual heroes but occasional representations of the ideal as it takes varying but recognizably similar guises. "The study of many individuals leads us to an elemental region wherein the individual is lost, or wherein all touch by their summits," Emerson writes; "no man, in all the procession of famous men, is reason or illumination of that essence we were looking for; but is an exhibition, in some quarter, of new possibilities" (*RM*, 32–33). The qualities of heroism abide forever, though the individual men who make them manifest do not: "the men who exhibit them have now more, now less, and pass away; the qualities remain on another brow" (*RM*, 33–34). Men of heroic stature were once "angels of knowledge and their figures touched the sky. Then we drew near, saw their means, culture and limits; and they yielded their place to other geniuses" (*RM*, 34). Still, though the individual hero fades, his singular achievement endures, setting a pattern for others to follow: "Every ship that comes to America got its chart from Columbus. Every novel is a debtor to Homer" (*RM*, 12).

The Emersonian hero is thus the individual who perceives a transcendental ideal and becomes what F. O. Matthiessen labels "a receptive channel for the superincumbent spirit,"[7] a voice giving expression to the "central man" he for the moment becomes. For Emerson, the voice of this "central man" was first Socrates; "Then the discourse changes, & the man, and we see the face & hear the tones of Shakespeare. . . . A change again, and the countenance of our companion is youthful & beardless, he talks of form & colour . . . it is the face of the painter Raffaelle." Other examples of the

---

7   Matthiessen, *American Renaissance*, 632.

central man's intrusion into history include Michelangelo, Dante, and Jesus: "And so it appears that these great secular personalities were only expressions of his face chasing each other like the rack of clouds."[8] All of these particular instances of the "single hero" share an apprehension of the transcendental ideal and the ability to make it manifest in the real world. An "effective, generative . . . constructive, fertile, magnetic" personality (*RM*, 7), the hero bears what Stephen E. Whicher calls "a necessary relation to virtue";[9] he is "enamoured of moral perfection,"[10] and acts within or on behalf of a human community.

But the heroic individual serves history not so much in what he accomplishes as in the testimony he offers to others of the possibility of heroic achievement, the hope of realizing, at least momentarily, a transcendental ideal. "I count him a great man," Emerson writes, "who inhabits a higher sphere of thought, into which other men rise with labor and difficulty; he has but to open his eyes to see things in a true light and in large relations, while they must make painful corrections, and keep a vigilant eye on many sources of error" (*RM*, 6). Most men, Emerson asserts in "Nature," suffer a serious defect in vision: "The axis of vision is not coincident with the axis of things, and so they appear not transparent but opake."[11] Heroes, however, are "a collyrium to clear our eyes from egotism and enable us to see other people and their works" (*RM*, 25). There is, of course, the danger that one is intimidated by the heroism of others, that "our delight in reason degenerates into idolatry of the herald.

8 Emerson, entry 130 (1846) in *The Journals and Miscellaneous Notebooks of Ralph Waldo Emerson*, volume IX, 1843–47, ed. R. H. Orth and Alfred R. Ferguson (Cambridge, Mass., 1971), 395. Subsequent references to Emerson's Journals are to the fourteen (projected) volumes of this edition, edited by William H. Gilman *et al.*, unless noted otherwise.

9 Stephen E. Whicher, *Freedom and Fate: An Inner Life of Ralph Waldo Emerson* (Philadelphia, 1971), 68.

10 Specifically, in this September 17, 1833, entry, Emerson asserts that Milton "was enamoured of moral perfection"; but, he continues, "Keeping my eye on this I understand all heroism" (*Journals*, IV, 87).

11 Emerson, "Nature," *Collected Works*, ed. Ferguson and Spiller, I, 43.

Especially when a mind of powerful method has instructed men, we find the example of oppression." "But," Emerson insists, "true genius seeks to defend us from itself. True genius will not impoverish, but will liberate" (*RM*, 18). Because "other men are lenses through which we read our own minds" (*RM*, 5), the hero can and should inspire men to heroic action of their own: "I cannot even hear of personal vigor of any kind, great power of performance, without fresh resolution" (*RM*, 14). Emerson concludes "Nature":

All that Adam had, all that Caesar could, you have and can do. Adam called his house, heaven and earth; Caesar called his house, Rome. . . . Yet line for line and point for point, your dominion is as great as theirs, though without fine names. Build, therefore, your own world. As fast as you conform your life to the pure idea in your mind, that will unfold its great proportions. (*Collected Works*, I, 45)

Finally the heroes perform, by proxy, what each individual is capable of doing himself: "In a century, in a millennium, one or two men; that is to say—one or two approximations to the right state of every man. All the rest behold in the hero or the poet their own green and crude being—ripened. . . . Each philosopher, each bard, each actor, has only done for me, as by a delegate, what one day I can do for myself."[12] Access to divine reason, or the transcendental ideal, is not the province of the chosen few; indeed, Emerson writes in a December 1834 journal entry, "Democracy, Freedom, has its root in the Sacred truth that every man hath in him the divine Reason or that though few men since the creation of the world live according to the dictates of Reason, yet all men are created capable of so doing" (*Journals*, IV, 357).

Implicit in Emerson's theory of heroism is a seeming paradox. Our heroes are those rare individuals who are able to perceive and for a while "represent" values permanently fixed in a transcendental dimension. They differ from most of us because they ascend to an ideal realm which, because the average man can perceive it only faintly and imperfectly, seems antithetical to the mundane world of mortal affairs. Yet, Emerson insists, all men are capable of realizing

12 Emerson, "The American Scholar," *Collected Works*, I, 65–66.

this same ideal, of bringing the transcendental into a mortal realm. Early in his career Emerson skirts this paradox by insisting on man's divinity; man is "a god in ruins," Emerson tells us in "Nature," but a god who if he but fulfills his own nature, properly focuses his potential, can recapture divine status. We must remember, however, that Emerson's most optimistic notes were struck rather early in his career in what were, for the most part, public addresses. Gradually we find emerging in Emerson's writing a strong undercurrent of doubt and pessimism. He is aware in June, 1838, that "This country has not fulfilled what seemed the reasonable expectation of mankind"; in the same vein he writes in June, 1847, "Alas for America as I must so often say, the ungirt, the diffuse, the profuse, procumbent, one wide ground juniper, out of which no cedar, no oak will rear up a mast to the clouds."[13] Emerson comes to feel acutely the discrepancy between his earlier ideals and the reality he daily confronts; hence he confesses in April, 1846, "I like man, but not men," and falls to such depths of depression that in 1850 he admits, "The badness of the times is making death attractive." As Stephen Whicher writes, "Through and under the vast claims of [Emerson's] faith runs a commonsense realistic perception of the actual state of affairs."[14]

The striking aspect of Emerson's lifetime preoccupation with great men or heroic personalities is that he is never satisfied with any of them. For Emerson there is only a heroic ideal, no true heroes; even the greatest of men fall short in one way or another since, as Sherman Paul points out, for Emerson "there were no finished souls."[15] Though quick to admire individual achievement, Emerson always pulls back from unequivocal endorsement of a particular man. There is always a defect or deficiency that undercuts heroic stature. After traveling through Europe—following much the same

13   Emerson, "Literary Ethics," *Collected Works*, I, 100; *Journals*, X, 79.
14   Whicher, *Freedom and Fate*, 69.
15   Sherman Paul, *Emerson's Angle of Vision: Man and Nature* (Cambridge, Mass., 1952), 168.

route as had Byron earlier—Emerson in his journals thanks God for having granted him the opportunity to visit with great men (Landor, Coleridge, Carlyle, Wordsworth); but, he writes in the September 1833 entry, "not one of these is a mind of the very first class. . . . Especially are they all deficient all these four—in different degrees but all deficient—in insight into religious truth" (*Journals*, IV, 78–79). The best poets of the age, "the poets that we praise, or try to, the Brownings, Barretts, Bryants, Tennysons, are all abortive Homers" (*Journals*, IX, 378). Thoreau, Emerson's friend who embodied the poet's doctrine of self-reliance, failed to achieve heroic stature in his mentor's eyes because his life was not "sufficiently active in the social sense." [16] Though Dante, Emerson writes in an 1867 journal entry, "still appears to me, as ever, an exceptional mind, a prodigy of imaginative function," he is "executive rather than contemplative or wise"; possessing "undeniable force of a peculiar kind," Dante does not exhibit "like Shakespeare, or Socrates, or Goethe, a beneficent humanity." [17]

One might argue that Emerson's personal aspirations to become the supreme poet of his age made him more finely attuned to the deficiencies of other artists—especially of those who were his contemporaries. Certainly, as Whicher claims, Emerson was fascinated by the achievement of great men, "with various large-scale abstract character-types—The Reformer, The Scholar, The Hero—shadowy outlines of the possible great emancipating roles he felt he had it in him to play, with God as his prompter" (65). Yet Emerson's impatience with the heroism of others transcends mere envy of great men. A close examination of *Representative Men* suggests that Emerson's disillusionment with the individual great man comes as a logical outgrowth of his heroic ideal.

Thomas Carlyle's *On Heroes, Hero-Worship, and the Heroic in His-*

16   *Ibid.*, 161.
17   E. W. Emerson and W. E. Forbes (eds.), *The Journals of Ralph Waldo Emerson* (10 vols.; Boston, 1914), X, 210.

tory (1841) provided Emerson the stimulus for *Representative Men*, for the American writer hoped to counter Carlyle's elitist sympathies by offering a more democratic view of heroic action.[18] After an introductory discussion of the nature of heroism and the function of the hero within human community, Emerson offers a series of six chapters on individuals who represent specific categories of endeavor: "Plato; or, The Philosopher," "Shakespeare; or, The Poet," "Napoleon; or, The Man of the World," etc. The structure of the book thus reinforces Emerson's "representative" theory of heroism; the individuals selected for analysis are important primarily as "types" who suggest the range of activity within a certain sphere.

Though each of the individuals given close scrutiny in *Representative Men* is chosen because he represents the closest mortal man has ever come to achieving the ideal within his sphere of activity, no one of them fully satisfies the demands of Emerson's heroic ideal. Plato, "the Philosopher," embodies the "culture of nations"; his sentences become "the corner-stone of schools . . . the fountain-head of literature" (*RM*, 39). Emerson admires Plato especially because he is able to reconcile the tension between fact and abstraction, society and solitude—something Emerson found so difficult to accomplish in his own life. Yet there is a serious defect in Plato: "Mounting into heaven, diving into the pit, expounding the laws of the state, the passion of love, the remorse of crime, the hope of the parting soul,— he is literary, and never otherwise"; consequently, Plato's philosophy lacks "the vital authority which the screams of prophets and the sermons of unlettered Arabs and Jews possess" (*RM*, 76–77).

The others selected as heroic types similarly have crucial defects. Swedenborg, the mystic, is defective in his "enthusiasm," and "his theological bias thus fatally narrowed [an] interpretation of nature" that, in last analysis, "is not human and universal" (*RM*, 121). Although Montaigne is better balanced, giving us a skepticism that provides a necessary check "against the exaggeration and formalism of bigots and blockheads," his intellectual predisposition renders

18   Matthiessen, *American Renaissance*, 632.

him incapable of the belief necessary to perceive the highest truths (*RM*, 171–86). In his journals, Emerson once pictured himself as the Goethe of America (VIII, 62); yet after extolling the virtues of Goethe, the representative writer, Emerson feels compelled to detail his shortcomings:

> I dare not say that Goethe ascended to the highest grounds from which genius has spoken. He has not worshipped the highest unity; he is incapable of a self-surrender to the moral sentiment. There are nobler strains in poetry than any he has sounded. There are writers poorer in talent, whose tone is purer, and more touches the heart. Goethe can never be dear to men. His is not even the devotion to pure truth; but to truth for the sake of culture. (*RM*, 284)

Emerson reserves for Shakespeare and Napoleon his harshest censure. Although he is the supreme poet, Shakespeare simply achieves beauty; he falls far short in his attempt to convey the truths of human existence: "As long as the question is of talent and mental power, the world of men has not his equal to show. But when the question is, to life and its materials and its auxiliaries, how does he profit me? What does it signify? It is but a Twelfth Night, or Midsummer-Night's Dream" (*RM*, 218). Emerson even chastises Shakespeare for dissipating his talents, for leading a life sharply at variance with the grandeur of his poetry: "Other admirable men have led lives in some sort of keeping with their thought; but this man, in wide contrast. . . . it must even go into the world's history that the best poet led an obscure and profane life, using his genius for the public amusement" (*RM*, 218). Napoleon, the "Man of the World," is perhaps the greatest heroic figure of the age. A distinguished statesman and unequalled military genius, Napoleon embodied the Europe of his time; but, Emerson tells us, "he is no hero" (*RM*, 225). He has in him "the qualities and powers of other men in the street" (*RM*, 225), but he lacks what for Emerson was the crucial element of heroism, moral sentiment: "Bonaparte was singularly destitute of generous sentiments. The highest-placed individual in the most cultivated age and population of the world,—he has not the merit of common truth and beauty" (*RM*, 253). In an April 1845 journal entry, Emerson writes: "The lesson [Napoleon] teaches is that which vigour always teaches, that, there is always room for it. . . . There is always room for a man of force." Yet, Emerson concludes, "A bully cannot lead the age" (*Journals*, IX, 192–93).

Emerson's developing pessimism regarding the possibility of heroism reflects his frustration at having failed in his self-appointed mission to become the great poet of the age. Sherman Paul writes that Emerson consciously tried to mold himself into the romantic heroic personality: his first trip to Europe "was in many ways a pilgrimage in which he followed Byron; and however mild it seems, his removal to Concord in search of the resources he needed was his *Sturm und Drang*, the assertion of the self he had to make" (161). The tension in Emerson between his desire for privacy and isolation on the one hand (which he thought necessary for the poet) and awareness of his obligation to community on the other generates what Whicher calls "a preoccupation with 'great action'" and great men (64–65). But in his thorough examination of "representative" heroes who offer patterns of great action, Emerson found "a self-projection of his own failures."[19]

Emerson's failure to achieve his ideal resulted from his inability to reconcile his concept of the poet with his understanding of the necessity for action within a human community. As poet, Emerson conceived of himself as "Man Thinking" and for most of his life thought that involvement with social issues was an abdication of responsibility to his ideal. Reflecting upon the 1830s and 1840s, Emerson writes that "the key to the period appeared to be that the mind had become aware of itself. Men grew reflective and intellectual." His generation differed from preceding ones that had "acted under the belief that a shining social prosperity was the beatitude of man, and sacrificed uniformly the citizen to the State" because it held firm the conviction that "the nation existed for the individual, for the guardianship and education of every man."[20] To reach its potential, the age needed the "great reflective Poet," a role Emerson

19 Paul, *Emerson's Angle of Vision*, 161.
20 Emerson, "Historic Notes of Life and Letters in New England," in E. W. Emerson (ed.), *Complete Works*, X, 326.

felt destined to assume. Committed to an ideal, transcendental realm accessible only through solitary contemplation, the poet had to extricate himself totally from the mundane world of daily affairs; hence, Emerson came to resent any demands imposed upon him by the pressing social issues of his time. In a letter to Thomas Carlyle, Emerson laments: "Though I sometimes accept a popular call, and preach on Temperance or Abolition of Slavery, as lately on the first of August, I am sure to feel, before I have done with it, what an intrusion it is into another sphere, and so much loss of virtue in my own."[21] Even after such friends as Alcott, Thoreau, Garrison, and W. E. Channing had become active in antislavery reform, the "poet of consciousness" remained aloof. He wrote in his "Ode" to Channing:

> I cannot leave
> My honied thought
> For the Priest's cant,
> Or the statesman's rant.
>
> ....
>
> If I refuse
> My study for their politique,
> Which at best is trick
> The angry Muse,
> Puts confusion in my brain.

As a member of the "aristocracy," Emerson believed that he had special obligations to fulfill: "The true aristocrat is he who is at the head of his own order, and disloyalty is to mistake other chivalries for his own. Let him not divide his homage, but stand for that which he was born and set to maintain."[22] Active involvement even in so just a cause as abolition would come at the expense of the poet's "special and lofty duties": "I have quite other slaves to free than those Negroes, to wit, imprisoned spirits, imprisoned thoughts . . . which, important to the republic of man, have no watchman,

21 Charles Eliot Norton (ed.), *The Correspondence of Thomas Carlyle and Ralph Waldo Emerson, 1834–1872* (3 vols.; Boston, 1883), II, 85.

22 Emerson, "Aristocracy," in E. W. Emerson (ed.), *Complete Works*, X, 57.

or lover, or defender, but I."[23] "But really a scholar," Emerson wrote in July 1846, "has too humble an opinion of the population, of their possibilities, of their future, to be entitled to go to war with them as equals. This prison is one step to suicide" (*Journals*, IX, 447). Groups representing prohibition, prison reform, women's rights, world peace, education for the blind, deaf, and dumb, penny postage, and a score of more eccentric causes repeatedly sought Emerson's support. Though he privately expressed sympathy for a variety of reform efforts, Emerson resented this philanthropic coercion: "Those who are urging with most ardor what are called the greatest benefits of mankind, are narrow, self-pleasing, conceited men and affect us as the insane do."[24] As poet, Emerson wanted to remain an "infinite spectator, without hurrying uncalled to be an infinite doer" (*Journals*, 1914 ed., III, 465).

The preferable alternative to group philanthropic action, Emerson thought, was individual improvement and expression. He wrote to Carlyle that if at any time he could "express the law and ideal right, that should satisfy me without measuring the divergence from it of the last Act of Congress."[25] Prostitution of justice occurs when men organize to bring it about; "Every project in the history of reform, no matter how violent and surprising, is good when it is the dictate of man's genius and constitution"; however, when adopted from another, reform becomes "very dull and suspicious."[26] The reforms, though they have their origins in ideal justice, "do not retain the purity of an idea" because "they are quickly organized in some low, inadequate form."[27]

Despite his aversion to active participation in reform causes,

23 Cited by Ralph L. Rusk, *The Life of Ralph Waldo Emerson* (New York, 1949), 368.
24 Cited by Harry J. Carman *et al.*, *A History of the American People* (2 vols.; New York, 1967), I, 539.
25 Cited by Marjory M. Moody, "The Evolution of Emerson as Abolitionist," *American Literature*, XVII (1945), 6.
26 Cited by Myrtle Henry, "Independence and Freedom as Expressed and Interpreted by Ralph W. Emerson," *Negro History Bulletin*, VI (May, 1943), 174.
27 Cited by Carman *et al.*, *History of the American People*, I, 539.

Emerson discovered that he could not resist the demands on his conscience engendered by the abolition movement. With passage of the Daniel Webster approved Compromise of 1850 and the ensuing enactment of the Fugitive Slave Bill, Emerson abandoned his characteristic detachment to join a radical and uncompromising crusade for total abolition.[28] His demand for an unconditional and immediate end to slavery—even at the expense of civil war—seems especially strident when compared to the prevailing, more moderate, antislavery sentiment advocating gradual emancipation and colonization of freed negroes.[29] Unacquainted with the concept of institutional power—its meanings, its uses, or its responsibilities— Emerson saw the slavery question not as a matter of institutional arrangements but, as Stanley Elkins contends, solely as a moral issue, "untouched by expediency, untarnished by society's organic compromises, uncorrupted even by society itself."[30] The poet never concerned himself with concrete plans for developing the slave's "infinite potentialities" when freed, or ways of integrating him into American society; rather, he ignored the social ramifications of the problem to focus exclusively on slavery as an abstract moral issue. Shortly after the outbreak of the war with Mexico, Emerson wrote that his concern with slavery was with "the morals of the system," and insisted that "the sentiment of right . . . fights against this damnable atheism" (Moody, 12). His belief that all men participated in the Over-Soul and were, in the end, inextricably related, forced upon Emerson responsibility for the sins of the slaveholder. Intensified by Emerson's former feeling of white supremacy and his refusal, prior to 1850, to become involved in the antislavery crusade, an immense burden of guilt fell upon the poet's shoulders: "I waked at night, & bemoaned myself, because I had not thrown myself into

---

28 Marjory M. Moody offers a detailed account of Emerson's role in the abolition movement in "The Evolution of Emerson as an Abolitionist."

29 David Donald, *Lincoln Reconsidered: Essays on the Civil War Era* (New York, 1956), 21.

30 Stanley M. Elkins, *Slavery: A Problem in American Institutional and Intellectual Life* (rev. ed.; Chicago, 1968), 27–34.

this deplorable question of Slavery, which seems to want nothing so much as a few assured voices" (*Journals*, XIII, 80). Later, Emerson admits to Carlyle that he began active participation in the abolition movement "without hope of effect, but to clear my own skirts."[31]

Emerson's involvement in the abolition movement taught the poet a painful lesson: the hero could not discharge his responsibilities simply by perception and articulation of the ideal. Though he liked to believe that thought was in itself the highest form of action, he came to realize that "there is somewhat not philosophical in heroism, there is somewhat not holy in it" (*Complete Works*, II, 249) and, as a result, drew a significant distinction between the saint, who worships "the moral sentiment as law" but "puts it far from him," and the hero, who realizes that he embodies the "moral sentiment" and so *acts* upon it (*Complete Works*, II, 250). Yet for Emerson, reconciling the ideal moral sentiment with the actual world of human affairs proved an impossible task: "The worst feature of this double consciousness is, that the two lives . . . which we lead, really show very little relation to each other. . . . One prevails now, all buzz and din; and the other prevails then, all infinitude and paradise; and with the progress of life, the two discover no greater disposition to reconcile themselves." For Emerson, Stephen E. Whicher writes, "The duality of his experience, condemning him to glimpses of a Kingdom to which he was entitled by his constitution, yet which he could not enter, seemed to him at first a vanishing anomaly, then a wild and bewildering contradiction, and finally an absurdity of fate which he must learn to accept as best he might" (70).

Most romantic artists and their fictional heroes encounter this same dilemma. His finely tuned sensibilities and mystical vision grants the Romantic access to a transcendental realm that commands his devotion and orders his life. Yet this access proves the Romantic's undoing, for he is unable to cope with a community firmly rooted in a mortal dimension at odds with the transcendental truth he per-

---

31 Norton (ed.), *The Correspondence of Thomas Carlyle and Ralph Waldo Emerson*, II, 201.

ceives. Consequently, most romantic heroes become tragic figures, doomed by their sensitivity and allegiance to an unrealizable ideal to a socially ineffectual life that ensures their demise. Obermann's confession of the failure of his quest exemplifies the despair that typically befalls the disillusioned hero: "The full force of the illusion lasted almost a month; a single incident dispelled it. It was at that moment that the bitterness of a pallid, rootless existence took possession of my soul."[32] To achieve heroic stature, the romantic protagonist must sustain his vision within a human community and, it is hoped, occasion a meaningful revolution; but in his attempts to do so, the would-be hero finds that he perverts the ideal so drastically as to make it more hideous than the abuses he hopes to correct (*e.g.* Ahab, Rappaccini, Napoleon), or that his quest is futile, rendering him a melancholy, ineffectual outcast (Werther, René, Harold). In either event, the tragic fact he discovers is that the heroic life is impossible. Byron's plea, "I want a hero," is, Harry Levin contends, "just as significant of its time as were the respective invocations of the *Aeneid* and the *Orlando Furioso* for theirs. It is the cry of a century which is often considered a century of hero-worship, the quest of an age forever seeking and never quite finding what Lermontov styled *A Hero of Our Time*."[33]

The romantics' discovery of the impossibility of heroism is crucial to the development of the anti-hero. If, as Lilian R. Furst claims, "the transformation of the hero into anti-hero is a process of reduction," then we might agree with her that the romantic hero stands "already well on the way to the modern anti-hero."[34] The heroes offered us by romantic literature fare rather poorly when juxtaposed to an Achilles, Hector, Aeneas, or Milton's Adam. But the heroic ideal against which the romantic hero is measured in many

---

32 Etienne de Sénancour, *Obermann* (Paris, n.d.), 45. "L'illusion a duré d'un mois dans sa force; un seul incident l'a dissipée. C'est alors que toute l'amertume d'une vie décolorée et fugitive vint remplir mon âme."

33 Harry Levin, *Contexts of Criticism* (Cambridge, Mass., 1957), 176.

34 Lilian R. Furst, "The Romantic Hero, Or Is He An Anti-Hero?" *Studies in the Literary Imagination*, IX:1 (Spring, 1976), 67, 53.

ways ties the romantic age more closely to the classical than to the modern. For not only has the twentieth-century intellectual abandoned the hope of heroic achievement, in seeming agreement with Prufrock that he is "not Prince Hamlet, nor was meant to be," but he has also lost faith in the validity of the heroic ideal itself. Chateaubriand's René might have resigned himself to his personal failings, but there is little doubt that he acknowledges the validity of the superior vision recognized and pursued by his sister and urged on him by Père Souël at the novella's close; he is disturbed and humiliated by the priest's censure, even if he lacks the strength to follow his counsel.[35] In the modern martyr drama, Edward Albee's *Tiny Alice*, the protagonist Julian finally "realizes his life-long religious wish" to die a martyr; but, as Karl Guthke asserts, "in the end he doubts the validity of the god to whom he is being sacrificed."[36] If, as W. B. Yeats writes in "The Second Coming," "the best lack all conviction," it is because they can find nothing worthy of belief, faith, or commitment.

The fact that no mortal can sustain a transcendental dimension does not, for the Romantic, imply the absurdity of that dimension. Indeed, Emerson's "great men" become anti-heroes only because they are measured against a clearly perceived heroic ideal and fall short. But the modern anti-hero typically is unable to find any redeeming vision. For Sartre's characters, Philip Thody writes, "the world as it exists is just not worth the trouble that the superior person would have to take if he were to set about dealing with it adequately."[37] In a similar vein, C. B. Cox suggests that a major problem in the twentieth century is that "humanism struggles without much confidence against a philosophical nihilism"; the anti-heroic artist, like Philip Larkin, may see the flaws in others, but he

---

35 Pertinent here is the fact that *René* was originally part of *Le Génie du Christianisme*, and intended as a caution against yielding to unfocused passion.

36 Karl S. Guthke, "A Stage for the Anti-Hero: Metaphysical Farce in the Modern Theatre," *Studies in the Literary Imagination*, IX:1 (Spring, 1976), 133–34.

37 Philip Thody, "The Anti-Heroes of Sartre and Camus: Some Problems of Definition," *Studies in the Literary Imagination*, IX:1 (Spring, 1976), 109–110.

"does not have the confidence in his own values which would allow him to interfere, to impose his own strong opinions on other people."[38] There may have been those in the Renaissance who, like Gloucester in *King Lear*, could say, "as flies to wanton boys are we to gods,/ They kill us for their sport"; but there was always someone like Edgar to counter, "The gods are just." There may have been those in the eighteenth century who could toy with the image of "un dieu qui se moque de l'homme"; but, as Guthke mentions, there was always a Samuel Johnson to label such images "absurd." Not so anymore: that image of the mocking god has become so widely accepted in modern literature and thought, Guthke asserts, that "the very question of theodicy has become absurd."[39]

Much of modern literature, in fact, results from the artist's groping for meaningful forms to express the absence of meaning or transcendent vision in modern culture. M. H. Abrams maintains that the romantic movement formed a watershed in the secularization of classical and biblical myths; what occurred was a "displacement from a supernatural to a natural frame of reference,"[40] and such occurrence profoundly affected the concept of heroism. For most romantics, however, this meant not so much a demotion of divinity into mortality as an elevation of man to the conditions of immortality through a discovery of the divine power harnessed within him. Filtered through the enervating gaze of literary naturalism, and subjected to the microscopic scrutiny of the social scientist, however, the "godlike" mortal of the romantics enters contemporary culture utterly bereft of any element of transcendence. The "natural frame of reference" liberated the romantic hero; that same reference trapped modern man within the stultifying laws of environment and heredity. And the twentieth-century artist has been among the first to note the change and its debilitating effect on creative achievement. Yeats, in "Sailing to Byzantium," abandons the "sensual mu-

---

38 C. B. Cox, "Philip Larkin, Anti-Heroic Poet," *Studies in the Literary Imagination*, IX:1 (Spring, 1976), 167.
39 Guthke, "A Stage for the Anti-Hero," 120–22.
40 Abrams, *Natural Supernaturalism*, 13.

sic" of "the young/ In one another's arms"—"those dying generations"—to seek the "holy city of Byzantium," an ideal realm where
as poet he can transcend his decaying culture and become a golden
bird on a golden bough singing "Of what is past, or passing or to
come." Eliot in *The Waste Land* laments the modern reduction of art
and culture to trivia—"O O O O that Shakespeherian Rag"—a process of reduction that goes hand in hand with the dehumanization of
life forces characteristic of the secular wasteland. Because he sees
art as the irreducible expression of being, Donald Davidson considers creative expression doomed in a civilization bereft of traditional
values, one that reduces "being" to basic brutish instincts.[41] William
Faulkner voices much the same theme in his Nobel Prize acceptance
speech, arguing that any art is "ephemeral and doomed" that accepts
the vision of man as an insignificant creature who simply endures
because he possesses a "puny, inexhaustible voice"; indeed, the artist
must celebrate and therefore help to preserve the heroic qualities of
man that have been "the glory of his past": love, compassion, sacrifice.

What is curious about the modern anti-hero is the absence of the
corresponding heroic figure against whom he is measured. Homer
may have given us the "anti-heroic" Odysseus but he also gave us
Hector. Milton creates Satan, but he also presents Christ and Adam.
The term *anti-hero* suggests that such a figure is the antithesis of the
traditional hero—a reverse mirror image, so to speak. Actually, the
hero seems to turn into the anti-hero by a process of reduction along
a sliding scale. The anti-hero of Dostoevsky's *Notes from Underground*, like the traditional hero, embarks upon a quest—to bump a
socially superior individual who, he thinks, has snubbed him. The
quest of course is so trivial as to be absurd; and Dostoevsky highlights the absurdity by casting the repeated approaches of the two
antagonists in terms of a medieval joust. The "anti-heroic" nature of
Dostoevsky's underground man is defined in terms of the medieval

---

41   Donald Davidson, "A Mirror for Artists," in *I'll Take My Stand: The South and the
Agrarian Tradition*, by Twelve Southerners (1930; rpt. New York, 1962), 28–60.

knight, just as Madame Sosostris, the modern fortune teller in Eliot's *The Waste Land*, is defined through juxtaposition to the ancient Egyptian prophetess. As we lose sight of the heroic image, as the culture as a whole denies the possibility of heroic achievement, the concept of the anti-hero becomes increasingly ambiguous. Sartre's anti-heroes, Thody asserts, are actually heroes; "metaphysical farce," Guthke informs us, has no use for heroes or non-heroes, only anti-heroes; Larkin's response, Cox insists, is the only honest one viable under present conditions.

The concept of heroism emerging from the literature of a particular age reflects basic cultural conditions and presuppositions. The discrepancy between the heroic ideal and the achievement of actual heroes suggests that the romantics in general, and Emerson in particular, serve as a transition between the classical or traditional view of heroism and the prevailing modern concept of the anti-hero. The romantic hero differs from his traditional antecedents in that he comes to realize the impossibility of sustaining a transcendental vision in a mortal realm. As a result he becomes disillusioned and ineffectual, generally retreating into a solipsistic world of the imagination governed by his transcendental vision but tragically isolated from human community. The romantic protagonist approaches heroic stature as he becomes differentiated from his fellows through his vision of an ideal that alone makes life meaningful; he falls victim to tragedy as his inevitable attachment to the ideal ensures his demise within the mortal realm to which he is inextricably bound. But the romantic hero differs fundamentally from the modern protagonist because he recognizes and pursues a transforming vision whose origin is, finally, outside the self. He might yearn for a return to an earlier Age (like the medieval) when cultural conditions were more conducive to heroic achievement, but he never adopts the cynical position that the transcendental vision is irrelevant or illusory, the fictive construct of his own overheated imagination. Indeed, always implicit is the assumption that the heroic ideal is real, has objective existence in a Platonic sense, and that his posture as anti-hero results solely from his personal inability to achieve it.

VIII

Conclusion

Any study of romantic heroism must confront the fact that the heroes of the 1770–1860 period in Western literature form a diversified group that defies any neat system of categorization. There are heroes of sensibility—like Werther, René, the Visionary of *Alastor*, or Childe Harold—who, bruised by too close contact with a harsh, closed, and coldly empirical world, retreat into the recesses of their *belle âme* in a doomed, narcissistic pursuit of transcendence. As Byron's Harold confesses, "But who can view the ripen'd rose, nor seek/ To wear it?" (III, xi).[1] Other heroes of sensibility—Endymion or Ishmael, for example—learn in the course of their wanderings that they must surrender the quest for transcendent love or knowledge and embrace the mortal dimension. Pechorin and, to a lesser extent, Don Juan, assume the posture of decadent dandy, lapsing into a state of perpetual ennui in a world of meaningless love affairs. Wordsworth's leech gatherer, Old Cumberland Beggar, and naïve child are heroes of nature, solitary and unspectacular figures who

---

1 References to Byron's poetry are to E. H. Coleridge (ed.), *The Poetical Works of Lord Byron*, and are cited parenthetically.

achieve solace in a benevolent natural world; "Michael," however, demonstrates that nature is not always so kind, for the old stoic shepherd is left to waste away, bereft of hope and abandoned by his son. Then there are those satanic remnants of the gothic tradition—Manfred, Ahab, Wieland—whose introspective search for knowledge or higher levels of awareness invariably results in destruction of human sympathy and warmth, and leads to a nightmarish imprisonment within the subterranean recesses of the self where one discovers an internal hell of mental anguish.

Other titanic spirits, like Faust or Prometheus, bring their personal quest for self-realization into harmony with a vision of communal regeneration; guided by providence, they become mythic embodiments of human consciousness who testify to romantic faith in man's ability to realize an heroic destiny. Hollingsworth and Pierre, however, stand as cautionary checks against the romantic expansionist impulse. Full of high purpose and noble intention, their quests for utopian communal life or justice and moral order fall prey to flawed human nature.

Thus the romantic age offers not the simple, consummate hero but varied, often contradictory modes or patterns of heroism. Yet from their exploration of the possibilities and pitfalls of self-consciousness, their portrayal of the quest for transcendence of moral limitation, artists of the period define what might be labeled the romantic heroic ideal. This ideal almost always involves, in its initial stages, introspection: a rejection of corrupted established authority and the sterile, rationalistic world order that provides it sanction; a plummeting of the interior consciousness in a desperate attempt to locate an authentic means of transcendence; and a reliance on the self—as transforming force, source of knowledge, or center of moral authority—that borders on solipsism. But, as Hartman, Abrams, Cooke, and others have argued, introspection is but a transitory phase, a middle strait in a larger passage; crucial to the heroic ideal is ultimate transcendence of self-consciousness, an absorption into cosmic consciousness that involves the hero's acceptance of communal responsibility. The enlightened individual must act to bring his peculiar glimpse of divine truth into a human arena so that all participate in his redemptive vision.

Most individual heroes of romantic literature fall short when measured against this ideal. Heroic if only because they refuse to rest content within the limitations imposed by the inescapable fact of their mortality, the various protagonists fall victim to self-consciousness. As Childe Harold confesses,

> —I *have* thought
> Too long and darkly, till my brain became,
> In its own eddy boiling and o'erwrought,
> A whirling gulf of phantasy and flame.
> (*Childe Harold's Pilgrimage*, III, vii)

Byron's phrase, "Too long and darkly," suggests that acute self-consciousness is not so much an avenue to heroism as it is a serious, potentially destructive, pitfall that must be either avoided or overcome. Some self-conscious heroes, like René or the Visionary of *Alastor*, find debilitating the narcissistic lure of solipsism; they become so infatuated with the loveliness of the taunting, divine vision of beauty within that they use it to buffer themselves from harsh reality and eventually wither. Indeed, Goethe, Chateaubriand, Shelley, and Byron all condemn their sensitive but ineffectual heroes; either in prefaces or in subsequent public disavowals of sympathy, these artists make clear the fact that the melancholy, world-weary wanderer fails to satisfy the demands of heroism. Other would-be heroes, like Byron's Manfred, whose "aspirations/ Have been beyond the dwellers of the earth" (II, iv, 58–59), become defiant in their self-imposed isolation, satanic figures who deny any bonds which might link them to other men: "My spirit walk'd not with the souls of man/ Nor looked upon the earth with human eyes" (II, ii, 49–50). Despite the zodiacal star's reminder that he is a "child of clay," Manfred steadfastly denies his humanity. To the solicitous Chamois Hunter's plea that he seek "the aid of holy men and heavenly patience" Manfred replies that such recourse is beneath him: "Preach it to mortals of a dust like thine,—/ I am not of thine order"

(II, i, 34–37). But Manfred's proud defiance proves to no avail, for like all mortals he too, Leslie Marchand notes, is "a slave to the limitations of the human condition."[2] He has no effect in human community.

Those romantic protagonists who become imprisoned in self-consciousness fail to achieve heroic stature in large part because they refuse to admit that transcendence of mortal limitation is not the sole aim of the heroic ideal. Neither an isolating commitment to a narcissistic ideal nor titanic pride in one's self-sufficiency serves to satisfy the age's insatiable demand for meaningful action that affects the course of history. The hero must not only transcend but also transform. He must come down from the mountain, leave the "painted ship on the painted ocean," or emerge like the butterfly from the cocoon of the self and immerse himself in human community, revitalize mankind with the power of his divine vision.

One striking feature of romantic literature is that so many protagonists distort, pervert, or simply fail to measure up to a heroic ideal. Such failure seems almost inevitable; the heroic ideal belongs to the realm of transcendence and man is trapped in mortal limitation. As a result, the artist seems often to define his heroic ideal by indirection or negative example. But the romantic artist does not surrender the possibility of heroism. Indeed, the intensity of the protagonist's struggle against limitation, his quest to experience and make manifest the transcendent dimension within a mortal sphere, serves as the gauge by which the degree of his heroism is measured.

Because he deemed the existing social, political, and moral orders antiquated and corrupt, the romantic hero—unlike his classical and Renaissance predecessors—could no longer serve himself or mankind by upholding or enforcing the standard of inherited tradition. Restless within the limitations imposed by the fact of mortality, he instead withdrew from the world in a militant search for transcendent vision. He differed from his heroic predecessors in that his activating vision of personal rejuvenation and communal good

2 Leslie A. Marchand, *Byron's Poetry: A Critical Introduction* (Boston, 1965), 121.

was personal and intuitive; he differed from his descendant, the modern anti-hero, in that he believed in the divine origin of his vision, the existence of a providential cosmic consciousness capable of transforming human life.

But this internal quest for higher states of consciousness, though indispensible, is but a single, preliminary aspect of the romantic heroic ideal. To achieve fruition, the hero must ultimately transcend self-consciousness itself. For some, notably Werther and the heroes of Keats's poetry, art affords release; the transforming power of the imagination operates on the materials of harsh reality and dissolves, for a time, all thoughts of self. In the realm of dance, music, or poetry Werther and his visionary, unobtainable love, Lotte, fuse; they are absorbed into the art form itself. Unfortuantely, however, art for Werther proves a "deceiving elf." He is unable to sustain the fleeting conditions forged through the aesthetic imagination and, like Endymion, makes the "homeward journey to habitual self." But for Goethe, art proves to be a more permanent means of transcendence, as it affords purgation of destructive, self-centered instincts. The liberating discipline of the art form enables the poet to objectify interior states of mind and thereby to transcend them.

Other heroes seek escape from egocentric self-absorption through various forms of religion as a focus of belief and aesthetic. Aware of the psychological and social havoc potential in the solipsistic stage of the heroic quest, romantic artists engage in a search for final transcendence of self into a meaningful and ordered pattern of existence. For a surprisingly large number, including Novalis, Kleist, Coleridge, Chateaubriand, Lamartine, and Franz Liszt, a providentially sanctioned religious order proves the means of overcoming spiritual despair. Those heroes who come closest to the romantic heroic ideal—Faust and Prometheus—transcend existential despair only as they are assimilated into a divinely orchestrated historical process. The hero must, M. H. Abrams argues, function "as an integral part of an organic social whole."[3] In accepting communal responsibility,

---

3   Abrams, *Natural Supernaturalism*, 200.

the hero fulfills God's providential plan, rejuvenates a decadent culture, and transforms his despair into a personal fulfillment granting serenity and hope.

The element of communal responsibility becomes especially pertinent in American romanticism. For the early puritans, the hero was a pilgrim on a specific errand; his progress toward private redemption was inseparable from his role in the community's fulfillment of a divinely ordained destiny. Later secular heroes, like George Washington, manifested a similar ideal: the heroic self fulfilled its nature only in relation to the providence that directed it and the nation that commanded its service.

Yet transcendentalism, the theoretical center of American romanticism, derived its force from a commitment to individual fulfillment; its hallmark was the Emersonian concept of self-reliance. The romantic writer in America turned to fiction in an attempt to dramatize the tension between the exercise of romantic will on the one hand, and the need for submission of the self to the demands of communal obligation on the other. Laboring under the shadow of the Puritan emphasis on man's innate depravity, American "dark" romantics such as Hawthorne and Melville called into question the premise of human and social perfectibility that, coming to the architects of the nation's political system from the preromantic idealism of the French *philosophes*, had sparked and sustained the "great experiment" in democracy that America became. Their work often parodied the transcendentalist social experiments and assessment of human nature and, with unwavering focus on the pervasive evil in the human soul, undermined any expectation of an improved or renovated human nature or social order. The self-reliant protagonist who engaged in an isolating quest for personal fulfillment—no matter how heroic he might seem—forfeited human compassion and posed danger to a social and political order dependent upon voluntary cooperation among citizens.

A fundamental problem in the romantic heroic quest becomes readily apparent in the protagonist's relationship to women. Typically the hero, desperate for an authentic love, commits himself to pursuit of a visionary female who is the earthly shadow of a transcendental ideal. A self-generated ideal, the woman takes her identity from the hero's intuitive conception of truth and beauty. She is, in other words, a narcissistic projection: an unattainable, disembodied goddess who consumes her lover. The hero becomes a supplicant to his created goddess, and engages in a sterile, narcissistic love that deprives the woman of identity and saps the male's virility. This exclusion of the vibrant feminine principle has profound social consequences since it removes from the community the procreative impulse that ensures its survival. Love can be for the hero a potentially redemptive force, but not if it is narcissistic; indeed, love serves the heroic quest only if—as with Faust—it enables the hero to transcend self-consciousness.

In American romantic fiction, sibling incest proves a significant variation on the theme of the woman as the male hero's narcissistic projection of interior consciousness. Incest for the American romantic artist, as for his European counterpart, symbolizes the narcissistic element in the solipsistic stage of the hero's quest. But in American fiction, incest is never rejuvenating; invariably, the incestuous love proves the hero's undoing. Mirroring the hero's psychological and aesthetic disintegration occasioned by total self-absorption, the effects of incestuous love point to a central tension in American romantic art between transcendentalism and Puritanism. The hero who turns inward to coddle the isolating impulses of the heart becomes trapped in the abyss of self and falls victim to a puzzling morass of sin and moral disorder. Furthermore, the theme of incest in American romantic fiction assumes political overtones: the national democratic ethos that encourages a relentless pursuit of individual self-fulfillment renders the hero at odds with a heroic ideal predicated upon acceptance of communal responsibility. If human nature is at heart base and disordered, then the utopian expectations of both transcendentalism and American democracy prove illusory and self-destructive.

The romantic concept of tragedy derives from an awareness that implicit in the heroic ideal is the inevitability that mortal man will fall short in his attempt to achieve it. The age was preoccupied with heroes, with the nature and possibility of heroic action; however, the romantics were rarely satisfied with either fictional or historical characters who pretended to heroic stature. The fate of Napoleon, of course, serves as a prime example. Full of hope and awe at Napoleon's quick and forceful rise to power from the ashes of the *ancien régime*, romantic artists recoiled in horror and disillusionment as they witnessed his egomania wreak havoc with all of Europe. Napoleon's fall and ignominious exile struck a blow to great expectations. But the fate of Napoleon served as an object lesson in the dangers present when the "great man" pursues his vision of personal fulfillment at the expense of the larger social order.

Emerson's *Representative Men* reflects romantic dissatisfaction with mortal quests to realize the heroic ideal. Each of Emerson's great men, as "a receptive channel for the superincumbent spirit,"[4] accomplishes much; yet all prove deficient in one way or another. History, in other words, offers no example of the single man who fully realizes the transcendental heroic ideal. Nevertheless, Emerson refuses to surrender the possibility of heroism; in fact, he strives to become the great poet of the age, the seer whose vision will kindle mankind's spiritual awakening. Yet Emerson too fails, in large part because he is unable to sustain his independent posture as "Man Thinking." Though Emerson liked to believe that thought was the highest and purest form of action, the pressing need for social reform—specifically abolition—pulled Emerson into a communal arena that, he feared, would prove toxic to his ambitions as poet. His involvement in the abolition movement taught Emerson that the hero owed his fellows more than perception and articulation of an ideal; he must embody the "moral sentiment" and "act" upon it. Unfortunately, Emerson discovers that the hero's "double-consciousness" can be debilitating: the "two lives" he must live—one of

4 Matthiessen, *American Renaissance*, 632.

the imagination, which grants him transcendent vision, and the other in human community, where he must try to impose that vision—"show very little relation to each other."

To achieve the heroic ideal, therefore, the romantic protagonist must sustain his transcendent vision within human community and thereby occasion regeneration of a decadent culture. But in his attempts to do so, the romantic hero either perverts the ideal so drastically that it becomes hideous and destructive, or he discovers that his quest is futile and retreats into the solipsistic world of the imagination. In either case, the tragic fact is that the heroic quest that the romantic protagonist finds irresistible proves impossible; his fascination with the ideal ensures his demise in the mortal realm to which he is inextricably bound. Yet in his recognition and pursuit of a transforming vision whose origin is outside the self, the romantic hero avoids the purposeless, despairing posture of the modern anti-hero.

Bibliography

Primary Texts

Augustine. *Confessions*. Translated from Latin by Vernon J. Bourke. Washington, D.C.: Catholic University Press, 1966.

Brown, Charles Brockden. *Wieland; or The Transformation: An American Tale*. Vol. I of *The Novels and Related Works of Charles Brockden Brown*. Edited by Sydney J. Krause, *et al*. 6 vols., projected. Kent, Ohio: Kent State University Press, 1977—.

Brown, William Hill. *The Power of Sympathy*. Edited by William S. Kable. Columbus, Ohio: Ohio State University Press, 1969.

Byron, George Gordon. *The Poetical Works of Lord Byron*. Edited by E. H. Coleridge. London: John Murray, 1905.

Channing, William Ellery. *The Works of William Ellery Channing, D.D.* Boston: American Unitarian Society, 1877.

Chateaubriand, Francois-René de. *Atala; René; Les Aventures du Dernier Abencerage*. Edited by Fernand Letessier. Paris: Garnier Frères, 1958.

———. *Les Natchez*. Edited by Gilbert Chinard. Paris: E. Droz, 1932.

———. *Mémoires d'outre-tombe.* 2 vols. Paris: C. Crouzet, 1859.

———. *René.* Vol. I of *Oeuvres romanesque et voyages.* Edited by Maurice Regard. 2 vols. Paris: Gallimard, 1969.

Coleridge, Samuel Taylor. *Coleridge: Poetical Works.* Edited by E. H. Coleridge. Originally published in 1912. London: Oxford University Press, 1973.

Emerson, Ralph Waldo. *The Collected Works of Ralph Waldo Emerson.* Edited by Alfred R. Ferguson and Robert E. Spiller. 12 vols., projected. Cambridge, Mass.: Harvard University Press, 1971—.

———. *The Complete Works of Ralph Waldo Emerson.* Edited by E. W. Emerson. 12 vols. Boston: Houghton-Mifflin, 1903.

———. *The Journals of Ralph Waldo Emerson.* Edited by E. W. Emerson and W. E. Forbes. 10 vols. Boston: Houghton-Mifflin, 1914.

———. *The Journals and Miscellaneous Notebooks of Ralph Waldo Emerson.* Edited by William H. Gilman, *et al.* 16 vols., projected. Cambridge, Mass.: Harvard University Press, 1971—.

Fichte, J. G. *Sämtliche Werke.* Edited by J. H. Fichte. 8 vols. Berlin: Veit und Comp., 1845.

Goethe, Johann W. *Der Junge Goethe.* Edited by Hanna Fischer-Lamberg. 6 vols. Berlin: Walter de Gruyter, 1963–74.

———. *Faust.* Translated from German by Walter Kaufmann. Garden City, N.Y.: Doubleday, 1961.

———. *Faust: A Tragedy.* Edited by Cyrus Hamlin. Translated from German by Walter Arndt. New York: Norton, 1976.

———. *Goethes Werke.* Edited by Erich Trunz. 14 vols. Hamburg: Christian Wegner, 1949–1960.

———. *The Sufferings of Young Werther.* Translated from German by Harry Steinhauer. New York: Norton, 1970.

Hardenberg, Friedrich von [Novalis]. *Novalis Schriften.* Edited by Paul Kluckhohn and Richard Samuel. 4 vols. Stuttgart: W. Kohlhammer, 1977.

———. *Novalis Werke.* Edited by Gerhard Schulz. Munich: C. H. Beck, 1969.

Hardy, Thomas. *Jude the Obscure.* Edited by Irving Howe. Boston: Houghton-Mifflin, 1965.

Hawthorne, Nathaniel. *The Centenary Edition of The Works of Nathan-*

iel Hawthorne. Edited by William Charvat, *et al*. 14 vols. Columbus: Ohio State University Press, 1962.

————. *The English Notebooks*. Edited by Randall Stewart. New York: Russell & Russell, 1962.

Heine, Heinrich. *Sämtliche Werke*. 7 vols. Philadelphia: J. Kohler, 1867.

Hölderlin. *Sämtliche Werke*. Edited by Friedrich Seebass. 4 vols. Berlin: Im Propyläen, 1943.

Hugo, Victor. *Oeuvres Complètes*. 45 vols. Paris: Ollendorff and A. Michel, 1904–1952.

————. *Victor Hugo: Poésie*. Edited by Bernard Leuilliot. 3 vols. Paris: Aux Éditions de Seuil, 1972.

Keats, John. *The Letters of John Keats*. Edited by Maurice Forman. Rev. ed. London: Oxford University Press, 1947.

————. *The Poems of John Keats*. Edited by M. Allott. New York: Norton, 1970.

————. *The Poems of John Keats*. Edited by Jack Stillinger. Cambridge, Mass.: The Belknap Press of Harvard University Press, 1978.

Koch, Adrienne, ed. *The American Enlightenment*. New York: George Braziller, 1965.

Lamartine, Alphonse de. "Avertissement de la nouvelle édition," *La Chute d'une Ange*. *Oeuvres complètes de Lamartine*. 41 vols. Paris: Chez L'auteur, 1860.

————. *Cours familier de littérature*. Paris: n.p., 1866.

————. *Méditations Poétiques*. Edited by Jean des Cognets. Paris: Garnier Frères, 1956.

————. *Oeuvres Poétiques Complètes*. Edited by Marius-François Guyard. Paris: Gallimard, 1963.

Lermontov. *A Hero of Our Time*. Translated from Russian by Paul Foote. Harmondsworth, England: Penguin, 1966.

Lewis, Matthew Gregory. *The Monk*. New York: Grove Press, 1952.

Melville, Herman. *Moby-Dick; or, The Whale*. Edited by Harrison Hayford and Hershel Parker. New York: Norton, 1967.

————. *Pierre or, The Ambiguities*. Edited by Henry A. Murray. New York: Hendricks House, 1949.

BIBLIOGRAPHY

Miller, Perry, ed. *The American Transcendentalists: Their Prose and Poetry*. Garden City, N.Y.: Doubleday, 1957.

Musset, Alfred de. *Le Confession d'un Enfant du Siècle*. Paris: Conard, 1937.

Norton, Charles Eliot, ed. *The Correspondence of Thomas Carlyle and Ralph Waldo Emerson, 1834–1872*. 3 vols. Boston: J. R. Osgood, 1883.

Poe, Edgar Allan. *The Complete Works of Edgar Allan Poe*. Edited by James A. Harrison. 17 vols. New York: Crowell, 1902.

————. *The Poems of Edgar Allan Poe*. Edited by Floyd Stovall. Charlottesville: University of Virginia Press, 1965.

Rousseau, Jean-Jacques. *Confessions*. Paris: Garnier, 1879.

————. *Les Rêveries du Promeneur Solitaire*. Paris: Éditions Garnier Frères, 1949.

Rymer, Thomas. *The Critical Works of Thomas Rymer*. Edited by C. A. Zimansky. New Haven, Conn.: Yale University Press, 1956.

Schiller, Friedrich. *Sämtliche Werke*. Edited by Gerhard Fricke and Herbert G. Göpfert. 5 vols. Munich: Carl Hanser, 1960.

Schlegel, Friedrich. *Kritische Ausgabe*. Edited by Ernst Behler, Hans Eichner, and Jean-Jacques Anstett. Paderborn: Schoningh, 1967.

————. *Kritische Schriften*. Edited by Wolfdietrich Rasch. Munich: Carl Hanser, 1964.

Sénancour, Etienne de. *Obermann*. Paris: Carpentier, n.d.

Shelley, Percy Bysshe. *Shelley: Poetical Works*. Edited by Thomas Hutchinson. Revised by G. M. Matthews. London: Oxford University Press, 1970.

————. *Shelley's Prose: or, The Trumpet of a Prophecy*. Edited by David Lee Clark. Albuquerque: University of New Mexico Press, 1954.

Thoreau, Henry David. *Walden*. Edited by Lyndon Shanley. Princeton, N.J.: Princeton University Press, 1971.

Washington, George. *The Writings of George Washington*. Edited by Worthington Chauncey Ford. 14 vols. New York: G. P. Putnam's Sons, 1889–93.

BIBLIOGRAPHY

Wollstonecraft, Mary. *A Vindication of the Rights of Women: Strictures on Political and Moral Subjects*. London: Johnson, 1792.

Wordsworth, William. *Wordsworth: Poetical Works*. Edited by Thomas Hutchinson, Revised by Ernest de Selincourt. London: Oxford University Press, 1969.

Secondary References

Abrams, M. H. "English Romanticism: The Spirit of the Age." Northrop Frye, ed. *Romanticism Reconsidered: Selected Papers from the English Institute*. New York: Columbia University, 1963.

————. *The Mirror and the Lamp: Romantic Theory and the Critical Tradition*. Originally published in 1953. New York: Norton, 1958.

————. *Natural Supernaturalism: Tradition and Revolution in Romantic Literature*. New York: Norton, 1971.

Adams, Henry. *The Education of Henry Adams*. Edited by D. W. Brogan. Boston: Houghton-Mifflin, 1961.

Auden, W. H. *The Enchafèd Flood; or, The Romantic Iconography of the Sea*. New York: Random House, 1950.

Babbitt, Irving. *Rousseau and Romanticism*. Boston: Houghton-Mifflin, 1919.

Ball, Patricia. *The Central Self: A Study of Romantic and Victorian Imagination*. London: Athlone Press, 1968.

Barnard, Ellsworth. *Shelley's Religion*. New York: Russell & Russell, 1964.

Barth, J. Robert. *Coleridge and Christian Doctrine*. Cambridge, Mass.: Harvard University Press, 1969.

Baym, Nina. "Portrayal of Women in American Literature, 1790–1870." Marlene Springer, ed. *What Manner of Woman: Essays on English and American Life and Literature*. New York: New York University Press, 1977.

Bell, Michael Davitt. *The Development of American Romance: The Sacrifice of Relations*. Chicago: University of Chicago Press, 1980.

————. "The Glendinning Heritage: Melville's Literary Borrowings in *Pierre*." *Studies in Romanticism*, XII (Fall, 1973), 741–62.

Bellows, Henry Adams, translator. *The Poetic Edda*. Princeton, N.J.: Princeton University Press, 1936.

Bercovitch, Sacvan. *The Puritan Origins of the American Self*. New Haven, Conn.: Yale University Press, 1975.

Bewley, Marius. *The English Romantic Poets*. New York: Random House, 1970.

Bloom, Harold. "The Internalization of the Quest Romance." Harold Bloom, ed. *Romanticism and Consciousness: Essays in Criticism*. New York: Norton, 1970.

————. *The Visionary Company: A Reading of English Romantic Poetry*. London: Faber & Faber, 1962.

Boas, George. "The Romantic Self: An Historical Sketch." *Studies in Romanticism*, IV (Autumn, 1964), 1–16.

Bodkin, Maud. *Archetypal Patterns in Poetry*. London: Oxford University Press, 1934.

Bonaparte, Marie. *The Life and Works of Edgar Allan Poe: A Psychoanalytic Interpretation*. Originally published in 1949. New York: Humanities Press, 1971.

Bowra, C. M. *Inspiration and Poetry*. London: Macmillan, 1956.

Bradley, A. C. *Oxford Lectures on Poetry*. London: Oxford University Press, 1909.

Bredvold, Louis. *The Natural History of Sensibility*. Detroit: Wayne State University Press, 1962.

Brombert, Victor. "The Happy Prison: A Recurring Romantic Metaphor." David Thorburn and Geoffrey Hartman, eds. *Romanticism: Vistas, Instances, Continuities*. Ithaca, N.Y.: Cornell University Press, 1973.

————, ed. *The Hero in Literature*. Greenwich, Conn.: Fawcett, 1969.

Brown, Herbert R., ed. "Introduction." *The Power of Sympathy; or, The Triumph of Nature*. By William Hill Brown. Boston: New Frontiers Press, 1961.

————. *The Sentimental Novel in America, 1789–1860*. Durham, N.C.: Duke University Press, 1940.

Bush, Douglas. *Mythology and the Romantic Tradition in English Poetry*. Cambridge, Mass.: Harvard University Press, 1937.

Butler, Eliza M. *Byron and Goethe: Analysis of a Passion*. London: Bowes and Bowes, 1956.

Campbell, Joseph. *The Hero with a Thousand Faces*. New York: Bollingen Foundation, 1949.

Carman, Harry J., *et al. A History of the American People*. 2 vols. New York: Knopf, 1967.

Chadwick, H. M. *The Heroic Age*. Cambridge: Cambridge University Press, 1912.

Chandler, Alice. *A Dream of Order: The Medieval Ideal in Nineteenth-Century English Literature*. Lincoln: University of Nebraska Press, 1970.

Cobban, Alfred. *Edmund Burke and the Revolt Against the Eighteenth Century; a study of the political and social thinking of Burke, Wordsworth, Coleridge, and Southey*. London: Allen and Unwin, 1960.

Comfort, Alex. *Art and Social Responsibility: Lectures on the Ideology of Romanticism*. London: The Falcon Press, 1946.

Cooke, Michael G. *The Romantic Will*. New Haven, Conn.: Yale University Press, 1976.

Cowie, Alexander. *The Rise of the American Novel*. New York: American Book Co., 1948.

Cox, C. B. "Philip Larkin, Anti-Heroic Poet." *Studies in the Literary Imagination*, IX (Spring, 1976), 155–68.

Creed, Elizabeth. *Le Dandysme de Jules Barbey d'Aurevilly*. Paris: Droz, 1938.

Crews, Frederick. *The Sins of the Fathers: Hawthorne's Psychological Themes*. New York: Oxford University Press, 1966.

Davidson, Donald. "A Mirror for Artists." *I'll Take My Stand: The South and the Agrarian Tradition*. By Twelve Southerners. Originally published in 1930. New York: Harper & Row, 1962.

Dédéyan, Charles. *Le Thème de Faust dans la littérature Européenne*. 2 vols. Paris: Lettres Modernes, 1959.

Donald, David. *Lincoln Reconsidered: Essays on the Civil War Era*. New York: Knopf, 1956.

Elkins, Stanley M. *Slavery: A Problem in American Institutional and Intellectual Life*. Rev. ed. Chicago: University of Chicago Press, 1968.

Engell, James. *The Creative Imagination: Enlightenment to Romanticism.* Cambridge, Mass.: Harvard University Press, 1981.

Estève, Edmond. *Byron et le romantisme française.* Paris: Boivin, 1929.

Fairchild, Hoxie Neale. *1780–1830, Romantic Faith.* Vol. III of *Religious Trends in English Poetry.* 6 vols. New York: Columbia University Press, 1939–68.

Fairley, Barker. *A Study of Goethe.* Oxford: Clarendon Press, 1947.

Ferry, David. *The Limits of Mortality: An Essay on Wordsworth's Major Poems.* Middleton, Conn.: Wesleyan University Press, 1959.

Fiedler, Leslie. *Love and Death in the American Novel.* New York: Criterion Books, 1960.

Frye, Northrop. "The Drunken Boat: The Revolutionary Element in Romanticism." Northrop Frye, ed. *Romanticism Reconsidered: Selected Papers from the English Institute.* New York: Columbia University Press, 1963.

Fulmer, O. Bryan. "The Ancient Mariner and the Wandering Jew." *Studies in Philology,* LXVI (1969), 797–815.

Furst, Lilian R. *The Contours of European Romanticism.* London: Macmillan, 1979.

———. *Counterparts: The Dynamics of Franco-German Literary Relationships, 1770–1895.* Detroit: Wayne State University Press, 1977.

———. "The Romantic Hero, Or Is He An Anti-Hero?" *Studies in the Literary Imagination,* IX (Spring, 1976), 53–67.

———. *Romanticism.* The Critical Idiom Series, Number 2. London: Methuen, 1969.

———. *Romanticism in Perspective: A Comparative Study of Aspects of the Romantic Movements in England, France, and Germany.* New York: Humanities Press, 1970.

Garber, Frederick. "Self, Society, Value, and the Romantic Hero." *Comparative Literature,* XIX (1967), 321–33.

———. *Thoreau's Redemptive Imagination.* New York: New York University Press, 1977.

Geist, Stanley. *Herman Melville: The Tragic Vision and the Heroic Ideal.* Cambridge, Mass.: Harvard University Press, 1939.

Gibbons, Edward. "Point of View and Moral in 'The Rime of the Ancient Mariner.'" *University Review*, XXXV (1969), 257–61.

Guthke, Karl S. "A Stage for the Anti-Hero: Metaphysical Farce in the Modern Theatre." *Studies in the Literary Imagination*, IX (Spring, 1976), 119–37.

Hamburger, Michael. *Contraries: Studies in German Literature*. New York: E. P. Dutton, 1970.

Hammond, N. G. L., and D. H. H. Scullard, eds. *The Oxford Classical Dictionary*. Rev. ed. Oxford: Clarendon Press, 1970.

Hankins, Richard. "Puritans, Patriots and Panegyric: The Beginnings of American Biography." *Studies in the Literary Imagination*, IX (Fall, 1976), 95–109.

Hartman, Geoffrey. "Reflections on Romanticism in France." David Thorburn and Geoffrey Hartman, eds. *Romanticism: Vistas, Instances, Continuities*. Ithaca, N.Y.: Cornell University Press, 1973.

———. "Romanticism and Anti-Self Consciousness." Originally published in 1962. Revised and expanded in *Romanticism and Consciousness: Essays in Criticism*. Edited by Harold Bloom. New York: Norton, 1970.

Heimert, Alan. "*Moby-Dick* and American Political Symbolism." *American Quarterly*, XV (Winter, 1963), 498–534.

Heller, Erich. "On Goethe's Faust." Victor Lange, ed. *Goethe: A Collection of Critical Essays*. Englewood Cliffs, N.J.: Prentice-Hall, 1968.

Henry, Myrtle. "Independence and Freedom as Expressed and Interpreted by Ralph W. Emerson." *Negro History Bulletin*, VI (May, 1943), 173–74; 185, 191.

Hirsch, David H. "The Dilemma of the Liberal Intellectual: Melville's Ishmael." *Texas Studies in Literature and Language*, V (Summer, 1963), 169–88.

Hoffman, Daniel. *Form and Fable in American Fiction*. New York: Oxford University Press, 1961.

———. "I Have Been Faithful to You in My Fashion: The Remarriage of Ligeia's Husband." *Southern Review*, New Series, VIII

(1972), 89–105.

————. *Poe Poe Poe Poe Poe Poe Poe.* Garden City, N.Y.: Doubleday, 1972.

Hoffman, Michael J. "The Anti-Transcendentalism of *Moby-Dick*." *Georgia Review*, XXIII (1969), 3–16.

————. "The House of Usher and Negative Romanticism." *Studies in Romanticism*, IV (1964), 158–68.

————. *The Subversive Vision: American Romanticism in Literature.* Port Washington, N.Y.: Kennikat Press, 1972.

Holmes, Richard. *Shelley: The Pursuit.* New York: E. P. Dutton, 1975.

Hook, Sydney. *The Hero in History: A Study in Limitation and Possibility.* Originally published in 1943. Boston: Beacon Press, 1969.

Jacobs, Robert D. *Poe: Journalist and Critic.* Baton Rouge: Louisiana State University Press, 1969.

Jost, François. *Introduction to Comparative Literature.* Indianapolis: Bobbs-Merrill, 1974.

Kayser, Wolfgang. "Die Entstehung von Goethes Werther." *Deutsch Viertejahrsschraft für Literaturwissenschaft und Geistegeschichte*, XIX (1941), 403–57.

Kempis, Thomas à. *The Imitation of Christ.* Translated from Latin by Leo Sherley-Price. London: Penguin, 1952.

Korff, H. A. *Geist der Goethezeit.* Leipzig: Koehler und Amelang, 1940.

Krieger, Murray. *Visions of Extremity in Modern Literature.* Vol. I of *The Tragic Vision: The Confrontation of Extremity.* 2 vols. Baltimore: Johns Hopkins University Press, 1960.

Lawrence D. H. *Lawrence on Hardy and Painting: Study of Thomas Hardy and to These Paintings.* Edited by J. V. Davies. London: Heinemann Educational Books, 1973.

Leonard, W. E. *Byron and Byronism in America.* New York: Haskell House, 1964.

Lerminier, Eugène. *Au delà du Rhin, ou tableau politique et philosophique de l'Allemagne depuis Mme de Staël à nos jours.* 2 vols. Paris: Bonnaire, 1846.

BIBLIOGRAPHY

Levin, David. *History as Romantic Art: Bancroft, Prescott, Motley, and Parkman*. Palo Alto, Calif.: Stanford University Press, 1959.

Levin, Harry. *Contexts of Criticism*. Cambridge, Mass.: Harvard University Press, 1957.

Levy, G. R. *The Sword from the Rock: An Investigation into the Origins of Epic Literature and the Development of the Hero*. London: Faber and Faber, 1953.

Lovejoy, A. O. "On the Discrimination of Romanticisms." *PMLA*, XXXIX (1924), 229–53.

Lowes, John Livingstone. *The Road to Xanadu: A Study in the Ways of the Imagination*. Rev. ed. Boston: Houghton-Mifflin, 1959.

Lucas, F. L. *The Decline and Fall of the Romantic Ideal*. Rev. ed. Cambridge: Cambridge University Press, 1963.

Lundblad, Jane. *Nathaniel Hawthorne and European Literary Tradition*. New York: Russell & Russell, 1965.

MacDermot, Violet. *The Cult of the Seer in the Ancient Middle East: A Contribution to Current Research on Hallucinations Drawn from Coptic and Other Texts*. Berkeley: University of California Press, 1971.

Magnuson, Paul. *Coleridge's Nightmare Poetry*. Charlottesville: University of Virginia Press, 1974.

Male, Roy. *Hawthorne's Tragic Vision*. Originally published in 1957. New York: Norton, 1964.

Manley, William. "The Importance of Point of View in Brockden Brown's *Wieland*." *American Literature*, XXXV (1963), 311–21.

Marchand, Leslie A. *Byron's Poetry: A Critical Introduction*. Boston: Houghton-Mifflin, 1965.

Matthiessen, F. O. *American Renaissance: Art and Expression in the Age of Emerson and Whitman*. New York: Oxford University Press, 1941.

McGann, Jerome. *Fiery Dust: Byron's Poetic Development*. Chicago: University of Chicago Press, 1968.

McIntyre, Clara. "The Later Career of the Elizabethan Villain-Hero." *PMLA*, XL (1925), 874–80.

Miller, Perry. "Emersonian Genius and the American Democracy."

New England Quarterly, XXVI (March, 1953), 27–44.

————. *Errand into the Wilderness*. Originally published in 1956. New York: Harper & Row, 1964.

————. *The Raven and the Whale: The War of Words and Wits in the Era of Poe and Melville*. New York: Harcourt, Brace, 1956.

Mogan, J. J. "*Pierre* and *Manfred*: Melville's Study of the Byronic Hero." *Papers in Language and Literature*, I (1965), 230–40.

Montgomery, Marion. *The Reflective Journey Toward Order*. Athens: University of Georgia Press, 1973.

Moody, Marjory M. "The Evolution of Emerson as an Abolitionist." *American Literature*, XVII (1945), 1–21.

Moorman, Mary. *William Wordsworth: A Biography, The Early Years, 1770–1803*. London: Oxford University Press, 1957.

Morrison, Claudia G. "Poe's 'Ligeia': An Analysis." *Studies in Short Fiction*, IV (1967), 234–44.

Murray, Henry A. "In Nomine Diaboli." *New England Quarterly*, XXIV (1951), 435–52.

O'Faolain, Sean. *The Vanishing Hero: Studies in Novelists of the Twenties*. Boston: Little, Brown, 1957.

Osborne, William S., ed. "Introduction." *The Power of Sympathy and The Coquette*. By William Hill Brown. New Haven, Conn.: College and University Press, 1970.

Parke, John. "Seven Moby-Dicks." *New England Quarterly*, XXVIII (1955), 319–38.

Patee, Fred Lewis, ed. "Introduction." *Wieland; or The Transformation Together with Memoirs of Carwin the Biloquist: A Fragment*. By Charles Brockden Brown. New York: Hafner, 1926.

Paul, Sherman. *Emerson's Angle of Vision: Man and Nature*. Cambridge, Mass.: Harvard University Press, 1952.

Pearce, Roy Harvey. "Hawthorne and the Sense of the Past, or, The Immortality of Major Molineux." *English Literary History*, XXI (December, 1954), 337–40.

Peckham, Morse. *Beyond the Tragic Vision: The Quest for Identity in the Nineteenth Century*. New York: George Braziller, 1962.

————. "Toward a Theory of Romanticism." *PMLA*, LXVI (1951), 5–23.

———. "Toward a Theory of Romanticism: II. Reconsiderations." *Studies in Romanticism*, I (1961), 1–8.

———. *The Triumph of Romanticism*. Columbia: University of South Carolina Press, 1970.

Perkins, David. *The Quest for Permanence: The Symbolism of Wordsworth, Shelley, and Keats*. Cambridge, Mass.: Harvard University Press, 1959.

Pochman, Henry A. *German Culture in America: Philosophical and Literary Influences, 1600–1900*. Madison: University of Wisconsin Press, 1957.

Porte, Joel. *The Romance in America: Studies in Cooper, Poe, Hawthorne, Melville, and James*. Middleton, Conn.: Wesleyan University Press, 1969.

Poulet, Georges. *The Metamorphoses of the Circle*. Translated from French by Carley Dawson and Elliott Coleman. Baltimore: Johns Hopkins University Press, 1966.

Praz, Mario. *The Romantic Agony*. Translated from Italian by Angus Davidson. Rev. ed. London: Oxford University Press, 1954.

Railo, Eino. *The Haunted Castle: A Study of the Elements of English Romanticism*. New York: E. P. Dutton, 1927.

Rank, Otto. *The Double: A Psychoanalytic Study*. Translated from German by Harry Tucker, Jr. Chapel Hill: University of North Carolina Press, 1971.

Ransom, John Crowe. *The World's Body*. Originally published in 1938. Baton Rouge: Louisiana State University Press, 1968.

Reed, Walter L. *Meditations on the Hero: A Study of the Romantic Hero in Nineteenth-Century Fiction*. New Haven, Conn.: Yale University Press, 1974.

Reiss, Gertrud. "Die beiden Fassungen von Goethes Die Leiden des jungen Werthers." Ph.D. dissertation, Breslau University, 1924.

Reiss, Hans. *Goethe's Novels*. Coral Gables, Fla.: University of Miami Press, 1971.

Richards, I. A. *Coleridge on Imagination*. Bloomington: Indiana University Press, 1934.

———. *Principles of Literary Criticism*. Originally published in 1925. New York: Harcourt, 1968.

Ridge, George Ross. *The Hero in French Romantic Literature*. Athens: University of Georgia Press, 1959.

Rose, Edward J. "'The Queenly Personality': Walpole, Melville and Mother." *Literature and Psychology*, XV (Fall, 1965), 216–29.

Rose, William. *From Goethe to Byron: The Development of 'Weltschmerz' in German Literature*. London: Routledge, 1924.

Rosenfeld, William. "Uncertain Faith: Queequeg's Coffin and Melville's Use of the Bible." *Texas Studies in Literature and Language*, VII (Winter, 1966), 317–27.

Roston, Murray. *Prophet and Poet: The Bible and the Growth of Romanticism*. Evanston, Illinois: Northwestern University Press, 1965.

Rusk, Ralph L. *The Life of Ralph Waldo Emerson*. New York: Columbia University Press, 1949.

Rutherford, Andrew. *Byron: A Critical Study*. Palo Alto, Calif.: Stanford University Press, 1961.

Sainte-Beuve. *Portraits Contemporains*. 5 vols. Rev. ed. Paris: Calmann Lévy, 1889.

Santayana, George. *The Genteel Tradition: Nine Essays by George Santayana*. Edited by Douglas L. Wilson. Cambridge, Mass.: Harvard University Press, 1967.

Schöffler, Herbert. *Die Leiden des jungen Werther: Ihr geistesgeschichtlicher Hintergrund*. Frankfurt a. M.: Vittorio Klostermann, 1938.

Schultz, Max. *The Poetic Voices of Coleridge: A Study of His Desire for Spontaneity and Passion for Order*. Detroit: Wayne State University Press, 1963.

Shumaker, Wayne. *English Autobiography*. Berkeley: University of California Press, 1954.

Simpson, Lewis P., ed. "Introduction." *The Federalist Literary Mind: Selections from the Monthly Anthology and Boston Review, 1802–1811, Including Documents Relating to the Boston Athenaeum*. Baton Rouge: Louisiana State University Press, 1962.

———. "John Adams and Hawthorne: The Fiction of the Real American Revolution." *Studies in the Literary Imagination*, IX (Fall, 1976), 1–17.

Spiller, Robert E., *et al*. *The Literary History of the United States*. 3rd ed., revised. New York: Macmillan, 1963.

Sypher, Wylie. *Loss of Self in Modern Literature and Art.* New York: Random House, 1962.

Tate, Allen. "Narcissus as Narcissus." *Essays of Four Decades.* Chicago: Swallow Press, 1968.

Thody, Philip. "The Anti-heroes of Sartre and Camus: Some Problems of Definition." *Studies in the Literary Imagination,* IX (Spring, 1976), 107–17.

Thompson, G. R. "The Face in the Pool: Reflections on the Doppelgänger Motif in 'The Fall of the House of Usher.'" *Poe Studies,* V (1972), 16–21.

Thompson, Lawrence. *Melville's Quarrel with God.* Princeton, N.J.: Princeton University Press, 1952.

Thorslev, Peter L., Jr. *The Byronic Hero: Types and Prototypes.* Minneapolis: University of Minnesota Press, 1962.

————. "Hawthorne's Determinism: An Analysis." *Nineteenth-Century Fiction,* XIX (1964), 141–57.

————. "Incest as Romantic Symbol." *Comparative Literature Studies,* XI (1965), 41–58.

————. "The Romantic Mind Is Its Own Place." *Comparative Literature,* XV (1963), 250–68.

Trilling, Lionel. *Sincerity and Authenticity.* Cambridge, Mass.: Harvard University Press, 1971.

Walzel, Oskar. *German Romanticism.* Translated from German by A. E. Lussky. New York: Frederick Ungar, 1965.

Warfel, Harry R. "Charles Brockden Brown's German Sources." *Modern Language Quarterly,* I (September, 1940), 357–63.

Warren, Robert Penn. "A Poem of Pure Imagination: An Experiment in Reading." *Selected Essays.* New York: Random House, 1958.

————. *Democracy and Poetry.* Cambridge, Mass.: Harvard University Press, 1975.

Wasserman, Earl. *Shelley: A Critical Reading.* Baltimore: Johns Hopkins University Press, 1971.

————. "The English Romantics: The Grounds of Knowledge." *Studies in Romanticism,* III (1964), 17–34.

————. *The Finer Tone: Keats' Major Poems.* Baltimore: Johns Hopkins University Press, 1967.

Wasserman, Renata R. Mautner. "The Self, the Mirror, the Other: 'The Fall of the House of Usher.'" *Poe Studies*, X (December, 1977), 33–35.

Wellek, René. *Immanuel Kant in England*. Princeton, N.J.: Princeton University Press, 1931.

———. "The Concept of Romanticism in Literary History." *Comparative Literature*, I (1949), 1–23; 147–72.

Whicher, Stephen E. *Freedom and Fate: An Inner Life of Ralph Waldo Emerson*. Rev. ed. Philadelphia: University of Pennsylvania Press, 1971.

White, Newman Ivey. *Shelley*. 2 vols. New York: Knopf, 1947.

Wilbur, Richard. "The House of Poe." Robert Regan, ed. *Poe: A Collection of Critical Essays*. Englewood Cliffs, N.J.: Prentice-Hall, 1967, 98–120.

Wilkinson, E. M., and L. A. Willoughby. "The Blind Man and the Poet: An Early Stage in Goethe's Quest for Form." *Studies in Honor of W. H. Bruford*. London: Cambridge University Press, 1961.

Winwar, Frances. *The Romantic Rebels*. Boston: Little, Brown, 1935.

Woodring, Carl. "The Mariner's Return." *Studies in Romanticism*, II (1962), 375–80.

Yeats, William Butler. *Samhain*. Number 5. Dublin: n.p., 1905.

Yoder, R. A. "The Equilibrist Perspective: Toward a Theory of American Romanticism." *Studies in Romanticism*, XII (Fall, 1973), 705–40.

Ziff, Larzer. "A Reading of *Wieland*." *PMLA*, LXXVII (March, 1962), 51–57.

Zumthor, Paul. *Victor Hugo: Poète de Satan*. Paris: Laffont, 1946.

Zwerdling, Alex. *Yeats and the Heroic Ideal*. New York: New York University Press, 1965.

Index